An Englishman Aboard

An Englishman Aboard

Discovering France in a Rowing Boat

CHARLES TIMONEY

PARTICULAR BOOKS
an imprint of
PENGUIN BOOKS

PARTICULAR BOOKS

Published by the Penguin Group
Penguin Books Ltd, 80 Strand, London WC2R ORL, England
Penguin Group (USA) Inc., 375 Hudson Street, New York, New York 10014, USA
Penguin Group (Canada), 90 Eglinton Avenue East, Suite 700, Toronto, Ontario, Canada M4P 2Y3
(a division of Pearson Penguin Canada Inc.)
Penguin Ireland, 25 St Stephen's Green, Dublin 2, Ireland (a division of Penguin Books Ltd)
Penguin Group (Australia), 707 Collins Street, Melbourne, Victoria 3008, Australia
(a division of Pearson Australia Group Pty Ltd)
Penguin Books India Pvt Ltd, 11 Community Centre, Panchsheel Park, New Delhi – 110 017, India
Penguin Group (NZ), 67 Apollo Drive, Rosedale, Auckland 0632, New Zealand
(a division of Pearson New Zealand Ltd)
Penguin Books (South Africa) (Pty) Ltd, Block D, Rosebank Office Park, 181 Jan Smuts Avenue,
Parktown North, Gauteng 2193, South Africa

Penguin Books Ltd, Registered Offices: 80 Strand, London WC2R ORL, England

www.penguin.com

First published 2013
1

Typeset by Palimpsest Book Production Ltd, Falkirk, Stirlingshire
Printed in Great Britain by Clays Ltd, St Ives plc

A CIP catalogue record for this book is available from the British Library

ISBN 978-1-846-14479-0

www.greenpenguin.co.uk

MIX
Paper from
responsible sources
FSC C018179
www.fsc.org

Penguin Books is committed to a sustainable
future for our business, our readers and our planet.
This book is made from Forest Stewardship
Council™ certified paper.

ALWAYS LEARNING   **PEARSON**

For Sequana

Acknowledgements

I would like to thank all the people who helped in their various ways with the events that led to the writing of this book, and it seems logical to do it in the order in which they come up in the story:

Nathalie, for pointing me in the direction of La Veules; Fyne Boat Kits, for the kit that started the whole thing off; Polly and Mark, for helping to launch it; the members of Rowing Club de Port Marly, for letting us do so; Andrew, for the barge advice; Lieutenant Olivier Dupas and Major Alain Roux and their colleagues of La Brigade Fluviale; Andy, for the ideas; Vincent, for leading me to Serge, and Serge, for taking me downriver on *Zen*; Ghislain, for introducing me to Bernard, and Bernard, for showing me round the YCIF; Sylvie, for introducing me to Dimitri, and Dimitri, for the trip to Triel; Christophe, for the amphicar; Dominique, for the river trip; Peter and Helen, for the St Crispin's day outing; J.-F., for welcoming me aboard *Hirondelle*; Andy, for the Le Havre info; and especially Inès, for coming along too and making the whole thing possible, Georgina Laycock and Jane Turnbull, without whom there would simply have been no book, and Marina Kemp for creating the final version.

'There is nothing – absolutely nothing – half so much worth doing as simply messing about in boats.'

The Wind in the Willows

Prologue

Twenty-seven minutes ago, I was standing at the source of the river Veules on the outskirts of Veules-les-Roses in Haute Nor-mandie: a man on a mission.

Veules-les-Roses lies some twenty-five kilometres west of Dieppe. There are pleasant houses faced with local flint, as well as some very pretty thatched cottages. Like any self-respecting French village (even one of just 600 inhabitants), Veules-les-Roses has a church, a *boulangerie*, a *pharmacie*, a post office and a couple of nice restaurants.

The Veules bursts from its source in a rocky bank and quickly joins up with streams from other nearby springs to form a broad expanse of water that is used for growing watercress. Ducks and coots abound. Further downstream, the river nar-rows and becomes much faster as it weaves between the houses, and the stream is dotted with water wheels. These mills were once used for grinding linseed or fulling cloth, but now, while the wheels still turn with the stream, none seems to do anything useful. Even in its faster-flowing sections between the mills the Veules is home to a surprising number of trout, all effortlessly holding position in the sunniest spots despite the current.

The village is attractive in the sunshine but, at first glance, it doesn't necessarily justify the two-hour drive to get here. The main reason for my mission lies in the fact that the Veules is one of the more notable *fleuves* in France. French makes a clear distinction between rivers that flow into other rivers or into

lakes and which are known as *rivières*, and those that flow into the sea. Such rivers, which include giants such as the Loire or the Rhône, are referred to in French as *fleuves*.

Twenty-seven minutes ago, I was standing by the source of the river. I'm now standing on a cobbled beach, my back to the brisk, cold wind, gazing at the Veules as it sweeps out of a narrow concrete gully and pours down to the sea. I have walked the river's entire length in less than half an hour. Had I not stopped to read the helpful tourist information signs spaced along the way I could probably have done it in under twenty minutes. For the Veules, at just 1,194 metres, is the shortest *fleuve* in France.

Today was really just a trial run to see whether I was able to explore an entire French *fleuve* from one end to the other. It is now time to try and fulfil my real mission – to explore something a little bit bigger.

I

Absolutely none of this would have happened if I hadn't decided to build a rowing boat.

Of course, I am not suggesting that it is in any way the boat's fault. Nevertheless, if it hadn't been sitting, newly finished, in the garage that New Year's Eve, the months that followed would very probably have been somewhat less eventful. In France, people don't seem to build boats in their garages. What's more, French people seem to find those who do so rather odd, especially if they also happen to be English.

It feels only fair to make clear from the outset that I am English despite the fact that I have been living in France for rather more years than might be considered reasonable, even by a huge fan of the place. The fact that I ended up here is entirely thanks to my wife. Many years ago, enjoying a peaceful but admittedly rather dull life in England, we both lost our jobs in the same month. While I understandably saw this as cause for concern, I was puzzled when Inès took the news more philosophically. Over the following weeks she carefully set about convincing me that we should make the best of a bad situation and use this unexpected freedom to up sticks and go and live in her native France. Just for a year, you understand: only a year. Inès took particular pains to point out that a year spent in a French office would look really good on my CV once we came back to the UK. In this, she may yet be proved right – one day. For the moment, twenty-five years on, I still live in France and I have a home-made rowing boat in the garage.

Everything came to a head on New Year's Eve. We had invited a group of friends round for the *réveillon* – the New Year's Eve meal. Traditionally, this should have involved: oysters, smoked salmon, foie gras, a roast and some very sweet pudding all washed down with copious quantities of wine. It hadn't been possible to prepare all that because I had been busy with the boat, so we had opted for a *fondue savoyarde* – the classic cheese fondue. This has the do-it-yourself aspect that always seems to make collective meals much more fun. About the only thing that we had kept from the list of classic essentials for a *réveillon* meal was the copious quantities of wine.

A cheese fondue is known in France as a *fondue savoyarde*, a name which gives a clue to its origin. It comes from the Savoie region of south-eastern France, down below Switzerland, an area notable for its ski resorts. When skiing holidays became popular in the 1950s, cheese fondues began to be eaten throughout France, but generally only in wintertime. It is the ideal winter dish because eating bread dunked in cheese is both warming and reviving after a long day in the snow, especially if it is accompanied by a local white wine such as Apremont.

You should allow 250 g of cheese per person made up of a mixture of Comté, Beaufort and Emmenthal, to which you add a decent slug of white wine, some kirsch and (unglamorous – but it makes a difference) a bit of corn starch.

There are two important things that you have to remember with cheese fondues. The first is to be generous with the garlic – not only rubbing the inside of the fondue pan with it but also chucking a good quantity of crushed garlic into the mix. This makes it taste better and also easier to digest. The second is to make sure you chop up your baguette at least eight hours in

advance, preferably the night before. This ensures that the bread has got dry and hard enough not to fall to pieces as soon as you dunk it in the melted cheese. Unfortunately, the fact that you should have done something the day before does tend to reduce the possibility of having a spontaneous and successful last-minute fondue evening.

The meal went by extremely cheerily, and, as midnight approached, the subject of the boat came up at last. All the various friends who were present had been following its progress with interest over the preceding months.

'Alors – où est-ce que ça en est?' – how's it coming on? – several people asked at once. When I admitted that I had actually finished it, there was a collective demand to be taken down to the garage to see it, despite the fact that there were only a few minutes left of the year. So, grabbing a couple of bottles of Champagne, I encouraged everyone to bring their glasses and follow me down to the garage. It is a common feature of French houses to have their ground floor on what is effectively the first floor. To come in, you have to go up a flight of steps from the front garden to reach the front door. The garage is then on the ground floor or in the basement, depending on how you look at it, typically together with a laundry room, a spare room and a cellar. A flight of stairs, which is usually hidden behind a door on the ground floor, leads to this lower floor, and it was down these that we all trooped with our glasses and bottles. Someone even thought of bringing the radio from the kitchen so that we could listen for the stroke of midnight.

Retrospectively, it seems a little odd to have gone through the New Year celebrations – 'Bonne année; bonne santé, plein de bonnes choses . . .' with the associated kissing of cheeks all round – in a very cold garage, but, as midnight chose to strike while we were down there, that is how it worked out.

Once the toasts and kissing were over, our friends started to have a proper look at the boat. It was a wooden, clinker-built rowing boat about seven feet long that I had built from a kit. It had varnished wooden panels that would shine in sunlight and golden wooden oars mounted in gleaming brass rowlocks. Even in the harsh light of the garage I thought it was a thing of beauty. Thankfully, our friends seemed to think it looked quite good too: there was much exclaiming and touching of the varnished wood. There was also quite a lot of speculation as to where I was going to launch it for the first time and what I would do with it afterwards. These were questions that I hadn't actually got round to thinking about at all: over the previous months all I had been preoccupied with had been finding the motivation to go down to the garage every evening to try to finish the thing.

I just smiled enigmatically in answer to their questions and said vaguely 'On verra' – we'll see. This was clearly a most unsatisfactory response in the eyes of our friends.

'You spend months building a boat and you don't even know what you are going to do with it now that it's finished,' they cried accusingly. 'C'est typiquement anglais!' Typically English not to know what you are going to do with a boat? How could they say a thing like that? Unfortunately, I couldn't come up with any kind of reply because they were right: I really hadn't the remotest idea what I was going to do with the boat now that I had finished it. Stalling for time, I said defensively 'Mais si, je sais!' – of course I know – looking desperately around the garage for some kind of inspiration as I did so. From where I was standing all I could see were a couple of grubby mountain bikes; my private stock of Shreddies; a purple sleeping bag that someone had failed to roll up and put back in its sleeve; my workbench, still littered with the detritus of boat building; and a pile of old books. On top of the pile was *Coming down the Seine*, the adventures of an Irish poet who had rowed down the Seine in the early 1950s.

Still waiting for an answer, someone said, 'Alors?' somewhat sharply. The only inspiration I could see was the book.

'Je vais ramer sur la Seine!' I was hoping that the idea of rowing about on the Seine would be enough to make them all leave me alone so we could go back upstairs into the warm and finish the Champagne.

Unfortunately, they weren't satisfied at all. 'Is that it?! Just row on the Seine a couple of times?'

I tried to justify myself by saying that of course I wasn't going to just row up and down a couple of times. 'Mais, pas du tout!' I was going to do much, much more than that. Waving my arms theatrically, I declared that I was going to maintain the great British traditions of exploring foreign lands and, where possible, claiming them in the name of the Queen, by fearlessly travelling down the nearby reaches of the Seine.

'Just the nearby reaches?' scoffed Christine, one of our more forceful friends and the wife of Siggi. 'I can't see the Queen getting all that excited about a few local reaches. You should row the whole way down the river from one end to the other.'

'I couldn't possibly row a little boat like this the whole length of the Seine. It would take months and months, and I'd probably sink. And anyway,' I carried on, in the tone of one who had come up with the winning argument, 'why on earth should I?'

This question had the opposite effect to the one intended and provoked a barrage of further suggestions.

'To continue the British traditions of nautical exploration that you have just been boasting about,' said one.

'To get fit!' said another.

'To discover the real France . . . whatever that is,' someone else suggested.

To my surprise Inès spoke up in support of this last idea by pointing out that travelling the length of a sizeable river like the Seine would surely cover a fair part of France and would therefore lead me to discover all sorts of interesting places along the way that I would probably never otherwise visit.

This was starting to sound quite tempting. 'That's all very well,' I admitted, 'but I still can't travel the whole length of a major river in just a little rowing boat.'

'We really think you should do it. In fact, we all challenge you to do so. But not just in your boat,' Christine allowed. 'You can use any other craft that are available, but it's up to you to find them. And if you don't manage to travel the whole way by the end of the year, you have to treat us all to more Champagne – a lot more Champagne,' she concluded, draining her glass as she did so.

The more I thought about it, the more I realized it would be a sort of quest. I have always secretly fancied taking part in one – walking the pilgrim's way to Santiago de Compostela or driving a battered old 2CV to Kathmandu: that kind of thing. But, apart from the fact that a decent quest tends to be somewhat time-consuming, one of the reasons why I hadn't ever undertaken one is that you can't really challenge yourself to one; someone else really has to do it for you. And, up until then, that kind of challenge had just never seemed to come up. Now that it had, I was surprised to discover how much I had been hoping for one to come along. And this wasn't just any quest; it was a quest to discover France! I really liked the idea: it had a nice ring to it. I also reckoned that it would be a fair bit easier than driving to Kathmandu and a lot less tiring than walking all the way to Spain.

But, hang on a minute, quest or not: wasn't this all a bit one-sided? What happened if I managed to reach the sea? Shouldn't *they* have to do something?

'Mais, si j'y arrive, vous allez devoir faire quoi?' I asked, trying desperately to salvage something from the situation.

'If you succeed, we will come to England with you on a reciprocal quest. Ours will involve trying anything English that you want – you know, all those things you are always going on about: Marmite, cricket, English wine, going upstairs on a double-decker bus, drinking horrible warm beer . . . Whatever you like.'

Well, that sounded as though it could be fun.

So we shook on it: I never could resist a challenge.

2

So, whatever possessed me to set about building a rowing boat in the first place?

Boats always seem to have been associated with happy moments in my life: learning to row with one oar on the Thames just below Folly Bridge with my dad when six or seven; learning to sail on the Salcombe estuary on school trips; sailing my venerable and decidedly leaky British Moth dinghy on the Thames by Port Meadow, and much more. But a childhood affection for boats doesn't really explain my sudden desire to transform a draughty suburban garage into a boat yard.

I'm almost positive it wasn't the result of a midlife crisis, not least because I have never heard of one based upon a modest wooden rowing boat. Such crises seem to require the involvement of oriental showgirls or shiny red sports cars at the very least. In fact, what I think led me to spend long hours battling with pieces of wood was the arrival of my new boss. My job at that time was fairly specialized and had required a fair bit of long-term training. My new boss, Thérèse, on the other hand, had no knowledge of it whatsoever. None of my colleagues could work out how she had come to be given the job until someone mentioned in passing that she was a very good friend of a man considerably higher up in the company hierarchy. 'Ah! Cela explique tout!' – that explains everything.

Hard as it may be to believe, in France the chances of getting on in a company thanks to the intervention of one's friends appear somewhat higher than they do in England. A clue to this lies in the fact that French has not one but two words that relate specifically to this kind of thing. For a start there is *piston* or *pistonner*, a word which can't be directly translated but which has to be explained as 'having friends in high places' or 'string-pulling'. Apparently, the expression comes from the fact that it is the pistons that get the engine moving. A second term, *copinage*, covers pretty much the same concept. This comes from *copain*, a slang word for friend. *Copinage* thus describes the lucky situation where you obtain something that you probably wouldn't otherwise have got, thanks to your friends.

Thérèse was a tall, rather strident woman who always looked like she had dressed in the dark, using clothes picked at random from someone else's wardrobe. But the problem wasn't aesthetic. The friction, and there really was a lot of it, arose due to her complete inability to grasp even the basics of the job. In order to give an idea of what I went through, let's imagine for a moment that my job at that time was that of a bakery manager.

Every Monday-morning meeting, week in week out, would have included a conversation along the following lines.

Thérèse (in a mystified tone): 'Now, about all this white powder that you keep ordering: what is it called again?'

Me: 'Flour.'

Thérèse (more mystified than ever): 'Flour, eh? Why have you never mentioned it before? Now, why do you keep ordering it? It is not as though we sell flour . . . do we? We're a bakery. What on earth do you do with it all?'

After several months of such conversations, it was clear to me and my immediate family that I needed a pastime to occupy me and keep my mind off my job.

Around the time in question there had been a report on the TV about some people who had spent what appeared to be a very happy time indeed rebuilding a wooden sailing dinghy that looked just like *Swallow* from the *Swallows and Amazons* books. I reckoned that something like that wouldn't tax my DIY skills too much and, more importantly, would keep my mind off work.

I originally set out to look for a second-hand wooden rowing dinghy. But my search ended up on the website of a small firm in Cumbria that made wooden-boat kits. A few clicks later I found myself looking at a series of golden wooden boats floating on calm, sunlit water. And with that, I had found my new destiny: I would build boats, or possibly at least one boat, from a kit. Wasting no time, I grabbed the phone. A very kind chap asked me several carefully worded questions and then steered me tactfully towards a model which was apparently the easiest one for a novice to build. It sounded perfect. There didn't seem to be any point in hanging about after that – once you have found your new destiny you might as well get started on it right away – so, with a brief wave of my credit card, I ordered it.

A couple of weeks later, an enormous cardboard box was delivered to our door – fortunately not by Marcel our postman on his bike but by two hefty guys in a big lorry. For some inexplicable reason, the men decided to carry it straight into our sitting room, rather than down to the garage. The box was at least seven feet long and much too heavy to carry downstairs once the men had gone, so we thought we would open it just where they had left it and then carry all the parts down to the garage later. Much cutting of bindings and slitting of tape revealed the stark reality of a rowing boat in kit form: a vast number of strangely shaped wooden panels of all sizes – far more than I had imagined – several pots of epoxy glue, a set of oars, some nice brass fittings and, right at the bottom of the box, an instruction manual.

It was actually quite fun to have all the pieces laid out on the floor in a giant jigsaw puzzle which made the room smell of sawn wood. In fact, it was so pleasant that I ended up leaving it all there for several days before finally carrying everything down to the garage. Somehow, having bits of boat littered all over the sitting-room floor seemed quite normal because bringing boats into the house was something of a family tradition. When I was a teenager, my battered old sailing dinghy, *Gyro*, twice spent the entire winter in my parents' dining room while I sporadically scraped and repainted her. The fact that I still have one of their dining chairs with smears of scarlet marine paint on its legs suggests that I didn't go to that much trouble to protect their furniture before starting work. Oddly enough, I don't remember that my parents complained that much at the time about being deprived of their dining room for so long. Actually, thinking about this properly now for the first time, I reckon that a possible reason why they didn't grumble more was because it gave them a perfect excuse for not having anyone to supper for the entire time the boat was in there.

When I first looked through the instruction manual, I noticed that it gave guidelines for the time needed for each stage of the assembly process: assembling the panels – four hours, gluing the joints – three hours, and so on. I can now safely say that a team of professional boat builders working on their seventeenth kit could perhaps accomplish the tasks in the recommended time. But, for a complete novice, it became quickly clear that a more accurate idea of the time required could be had by keeping the manufacturer's figures but simply substituting 'weeks' for 'hours'.

As well as taking a lot longer than expected, the building process proved to be far more solitary than I had envisaged.

When I first started the kit I had vaguely assumed that family and friends would come and give me a hand now and again. In fact, no one really came down to the garage at all except on the rare occasions that I desperately shouted for help with holding something or with turning the boat over. I recently asked my family why they hadn't come down to the garage more often and was told that it was because they were all quite convinced I was happy doing it all by myself. So much for inter-family communication. Unfortunately, from this I assumed that they hadn't wanted to come downstairs for fear that they might somehow get in the way or disturb me. Wanting to know if this was so, I foolishly pressed for further details. That was when they spoiled it all by admitting that not only had they all been very happy indeed to be left in peace upstairs while I spent all my spare time downstairs, they had even taken turns to bring me cups of tea and slices of cake to make sure I didn't come back up too soon.

The only time that several people came to chat on the same day was when I took the half-assembled boat outside the garage and set about ironing it.

I had unexpectedly discovered at one crucial point in the assembly process that some of the planks weren't as bendy as I needed them to be. The only way I could think of to make them supple enough was to steam them. So Inès and I carried the boat outside and I spent the next hour or so wandering up and down the planks with our iron pumping out steam for all it was worth. The sight of an Englishman brandishing a steam iron over some pieces of wood caused several neighbours, as well as one unknown passer-by, to come and ask what on earth I was up to. They all ended up staying for a chat. That is very probably the day of the building period that I remember the most fondly.

Of course, there were times when assistance was readily offered and even more readily accepted. At a later stage in the assembly process I found that I needed to get all the planks of the hull lined up exactly in their proper places in order to be able to start glueing the whole thing together. But the planks just wouldn't go where I wanted. In desperation, I called my friend Siggi, who is a German DIY expert. Siggi turned up with several long, blue, belt-like straps. Once wrapped at strategic points around the boat, these allowed us to pull the planks into their proper places. Unfortunately, even when surrounded by straps, the planks still did their best to put up a fight. Trying to get the better of them revealed an interesting facet of international cooperation. While we were happily putting the straps into position and things were going well, Siggi and I chatted calmly, as we generally do, in French. But when things started getting a bit tricky – especially during a mad moment when we were both frantically pushing and pulling the various lengths of wood, heaving on the straps all the while – and fingers started to get painfully trapped under the tightening webbing, we each started shouting in our mother tongues: 'Pull! Quick! Push that bit there! Ow! Mind my fingers!' and 'Mensch! Ist der so ungeschickt, der hat ja wirklich zwei linke Hände!'*

Everyone reverts to their mother tongue when they count, pray or swear. In my experience one's own language is the only one which guarantees the release of built-up tension in a stressful situation, especially one in which your fingers are being squashed. On the other hand, it is not really the best means of communicating between two people of different nationalities. Not speaking any German, I had no idea what

---

* My God! He's so clumsy – you'd think he'd got two left hands.

Siggi was yelling about – although I could guess. But, whatever it was, we eventually managed to defeat the planks.

The final part of the assembly process was rather easier, involving endless sandpapering of the whole boat, making the rough planks smooth as proverbial silk, followed by the pleasing application of coat after coat of transparent epoxy and varnish.

Once finished, the boat looked pretty good. Of course, if you looked too closely you could spot the occasional clue that it had been built by an amateur. The wooden panels were held together with what the instruction manual referred to as 'fillets': lengths of epoxy resin glue. On the manufacturer's website are pictures of boats made in their own workshop. These boats have fillets that are straight and thin and almost unnoticeable. How on earth their boats stay in one piece with such miserly quantities of glue to hold them together is a mystery. The fillets I made had spread across the inside of the boat like runny toffee spilt on a stove. Beautiful, they were not, but at least they looked reassuringly strong.

The next logical step was to find out whether it actually floated. But where do you launch a home-made rowing boat for the first time? It was far too big for the bath and we don't know anyone with a swimming pool. As I wasn't sure it was actually going to float at all, it seemed a good idea to try and find somewhere relatively safe to launch it. Inès and I therefore spent most of the next two weekends driving about the *département* looking for a nice gentle stream or even a decent-sized duck pond that might fit the bill – but in vain. The lack of a launching site, added to the cold January weather, diminished my enthusiasm to such an extent that the boat languished in the garage for several weeks.

We had almost forgotten about it altogether when some

friends from England came to stay. When Polly and Mark discovered that there was an unlaunched, homemade rowing boat sitting in the garage, they insisted that we do something about it as soon as possible and preferably before they went back to England. Mark came up with the splendid idea of looking for a rowing club on the Seine, because any such club would have a slipway or a jetty that they might let us use if we asked nicely.

The next day was a Sunday, a day any rowing club should be open, but probably not too busy. So, with the boat sitting proudly on the roof rack of Polly and Mark's car, we set off to try the Port Marly rowing club. The club lies on a quiet stretch of the river which is sheltered by a long island. Rather than just turn up with the boat, we thought it might be a good idea to go and see what the people from the club thought about letting some non-members use their jetty for a launching ceremony. We came upon several fit-looking rowers in very professional-looking kit who were getting ready to set off in a couple of sculls. Our initial requests to use their facilities didn't meet with much enthusiasm. They looked decidedly sceptical and made it clear that we would just be getting in their way. 'But I built the boat with my own hands!' I cried, stretching out the hands in question to give weight to my argument. This got a far more positive reaction: two of them asked if they could come and see it. The sight of the boat gleaming in the sunshine on top of the car clearly improved our chances, but, before agreeing to anything, they asked whether we knew anything at all about rowing. It was obvious from the way they asked that they weren't so much concerned with our rowing skills as keen to ensure that they wouldn't have to come and rescue us if anything went wrong. 'Mais, lui, il est de Cambridge, et moi, je suis d'Oxford,' I replied, in the confident tones of one who was explaining everything. As trump cards go, the fact that Mark lived in Cambridge while I came from Oxford was clearly the perfect one to play with rowers from any nation. They had even heard of Le Boat Race, though we didn't go so far as to try and claim that either of us had actually rowed in it.

After some muttered discussion among the rowers, it began to look as though we were going to be allowed to launch the boat after all. Taking it off the roof rack, the four of us carried the boat proudly towards the long wooden jetty that lay along the bank of the river. By the time we got there, the rowers had clearly warned the other club members about 'les Anglais d'Oxford et de Cambridge'. A worrying number of them had come out of the clubhouse and had actually lined up along the bank to watch. I tried to ignore their distinct moment of collective scepticism when they got their first proper sight of the boat.

A traditional French launching ceremony is similar to a British one in that it involves whacking the boat on the bow with a bottle of Champagne and sending it sliding down a slipway. However, the words used are slightly different. The French person wielding the bottle has to ask God to 'Daignez par votre sainte main, Seigneur, bénir ce navire et tous ceux qu'il portera' – deign by your hand, Lord, to bless this ship and all who sail in it. Given that the French words for boat and ship – *bateau* and *navire* – are both masculine, there is no equivalent of the English habit of calling ships 'she'.

Traditionally, in the UK, it is the Queen who is called upon to name important ships; in France it often falls to the President's wife. *Le France* – France's greatest transatlantic liner – was launched in 1960 by Mme Yvonne de Gaulle. Her husband,

President Charles de Gaulle, accepted an invitation to speak after his wife, apparently because it would give him a unique opportunity to cry: 'Vive *le* France; vive *la* France!'

Unfortunately, in the excitement of setting off that morning we had forgotten all about the Champagne. As it turned out, this wasn't really a problem, because the club didn't actually have a slipway at all. So, rather than have any kind of formal launching ceremony, we ended up just carrying the boat onto the jetty and plonking it in the water. Once in the water, the boat just sat there, not doing much apart from bobbing about a bit, with everyone looking on in complete silence. The moment clearly called for some kind of guidance, so I cried 'Il flotte!' For float it clearly did. At this, Inès, Polly and Mark cheered, whereupon all the rowing club people started clapping enthusiastically too. 'Fluctuat nec mergitur!' cried one of the rowers. This is the motto of the city of Paris, which features on the city's shield under a picture of a boat. It roughly means 'It pitches up and down, but does not sink.' It was so appropriate that I really wished *I* had thought of saying it.

The boat had been in the water for almost a minute by then and, to my understandable relief, there were no signs of any leaks: my generous use of glue was clearly paying dividends. It was perhaps time to put my boat-building ability to the ultimate test by getting aboard for the first time. I tentatively slipped onto the thwart, slightly anxious that any mistakes I might have made were about to be brought spectacularly to light in front of a group of experts. Thankfully, while the boat settled a little in the water, there were no alarming creaks or groans from any of the planks and still no signs of any leaks. In fact, despite being relatively light, once it was in its element for the first time the boat felt reassuringly strong and sound. 'Alors, vous allez l'essayer?' another of the rowers inquired. Of course I was going to try it. I slipped the oars into their beautiful brass rowlocks, gave a proud salute and pulled away from the jetty. A photo was taken just as I rowed away. The boat looks wonderful, of course, with its gleaming wood and golden oars, but I especially like it because I have the happiest grin of any photo I have seen in recent years. I had built a boat, and it actually floated – who wouldn't have grinned?

3

So, having shown, to my considerable relief, that the boat floated, I could now sit back and start thinking about my quest.

At least I had picked a popular river to explore, because everyone knows the Seine. Of course they do: it is the river that flows through Paris. Anyone who has visited the Eiffel tower, the Louvre or Notre Dame will very probably have come into contact with the Seine at some point. Indeed, it is very hard for a conscientious tourist to fully discover Paris without crossing and recrossing the river several times a day. Its wandering course through the city and the adjoining counties is so well known, and so instantly recognizable, that the Parisian mass transit authority – the RATP – puts the meanders on its maps and even uses it as part of its logo.

While everyone knows that the Seine flows through Paris, it seems that people are less sure about where it comes from or where it goes afterwards. I can say this with a fair degree of confidence because part of my research for the quest involved giving French people a blank map of France and asking them to trace the course of the Seine. My simple request provoked a wide range of reactions: several of the people I asked went to pieces right from the outset and simply drew a vague squiggly line across the top half of the country. The left-hand end of their lines entered the sea in a huge range of locations anywhere from Bordeaux to Dieppe. It seems hard to explain inaccuracy on so spectacular a scale because the Seine, once it leaves Paris, is anything but inconspicuous. It is a couple of hundred metres wide: it is a big river. It is also very bendy so, whichever road you take going generally north-west away from the city, you are fairly sure of crossing it, or at least running beside it, at least once. Parisians love to drive out to Normandy at the weekends, and the main roads and motorway that lead you there all encounter the Seine on numerous occasions. Downstream of Paris, it's a river you can't really miss.

More logical candidates, faced with filling in their maps, started off by locating Paris. To do this, they stared hard at the map's outline and, after considerable reflection, put a tentative dot somewhere in the Ile de France region. The more assiduous ones tried to line up their thumbs with easily identified landmarks on the map to better judge the city's location. Having more or less successfully located the capital, they then drew a wiggly line out towards the Normandy coast. So far so good; but what about the bit before Paris? Where does the Seine actually come from? That seemed troublesome for everyone that I asked. I was offered Seines with their source in Dunkirk and others that doubled back and headed purposefully towards Orleans or even all the way down to Tours. Very few people indeed got it anywhere near right.

But, even if they didn't know exactly where it flows, most people can recall their first-ever sight of the Seine, something that very often seemed to have occurred during a fondly remembered family visit to Paris. I certainly remember the first time I saw it – it wasn't on a family visit, it was the day the barge crashed. I was eighteen and had spent the previous month doing the washing-up in the café of an Oxford motel in order to pay for my trip. I left my parents' house on a freezing January day with a rucksack, very little money and no warm clothes whatever to spend a week with some friends of theirs in Paris – Léah and Marcel – who I barely knew, but who I would like to thank now, somewhat belatedly, for having me.

The plane had landed in Orly, and I had managed to find the bus to Les Invalides in central Paris without too much trouble. Once there, I decided to walk all the way to Léah and Marcel's flat, which was in Argentine in western Paris, rather than catch the Métro. Setting off in the direction of the Champs-Elysées, I found myself a couple of hundred metres later on the Pont Alexandre III with one of the most beautiful views I had ever seen. The Seine, the Grand Palais, the top of the Eiffel tower, part of the Louvre and even the top of the Concorde obelisk; had it not been so cold I would have spent the whole afternoon just marvelling at it all. The river looked so wonderful that I decided to go down onto the quayside to walk some of the way towards Argentine. Wandering along the towpath, I was particularly captivated by some huge sand barges – vast, slab-sided, metal craft – that were sweeping round the bend towards the Eiffel tower, throwing up a huge wash behind them. I remember thinking that it must be hard to steer something so massive and unresponsive. Pausing to sit on a bench, watching the river and the various passing boats, I fell to wondering what it might be like if one of the big barges misjudged the bend and hit the quayside. I reckoned that it would probably make a size-able bang.

The captain of a barge which was heading steadily down the right-hand side of the river towards the Eiffel tower seemed suddenly, and for no apparent reason, to decide, just as he got level with my bench, to slow down and then swing over to the opposite bank, presumably to moor there. He swung the barge into a tight left-hand turn, but it quickly became apparent that he had underestimated either his speed or the width of the river. He thus found himself travelling more or less at right angles to the current, still at a modest speed, heading straight for the wall of the opposite quay. I could see him in his cabin, frantically spinning the wheel the other way, trying to turn back down the river. But he had left it too late.

Even though the barge was on the other side of the river, the crashing, clanging, wrenching noise as it smacked into the quay wall and scraped along it was surprisingly loud. Luckily, both the barge and the quayside appeared to be solidly built, so the barge just rebounded a short distance and then just carried on down the river. It didn't seem to have been damaged but did seem to be going a fair bit more cautiously than before.

The whole event was most unsettling: I had only been in the city for half an hour and already I had brought about a major shipping incident, seemingly just by thinking about it. This is not the sort of thing that anyone would reasonably want to repeat so, in the many years I have lived in and around Paris, I have been very careful never to envisage any other kind of boating accident, a practice that has happily ensured safety on the river to this day.

Incidentally, I don't remember much about Léah and Marcel's flat except for the fact that their loo-roll holder played a tune (that I could whistle for you now if asked) each time anyone pulled it.

The Seine might be a well-known river but, faced with the task of exploring it in its entirety, I could see that I needed some sort of a plan. My initial research was limited to the basic essentials. It is a long river, 776 kilometres – about 470 miles – long, far longer than any in the UK: it is over twice the length of the Severn or the Thames and twelve times that of the river Cherwell in which I learned to swim by being dangled in it on the end of a rope when somewhat younger. Further research showed that the source lies somewhere in Burgundy, a good three-hour drive to the south-east, while downstream of Paris the Seine eventually reaches the English Channel at Le Havre, two hours along the motorway to the north-west. The nearest point on the Seine lies just down the road, a mere four kilometres from our house. The only reassuring aspect I could find in the idea of attempting the trip was that if I got fed up about halfway along, at least I'd be only four kilometres from home.

A bit of background reading . . .

I spent a long while staring at the map. The first thing that struck me was how bendy the river was. Indeed, pretty much the whole length of the river from source to sea was one continuous series of bends. While you could argue that rowing down a dead-straight river might become a bit boring after a while, the presence of so many bends was going to make the river journey far, far longer than might be expected from just measuring the direct distance from the source to the sea. Clearly, I was going to have to spend a lot longer in boats than I had anticipated. My second observation was equally worrying: all the wonderful towns and places in France that I had never got around to visiting but which I one day hoped to do so – Carcassonne, Vézelay, Albi, Colmar, the Verdon gorge and others – were conspicuous by their absence along the Seine's route. With that I went to find my trusty Michelin Green Guide to France. This has a map of the whole country with all the three-star 'worth a journey' places highlighted in green. As far as I could see from the map, before and after the greater Paris region there was something of a shortage of cultural centres, crusader castles, snow-capped mountains or gastronomic paradises. Running my finger along the course of the Seine, there wasn't a single green name at all along the first third of the river with only a town called Troyes getting two stars, as it is apparently considered as 'worth a detour'. The Paris region was, unsurprisingly, rich in three-star attractions, but things tailed off sharply downstream of the capital. Following the river on the map down to the sea, only Rouen and somewhere called Jumièges were considered as meriting a trip in their own right.

What sort of places, I wondered, was my quest going to take me through?

The time spent staring at the map did at least seem to show that the river could be broken down into three distinct sections: from the source to Paris; the Paris area; and the stretch from Paris to the sea. And with that, I had a plan! I would do the journey in the three stages, using the rowing boat wherever possible and other means of transport, assuming that I found them, for the rest. Clearly, the stretch from the source towards Paris, the part that would most likely involve using the boat, couldn't really be done on my own. I was going to need help getting the boat in and out of the car. A bit of moral support would also probably be much appreciated. And someone to sort out any problems that might arise with the locals. In short, a supportive sort of person who speaks French like a native. 'How would you fancy a few days in Burgundy?' I asked Inès.

I have come to appreciate that it isn't always easy for a charming and well-brought-up French woman to endure married life with an Englishman. However, in Inès's well-honed search for a peaceful life, she has learned to put up with her husband's occasional moments of extreme Englishness, and indeed can often turn them to her advantage. On learning that her husband was planning to spend most of his free time for the foreseeable future travelling the length of a sizeable river, Inès's reaction was: 'Si ça lui rend heureux, pourquoi pas?' – if it makes him happy, why not? But, as I later discovered, she went on to think: 'Au moins, quand il a un but, il est généralement de meilleure humeur' – at least, when he has a goal in life, he is usually in a better mood.

4

I have made much of the fact that I am an Englishman living in France. Given this, what sort of welcome should I expect from the locals as I travelled along the river? Whatever sort it proved to be, it would probably be completely different if I came from any other country except England. The fact that I am English makes matters just that little bit more complicated because, unlike many other countries, the French and the English have plenty of things in common. What's more, these are things that they feel violently differently about. And having things in common complicates any relationship.

For a start, England and France have history in common; quite a lot of history in fact. Much of this history involves the vast number of battles, campaigns and century-long wars in which both countries have taken part. This is the sort of thing that, you might assume, would form a lasting bond between any two peoples. Unfortunately, up until 1815, pretty much all the battles in which they took part found the two countries not bonding on the same side but doing their best to wipe each other out from opposing ones.

The millennium that starts from the successful Norman invasion of 1066 has been filled with numerous examples of Anglo-French conflicts. Before the invasion, both countries were far too busy fighting off the Vikings to allow themselves the luxury of fighting each other. Then came the Crusades. Once they were over (and when, ironically enough, England was already ruled by the French) the two countries were at last free to get down to some decent cross-Channel fighting.

From the end of the Crusades to the defeat of Napoleon, there was never a century that didn't feature a good war, some of which lasted longer than others. The Hundred Years' War kept both countries busy from 1337 to 1453, though it did include the occasional period when no actual fighting took place, even though peace hadn't been officially declared either. In the seventeenth century the French took the Dutch side in the Anglo-Dutch War, then went on to make a bit of a habit of teaming up with whichever country was currently at war with England, notably in the War of Spanish Succession and the War of American Independence. Things came to a climax from 1792 to 1815, thanks to the efforts of Napoleon, in a series of battles into which the two parties managed to drag most of the rest of Europe and even Russia.

Since 1815, there have been wars in which France and England have found themselves in the unaccustomed position of participating shoulder to shoulder rather than face to face. These, obviously, were a question of necessity rather than choice: the two countries suddenly found themselves facing a common foe. However, becoming partners through obligation is not quite the same as one of the countries thinking: 'I am in a bit of a tricky spot here, what I really would like is to have the English/French on my flank: at a time like this, they are people who you can really rely on.' On the military front, therefore, they appear to be two countries separated by a common history, though, over the past 200 years or so, the temporary cessation of hostilities means that, at least, things shouldn't be getting any worse.

The two countries have some geography in common too. They both have marine boundaries along the same stretch of sea, although you wouldn't necessarily know it if you just heard them talking about it. For the French, it is *la Manche* – the sleeve – a rather dismissive word that sums up their indifference to the expanse of water in question. It is cold, grey, tidal, full of uninteresting ships and doesn't have that much in it that is worth eating. Why would they bother with it? There are warmer, bluer seas to the south where it is fun to go on holiday, or seas along the Atlantic coast with long beaches and waves where you can surf, or, best of all, seas from Normandy to Brittany with beaches that are stuffed full of free shellfish of all sorts. Those are the sort of seas that you can get excited about. But *la Manche*? If they had thought for a minute that it had any real virtues, the French would have laid claim to it long ago.

For the English, it is not the same at all: their Channel marks the principal starting point for foreign lands. Many English people are, of course, aware that other countries lie beyond the Atlantic or even across the North Sea, but they are just too far away, or in some cases far too foreign, to even think about. And, more importantly, you can't see them. France, on the other hand, is just over there; it is visible. If you stand on a hill by Dover and squint hard, you can see the clock tower in Calais. That is very exotic indeed.

When it comes to 'abroad', the French are spoilt for choice: they can travel in less than a day to any of seven foreign countries without even getting off the motorway. What's more, they don't have to wait for a clear day to stare across a stretch of sea and spot 'abroad', they can just stand at any of their frontiers and there it is, generally just the other side of a river. Indeed, I have seen my son, sitting on a brasserie terrace in France, throw sugar cubes across a stream to his sister, who had decided to go and drink her coffee in Spain. With all these easily available potential foreign destinations the French feel less of a need to cross an unwelcoming stretch of cold sea just to get to yet another country.

For the English, the fact that the Channel is the gateway to the rest of the world, coupled with the fact that it is just wide enough to be exciting, but not too wide that you can't see the other side, means that crossing it by any means available has always seemed a tempting prospect. Thus, a variety of English people have gone to great lengths to become the first to cross the Channel by all sorts of different means, while the only first crossing of note that was made by a French person was the flight by Blériot. It's telling that Blériot made the trip, not because he was desperate to visit England, but simply to win a sizeable cash prize which had been offered by a newspaper.

Apart from history and geography, what other common characteristics separate the French and English? The list of things I could deal with here is very long, but, as I have a river to explore, I will just pick one of the more obvious ones: queuing. It is said that the English love to queue. This is a good thing because they do it a lot and really have quite a talent for it. Indeed, as George Mikes pointed out, 'An Englishman, even if he is alone, forms an orderly queue of one.' As they like queuing so much, any arriving English person, finding himself faced with an existing line of people, will have no other thought but to join it at the back. There is thus very little queue-jumping in England. Conversely, it is often said that, for the French, to see a queue is to try and jump it. There may be some slight grain of truth in this allegation. For example, if the queue is at a cinema, theatre, sports ground, rock concert venue, public building, passport counter, bar, airline check-in counter, railway ticket office, supermarket check-out, income tax building, newspaper stand, the open doors of a Métro . . .

then any arriving French person will not hesitate to jump the queue. Indeed, not trying to jump the queue in such circumstances would very probably cause them real pain.

To this brief and restricted list must of course be added any sort of queue, however short or temporary, that involves any kind of motor vehicle. Such motorized queues have, quite understandably, to be jumped in the most aggressive of manners. That is the way of things. But those are just the exceptions. Providing you stay in your hotel room all day, you will hardly ever encounter queue jumping in France. Should you feel the need to venture outside, I can assure you that, apart from the examples already given, the French are capable of queuing in the most disciplined manner, often for long minutes and always in high good humour. Examples? You would like some examples? Nothing could be easier: the queues for a baker or any counter at a food market. Whenever there is good food at stake, French people will be happy to queue and, what's more, do it in a most disciplined manner. At the cheese counter of a market, for example, there is an atmosphere of peaceful anticipation. Those choosing their cheese take their time, ask to be shown various possible alternatives, hesitate, ask for more information and finally exchange a few words while hunting for their money. During all this time, those waiting never raise a hackle. All is calm. It is the same at a good baker: good bread and exquisite cakes are worth queuing for.

So, returning to my original question, as an Englishman exploring a French river, how should I expect to be received by the locals?

To answer this, we first need to know how easy it is, when I strike up a conversation with an unknown French person, for them to spot that I am English. If you imagine that the situation is reversed and you find yourself confronted with a stranger who, unbeknown to you, is French, how many words will have to be exchanged before you start to wonder whether perhaps the person is foreign? Depending on how well he speaks English, more or less time will pass before you decide that he has some kind of accent, with a bit more time being necessary for you to positively identify the accent in question as a French one. The fact that some of the words used may not quite fit the context may also provide valuable clues. In my case, even after all the years I have spent living and working here, it rarely takes more than ninety seconds before I get spotted for what I am. Of course, there are exceptions: if the encounter takes place in a blacksmith's forge, a night club in full swing or on the deck of a ship in a storm, the overwhelming noise will extend the detection period, though not indefinitely.

Geography can play a part here too. If the conversation takes places somewhere like Marseilles, where the locals have a very strong accent of their own, they will spot my accent but not see it for what it is. Very often they will assume not that I am English but that I come from *le nord* – somewhere in the vast reaches of France that lie generally to the north of them.

So, at best two minutes into a conversation with someone, whoever it is will be fairly sure that the stranger he is talking to is English. And then what? Will this influence the way the rest of the conversation goes? In my experience, hardly at all. Despite all that you read in the newspapers, there is very little animosity shown towards the English by the French. This doesn't mean that they don't occasionally drive me mad with their inane questions about all aspects of life in England, because they do. But in all the years spent in France, I can't think of an example of a single situation where things have degraded simply due to my nationality.

In fact, being English can get you out of trouble more often than it gets you into it. I was once supposed to take part in a sporting event for which the participants had been told to bring along a medical certificate showing that they were *apte* – healthy enough – to take part. I had the certificate but had somehow forgotten it at work. Once the organizer discovered I hadn't got it with me, a long period of increasingly desperate negotiation began. Things were going very badly, so I asked to speak to the chap's boss, a man who, to my surprise, was actually summoned. Having heard the facts, he also refused to let me in. In desperation I played the only card I had left. 'Mais . . . je suis anglais!' The moment they turned to look at each other, shoulders slumped and sighing theatrically, I knew it was going to be OK. 'Et, en plus, il est anglais,' the boss said to his acolyte. It was the 'Et en plus' – and to cap it all – bit that was the key. Here is this bloke who is so gormless that he turns up without the only thing that he had been told to bring at all costs, and then he goes and wastes ten minutes of our valuable time arguing about it. And now, to cap it all, he's told us he is English. English! If that doesn't take the biscuit. Thanks exclusively to my being *anglais* and thus not like other folk, I was allowed to take part.

Incidentally, I have been using the terms 'England' and 'English' here as a sort of shorthand for any or all of the people of the United Kingdom. Long and painful experience has shown that, while many French will admit to having heard of words like England, Great Britain and, in exceptional cases, the UK, they are not all that clear what they actually refer to. If you show them a map and actually manage to keep their attention long enough to get them to look at it, most are woefully incapable of finding any of the places on it. At best, they tend to just flap their hands over large areas of Western Europe, often as far up as Lapland, confident that, whatever it is they are being unfairly asked to point to, it must be around there somewhere. To see that this really is so, you just have to chat with a French person about their summer holiday in Scotland. When you show interest and press for more details, such as where exactly they have been, they will tell you, in all seriousness, that the Scotland they have just spent two weeks travelling round was somewhere in Wales. Ignorance on this scale may be wounding for the British, but if you tell the story to another French person, they won't find any aspect of it strange at all.

Of all the countries making up the UK, it is Scotland which is viewed the most favourably; where, for once, a long history has a positive effect. Back in 1295, Scotland and France were both finding the English rather tiresome – some things never change – so they decided to join forces. The two countries formalized their association by something that became known as the Auld Alliance. The formal effects of this lasted until the sixteenth century and are still seen in events like the Six Nations Rugby tournament, where the Scots enjoy a special treatment from French fans and media alike.

A final indication of how England is viewed lies in the fact that she is not always referred to by her proper name. If the person mentioning it is in a rare good mood, then they may well use the proper term – *l'Angleterre*. If, however, something has irritated them – anything to do with politics, economics, sport, food, the weather or even the holiday they spent there when a child is often reason enough – then the country of my birth will become *la Perfide Albion* – Perfidious Albion. England was originally known as 'Albion' by the Greeks and the Romans, possibly due to the white cliffs, but it was the French who felt they had to add a critical adjective. If questioned on the need for such an unflattering term, French people can come up with numerous examples of English perfidy over the centuries, many of which stand up to detailed examination. Indeed, hard as it may be to believe, the English have been quite embarrassingly perfidious on more than one occasion. Rather than give examples here, I shall trust to luck and hope that a suitable instance presents itself along the river.

Any Frenchman reading that last sentence would probably consider it a foregone conclusion.

It is time to find out if they are right.

Part 1:
The Source to Paris

5

Being only seven feet long, the boat is small enough and light enough to easily fit on a car roof rack, assuming we actually had one. Unfortunately, we don't. Luckily, rather than go out and find a suitable roof rack, I was able to borrow a brand-new people carrier from work. Careful measurement both of the boat and of the inside of the people carrier had seemed to show that one would just fit inside the other. When it was time to set off, the boat did just about fit in the back, but, in order to shut the rear door, I found I had to drive with the seat jammed so far forward that my chin stuck out well over the dashboard and the ignition key dug well into my leg.

A near-four-hour drive, round the Périphérique and down a long stretch of the A5 motorway, found us in the middle of nowhere with no water to be seen, not even a bucketful. Surely on any reasonable list of requirements when looking for a good spot to start a river trip that of at least a modest quantity of water must feature prominently? Perhaps not necessarily in first place, but definitely up there in the top three. (The other two requirements are, of course, a packet of plain chocolate digestive biscuits and a boat.) Unfortunately, the first few minutes that we spent wandering about the site of the source of the Seine failed to reveal any water at all.

If finding water at the source of a large river was proving difficult, finding the *site* of the source in the first place hadn't been that easy either. The source lies in Burgundy near the main road that heads south from the town of Châtillon-sur-Seine towards

Dijon. About thirty kilometres from Dijon is a sign that is both small and set back from the road. Most people travelling down the road very probably don't even notice it. It points to the D103 and reads simply 'Source de la Seine 2'. There is an 'i' to show that there is an information booth nearby as well as a rosette symbol to show that the site is considered to be a tourist attraction.

We almost missed it altogether. At a point that was as unremarkable as it was in the middle of nowhere we caught sight of a small sign that read simply 'Site des sources'. It didn't even say what the source was of, it just pointed away from the road through a small gate. There was no car park, just a vague strip of flattened earth beside the road, so we left the car there and walked over to the sign. Some steps led down from the gate towards an expanse of grass which was limited on one side by the road and on the other by an area of woodland. Two or three picnic tables were set out on the grass, but there was no water to be seen anywhere.

There didn't seem to be any other signs anywhere, so we just wandered vaguely around until we stumbled across the information booth that had been promised back on the main road. This proved to be something of a disappointment: it was nothing more than a plain garden shed. There was a notice board fixed to the shed wall, but it didn't actually have any notices on it. Closer examination of the shed door showed that it wasn't locked but was just held closed by a large lump of limestone that had been leaned against it. It seemed silly to have come all this way and not have a quick look inside, so I pushed the stone aside and opened the door. We were rewarded by the sight of a single, forlorn-looking plastic chair and two tourist posters showing some of the wonders that are to be found in Burgundy, none of which was the Seine. And that was all there was.

Undaunted by this lack of helpful information, we abandoned the booth and set off to find the source all by ourselves. There was a rough path near the shed which led away towards a small meadow. Once out on the grass we could just make out, from the occasional glint of water and the presence of a few reeds, that the centre stretch of the meadow was possibly a tiny bit damper than the rest of it. Away to our left was a small, hump-backed footbridge that seemed to span part of the damper stretch. The point of putting a bridge there seemed debatable: anyone who wanted to get to the other side of the meadow could just walk straight across, jumping easily over the squelchiest bits, without any need to make a wide detour to go over the bridge.

At the far end of the meadow to our right there was what appeared to be a cave. Getting closer, we could see that it was a cross between a Victorian folly and a grotto and that it housed a statue of a reclining female figure. Seen from close up, the

figure was remarkably attractive, lying on one elbow in the classic pose with a crown of lilies on her head and a bunch of grapes held in her right hand. For a simple, weathered limestone statue, she really was surprisingly pretty. And, more importantly, there was water. At last!

The statue's head was turned to look down into the small pool below her. At first glance the water appeared quite still but, after I had stood there for a while, I noticed that it occasionally bubbled fitfully like a defective Jacuzzi. This feeble bubbling was seemingly the source we had come all this way to see, for the statue was that of Sequana, the Roman goddess of the Seine.

Sequana's relationship with the Seine is explained by the fact that she was originally a water nymph, the daughter of Bacchus (which also explains the bunch of grapes the statue is shown holding). Being very beautiful, she caught the roving eye of Neptune, the sea god, who promptly decided to make off with her. Rather than accept Neptune's advances, Sequana promptly fled from her home in Italy. Pursued by Neptune, she travelled a huge distance and ended up in Burgundy, where, just as Neptune was about to grab her, she was saved from this terrible fate by being transformed into a river by Bacchus and his friend Ceres. From her name Sequana comes the modern-day name of the river, Seine.

First the Gauls and later the Romans believed that the source had curative properties. The Gauls threw coins in the spring and offered ex-votos to the original statue of Sequana, which is now in a museum in Dijon. Recent excavation revealed nearly a thousand of these engraved metal plates, many of which had images of the disease or ailment for which a cure was being sought. The more pragmatic Romans, rather than throw coins in the water, simply built baths nearby to make the best use of the water's healing properties.

The name Sequana originally derives from an earlier Celtic word, *squan*, which means snake-like or serpentine. This, given the astonishing numbers of bends that the map showed to be waiting for me downstream, seemed worryingly appropriate.

But where exactly is the source? Well it seems that it isn't really anywhere particular at all.

Most reference works just say that the source is on the Langres plateau. Pressing for more details usually reveals that the source is either in St-Germain-Source-Seine or, according to more recent works, in Source-Seine, which is apparently the new name for the *commune* in which the source is located. But Source-Seine hamlet, such as it is, lies a fair way up the road from the grotto with the statue, while the village of St-Germain-Source-Seine is further along from there. There doesn't seem to be a name just for the actual place where the source of a major river is located. Am I the only one to find this odd? Incidentally, the inhabitants of St-Germain-Source-Seine – who can't be all that numerous – rejoice in the name of *Séquanigerminois*.

Only two things about the source seem fairly certain: it lies, as every French schoolchild is expected to know, on the Plateau de Langres, and the source itself actually belongs to the Mairie de Paris. It seems that in the 1830s the city of Paris decided that, as the Seine flowed through their city, they really ought to own its source. Baron Haussmann – he who redesigned the shape of Paris under Napoleon – seems to have been the driving force behind the original idea. The actual sales contract was only signed much later – in 1864. While it is clear that Paris Municipal Council bought it, it is not clear who actually sold it to them, even less how much it went for. Having acquired the source, the city of Paris arranged for the grotto to be built and commissioned the statue. Strangely enough, now that the city of Paris owns the source, no one seems to know what they actually do with it. There is no mention of the city at the source, and I've never seen any reference to the source anywhere in Paris. I suppose there's not really that much you can do with a small pond of water a few hundred kilometres away apart, perhaps, from bottling some of it and selling it for an inflated price.

There wasn't a lot to do at the source, although this was possibly because we had gone there out of season. We had tried to follow the river – if you can call a squishy strand of meadow a river – downstream on foot but had been barred from doing so by a series of fences. The only thing left to investigate was the little footbridge. This, the very first bridge over the Seine, is called Le Pont Paul Lamarche in honour of the man who not only looked after the site for many years but was also the first person from the locality to reach the age of 100 – a *Séquanigerminois centenaire*, then. The bridge is shaped like a real stone bridge but, being only eighty centimetres or so high, looks more suited to a model village than to crossing a major river.

6

Things never seem to go the way you plan. Before setting off, I had somehow assumed that, at most a couple of kilometres downstream from its source, the Seine would be wide enough for me to row on and that the boat could be launched without too many problems. What's more, I had imagined that, once on the water, I would be free to row a few kilometres down-river before being picked up in the car at a prearranged spot by Inès in her role as support crew and then being whisked off for a reviving drink or a meal somewhere.

But it wasn't like that at all. From the source to Châtillon-sur-Seine a good fifty kilometres downstream, the river is hardly ever wide enough to launch a boat on, let alone row on at all. Even a small rowing boat like mine requires a width of water of over four metres because each oar is 2.1 metres long. I have to confess that I now know exactly how long the oars are because it says so on the labels. However much you enjoy row-ing, and however scenic the river, there comes a point where the activity starts to lose a little of its original spice and you find yourself in a mild state of boredom in which you will hap-pily read anything, absolutely anything there is to hand, even a label on an oar. If a few pleasant hours in a rowing boat lead to such an enthusiasm for reading matter, whatever must happen to round-the-world sailors after they have been at sea on their own for months? No wonder Ellen MacArthur ends up giving names to every bit of gear on her boat.

So, rather than a young river which I could explore in the

boat, what we followed down to Châtillon was more a large stream, fast-moving in places, sluggish in others. Along the faster stretches we often found the ruins of old mills. These had apparently been used right up until the 1950s for milling flour or for grinding seeds for Dijon mustard.

Even though it wasn't possible to row on the stretch of the river near the source, the first day wasn't completely wasted, because we did encounter a vastly superior breed of *lavoir*. In our village there is a carefully preserved *lavoir* – an old-fashioned outdoor laundry. It is a simple structure, just six square wooden pillars that support a tiled roof which shelters a washing area. Almost up until the Second World War the washing was done by the ladies of the village, who squatted down and dunked the clothes in the stream that even now flows down a channel in the middle of the floor. Our village *lavoir* is fairly unremarkable: it looks pretty much like those found almost anywhere in northern France.

The *lavoirs* in this part of Burgundy aren't like that at all: nearly every small village seems to boast a magnificent structure far too grand for just washing clothes in. The first one we saw near the source of the Seine was so impressive I thought it was a well-preserved Roman villa. It was in the centre of a small village with the improbable name of Billy-Lès-Chanceaux, where it dominates the centre square. Made of weathered, golden stone, it is a sizeable structure which has six classical-looking pillars that form an open front. The roof, covered in dark-red terracotta tiles, is supported by a complex array of oak beams. A low wall across the front of the *lavoir* has a short but formal flight of stairs leading down to a rectangular washing area. There are well-tended flower beds all around the walls and a splendid bronze statue of a swan stretching its wings set in the middle of the front. The building dates from

1854 and is fed by two streams, the Teuchey and the Savonneaux. It is perhaps a pity that the stream isn't called Savonneux and not Savonneaux, because *savonneux* means 'soapy'.

Not all *lavoirs* – I'm hoping I'm not trying your patience with this – are fed by streams: some are fed simply by rainwater that is collected by a broad, sloping roof. These, apparently, are known as 'impluvium' *lavoirs*. Less pleasant to use must have been 'tunnel' *lavoirs* that are set directly into a rock face above a stream.

Nearer the source is the hamlet of Courceau, which has the first *lavoir* watered by the Seine on its journey north. This is a proud boast that I am forced to make on its behalf, because no one in the village apparently thinks that this is important enough to deserve a mention. The Courceau residents, of whom there can't be all that many, given the size of their hamlet, are clearly fond enough of their *lavoir* to have just given it a thorough spring clean. The stones have had a good going-over with a sand-blaster, and the roof tiles are all brand-new.

The Courceau *lavoir* stands beside a bridge that has the first of an unknown number of small signs beside it. The sign was something that I was going to get to know all too well in the following months. It is a rectangular black metal plate with the words 'La Seine' in lower-case white letters. To the left of the words are three white wavy lines, one above the other, to represent flowing water. The fact that there are only three wavy lines is extremely annoying. If only they had put four I could have taken a nice photo of my hand on the sign, giving the impression that I had just traced the lines with my fingers dipped in paint. I tried several permutations of fingers and thumb, but, whichever way I did it, it just looked silly. For a while I even contemplated adding a fourth wavy line myself to make the picture work, but there wasn't really any room on the sign.

From Courceau we followed the river onwards towards Châtillon, vainly looking for a spot where we could launch the boat for the first time. But before getting to Châtillon, the road led us through the village of Nod-sur-Seine. I spent the time between spotting the first sign to Nod and actually getting to it speculating on possible names for its inhabitants. They turned out to be called *Bellenodiens* and not 'Noddies', as I had perhaps optimistically imagined.

Nod-sur-Seine, which lies about thirty kilometres from the source, is notable because of the events that took place there in 1944. In the summer of that year, there were not one but two *débarquements*, or Allied landings, in France. The first was obviously the Normandy landings in June 1944. But two months later, in August 1944, there was the *débarquement de Provence*, where a second allied invasion force landed from the Mediter-ranean with a view to forcing the Germans to fight on two fronts. The two armies advanced slowly through France and finally met up on 12 September 1944, in Nod. To mark the occa-sion there is a monument in the village centre which is flanked by a Willys Jeep and a US half-track of the type used at the time.

By the way, please don't make the same mistake I did – the name of the village is pronounced 'Noh', not 'Nod'.

A short distance from the monument, on what looked like a school sports field, we could see a crowd of people milling slowly about. I sniffed the air, then checked my watch: 11.30. 'Oh look! There's a *brocante* just over there. Do you think we have time for a quick look?' Inès sniffed the air suspiciously, checked *her* watch, gave me what can only be described as an old-fashioned look and agreed.

A *brocante* is a French jumble sale. They are essentially simi-lar to a car boot sale in the UK – though such things are almost unknown in France – but where the goods for sale are set out on lines of trestle tables rather than emerging from a car boot. Clearly, many of the things for sale will be typically French, notably books and magazines as well as sixties and seventies pop records featuring French artists that are very probably not everyone's cup of tea. While the records on offer may be best avoided, the *bandes dessinées* – cartoon books – are often a much better bet. You can often find well-cared-for examples of Tin-tin, Astérix or Lucky Luke books at knockdown prices. For the rest, however, the general jumble will be much the same as it is anywhere else.

So why my enthusiasm for going to wander round a *brocante* in an unfamiliar village, when there was nothing that we especially wanted? The clue to the answer lies in the smell of grilling meat that I had picked up on the wind: where there is a *brocante*, there is almost always a stall in a corner somewhere selling *merguez*. *Merguez* are long thin sausages that are best cooked on a grill. *Merguez*, coming originally from North Africa, are spicier than normal European sausages. Any self-respecting *brocante* will have a large grill set out over glowing coals, or, at a pinch, over a gas burner, with a shifty-looking chap in a bright T-shirt standing nearby, periodically turning over an array of sausages. At an adjacent table, an acolyte will be chopping baguettes into lengths and splitting them along one edge. Beside him there should be either a proper drinks cooler or, failing that, a plastic dustbin with cans of beer and soft drinks chilling in iced water. If it is a really sophisticated operation, there will be beer on tap and a chip fryer. Plastic tubes of ketchup and mustard should also be scattered about within easy reach.

Few things on earth, or, perhaps, few things that you can eat while standing in a French field with a jumble sale going on around you, can be better than a well-grilled *merguez* – you have to specify when ordering that you like them well-grilled – in a length of baguette washed down by a plastic glassful of gassy beer. Trust me: things really don't get much better than that. To make the whole experience perfect that day, I was lucky enough to get to the *merguez* stall just before the lunchtime rush really started.

7

And with the boat bone-dry in the back of the car, we found ourselves in Châtillon-sur-Seine, where we had booked a hotel for a few days. Despite being the largest place between Dijon and Troyes, Châtillon is little more than a small market town. Its most useful feature lies in its location, fifty kilometres from the source, which allowed us to make forays of discovery both upstream and downstream of the town.

As the Seine forms a whole third of the name of Châtillon-sur-Seine, one could be forgiven for assuming that it must feature prominently in the lives of the inhabitants. But we quickly realized that the locals hardly seem to be aware of the Seine at all. For a start, despite the fact that the river traverses the entire town centre, you can't really see it. For most of its length the Seine either is underground or flows through a gully which lies well below eye level. Even if you take the time to lean over the wall and look down into the gully, there is not much to see. The river here is only a few metres wide and about 15 centimetres deep. Judging the depth of the water is easy enough: all you have to do is look at the birds. Swans just lurch along, their webbed feet dragging up clouds of mud, while ducks manage to dabble on the bottom simply by stretching their necks. Despite being a good way from its source, the Seine is clearly still in its infancy here.

Walking beside a stretch of river that flows in a gully through the centre of the town, we came across a second statue of Sequana. However, if it hadn't had her name underneath we would never have realized who the statue was supposed to represent. Rather than the sylph-like reclining figure that graces the source, this one is just a simple bust. More importantly, it has clearly been sculpted by someone who had never actually seen the delightful Sequana, for he has given her most unflattering chubby cheeks. And, as though that wasn't insult enough, the sculptor has kitted her out in some kind of thick woolly cardigan. If this statue really is true to life, which I for one doubt most strongly, notably due to the fact that Sequana was transformed into a river at an early age, the only possible explanation is that river goddesses must age just like everyone else. Surely, if that's the case, it must take some of the fun out of being a deity?

Continuing our wander around Châtillon, we discovered that another reason why the Châtillonnais don't take much notice of the Seine is because it is upstaged by its local cousin.

When the locals talk about *their* river they aren't thinking of the Seine but of the Douix, a river that rises in the middle of the town. I had read the name in guidebooks but hadn't actually heard it pronounced. Unfortunately, my tentative attempts to pronounce the name were met with outright ridicule by the first local I tried it on.

Getting the name of the river wrong is just one of endless examples of how difficult it really is to learn a foreign language. Even now I have lived in France for over twenty years it is still distressing to discover how frequently I find myself faced with things that I don't understand or simply find myself doing wrongly. And it is generally the minor things that cause the most problems. At work I can generally manage to talk fairly easily about my job. But put me up against trivial things like names of fish or trees or even those of childhood diseases and I can still get them worryingly muddled up. Worse, even if I know the right word, I can still occasionally manage to wrest defeat from the arms of victory by pronouncing it wrongly. So it was with the Douix, which isn't pronounced like 'Twix' at all. It would seem that you are supposed to pronounce it 'Dou-y'. Well, who would have guessed?

The Seine would do well to take lessons from the Douix on how to become a decent-sized river in the minimum of time. The Douix may have heard of rivers that bubble limply out of the ground and then drizzle along for miles, but it clearly wants nothing to do with the idea. In the side of the hill at the edge of the town is a cliff face with a small cave formed at its base. A notice fixed to the rock at the mouth of the cave warns potential cavers that, if they plan on diving in the pond and swimming on to explore the inside of the cave – which apparently extends back some considerable distance – they must leave a team member on watch outside the cave. The notice is a typical French formal affair littered with official-sounding legal terms like *arrêté* and *abrogation* and makes references to articles of law such as L2212 of something called Le Code Général des Collectivités Territoriales, whatever that may be. It seems that, whatever it is, prospective cavers would be well advised to take heed of it.

Quoting L2212 on a sign like that is just another example of the French passion for formalizing things. You only have to look at the reserved seats in public transport such as the Métro to see that, as my old boss used to say, 'Il va sans le dire; mais il va beaucoup mieux en l'écrivant' – it goes without saying, but it goes even better if you write it down. But the sign you can see on the carriage wall does seem a little over the top: it lists those people who are entitled to claim the reserved seats and, what's more, it does it in strict order of priority. Someone has carefully established a hierarchy setting out which people are allowed to sit down, while others have to stay swaying in the aisles. According to the list, war wounded get first choice, while people who got their injuries at work have to wait their turn. Pregnant women come about halfway down the list, just before people with very small children, while elderly people of seventy-five or over, perhaps somewhat unfairly, bring up the rear. There aren't that many of the special seats in a Métro carriage, so you occasionally see two or more people from the list of categories who each want to sit in the same spot. To see who gets the seat, they first have to establish their respective positions on the list to the satisfaction of the others and then see who comes out the highest.

It is not uncommon to see a brief but surprisingly tense game of 'Métro whist', where two or three people contesting the same seat produce laminated cards from their wallets, play them and see who wins. An old man plays first: keen to sit down, he produces his 'elderly person who has difficulty standing' card and plays it confidently. His confidence is misplaced because a younger chap who is also contesting the seat promptly produces an 'injured at work' card, which, despite the age difference, easily beats the old man's opening bid. The younger chap smiles at the old fellow's misfortune, but, before he can claim the seat, a creased and faded card is flicked in front of his face. It is held by an even older man who has been standing in the background, ramrod straight, waiting his turn. He has played a military card that trumps almost anything. Knowing he has won the trick, the older man nods stiffly and sits down.

Oblivious to the nearby formal sign, the Douix bursts forth out of the cave with surprising, un-Seine-like enthusiasm. There is no drizzly stream but a large, clear pond in front of the cave from which a young river flows enthusiastically over rocks. Wagtails dart from one side of the pool to the other while ducks swim in and out of the cave. It is all decidedly picturesque. Fifty metres from the cave mouth the river is already ten metres wide and flowing purposefully. But, unfortunately, the Douix's enthusiasm and impetuosity don't last long. A mere hundred and twenty of my paces from the rock face, the Douix encounters the Seine. And that, for our friend the Douix, is that. The Seine, on the other hand, benefits considerably and leaves Châtillon a much deeper and broader river than when it arrived.

Having seen most of what Châtillon had to offer, we headed back to our hotel. This wasn't one of a modern, rather bland chain, but rather was one of those small, old-fashioned hotels that you find in quiet French towns. It had clearly been run by the same family for decades. Such hotels generally have somewhat staid names like L'Hôtel du Commerce, if they are near a market, or L'Hôtel de la Gare, if located opposite the railway station. Ours was in the centre of the town and was thus, somewhat unimaginatively, called L'Hôtel du Centre.

Sitting in our room, recovering from the first day of discovery, I was struck by how you could instantly be sure that the room you were in was in a small French hotel and nowhere else. A brief glance at the bed gave the first clue: there was a *polochon* – a bolster – instead of a pillow. This always strikes me as a cruel device which seems to have been devised with two main aims. The first is to give you a very stiff neck should you be foolish enough to try to sleep on it. How anyone is expected to drift comfortably off to sleep with their neck jammed at a forty-five-degree angle against a log wrapped in a pillowcase is beyond me. But if you set about unravelling the bolster from all its convoluted wrappings in the bottom sheet of the bed before chucking it triumphantly on the floor, you will discover its second function. This is to make you appreciate how difficult the job of a chambermaid really is. For, when you set out to remake the head of your bed and tidy up the length of unrolled sheet, you find that somehow, when you tuck it all back in, it doesn't look anywhere as neat as it did when the chambermaid did it. Happily, you can cheer yourself up by looking around the room for the special cupboard that should be there somewhere and which has a nice soft proper pillow waiting for you on the top shelf. Putting a proper pillow on the bed instantly makes you feel more comfortable, even though you know that you are going to spend the rest of your stay tripping over the accursed bolster that you have left lurking on the floor. Incidentally, a French pillow fight is called *une bataille de polochons*. A bolster takes a fair bit of wielding, but, in my thankfully limited experience of these things, once someone actually gets it swinging, it can cause a far more painful blow than a simple pillow.

Further clues to the Frenchness of the bedroom lay in the cream-coloured light switches that turned on with a feeble ping rather than a decent click, the cast iron radiator and the white, ridged bedspread. Of course, there were sheets and blankets, not a duvet, beneath the bedspread. The final clue lay in the windows: they were two-part windows that opened inwards. Each window part had its own white net curtain pulled sideways near the bottom by a frilly tie. There was also a complex rod and lever arrangement to creakily open and close the windows. The windows had to open inwards because, like almost all windows in France, they were fitted with shutters. The fact that the windows open that way means that a common UK window feature is almost unknown in France: the window sill. Most UK houses have window sills in most rooms. Window sills are brilliant things: they are the perfect storage places for knick-knacks, half-finished mugs of coffee, vases of flowers and domestic pets. Having shutters is all very well, but the absence of a window sill forces French people to find other, far less satisfactory places to put their various bits and pieces.

Oh yes, and, as we were in France, there was no question of the room containing a kettle, even less a decent selection of teabags.

Châtillon is famous for something called the Cratère de Vix. This is not a large circular hole in the ground, as I perhaps foolishly assumed, but a huge Bronze Age vase originally made in classical Greece. It was found in the tomb of a woman known as La Dame de Vix, and the tomb's contents now form the heart of the local museum. I was quite keen to have a look, but unfortunately the museum was closed for renovation. So we went to the local market instead.

At first sight, the market had nothing to distinguish it from any other that you can find throughout France. There were the usual fruit and vegetable stalls, as well as butchers selling various cuts of meat, including those incredibly neat joints that are all carefully tied up with immaculate white string. There were cheese sellers, ever ready to help you pick the sort of cheese you fancy and then help you to find the exact specimen that would be perfect for the moment you are planning on eating it. A little further along, a specialized stand offered olives, whether black, green, stuffed or spicy, as well as selections of *tapenade*, a savoury paste made from olives and capers and, occasionally, anchovies that is delicious when spread on fresh bread.

From all sides we could hear the stallholders' question: 'A qui le tour?' – who's next? – and their encouraging cries of 'Et, avec ceci . . . ?' – and what else would you like? – to urge customers into a further, unplanned purchase. But, in one corner, there was a very small stand that had a disproportionally large group standing round it. There didn't seem much being offered for sale, just four or five small prune-like objects on little dishes. Pushing closer revealed that they weren't prunes at all but truffles, and not just any truffles: these were truffles which had come all the way from Périgord in south-west France. Périgord is generally recognized as being the spiritual home of the truffle. Indeed, *truffes* are often referred to as being the black gold of Périgord, a reflection of their rarity and their astonishingly high price, which can occasionally touch 500 euros per kilo.

I first properly encountered truffles when staying with friends who are quite simply mad about them. More exactly, they are mad about any dish containing even the slightest trace of the things. In the course of our stay we were lucky enough to be presented with such wonders as *omelette aux truffes* – a creation which appeared to have been made from almost equal proportions of eggs and truffles – and *beurre aux truffes* – a bowl of speckled-looking butter that we were encouraged to spread extremely generously over plain boiled potatoes. It has to be said that the simple presence of a few slices of truffle transforms a plain omelette, and especially a plate of buttered boiled potatoes, into something from another culinary dimension. No wonder Brillat-Savarin, the eighteenth-century epicure, called them 'les diamants noirs de la cuisine' – cookery's black diamonds.

But where do truffles come from? In our friends' case, their truffles came from their next-door neighbour, a shrewd-looking chap in his fifties called Régis, a man with the air of one who can get the good things in life without having to try too hard. When I chatted to him over an *apéro* one evening, Régis explained that people used to use a trained pig to root out truffles (which, as you probably know, grow underground, generally near oak-tree roots). The disadvantages of using a pig are numerous: first, obviously, you have to have a pig and have somewhere to keep it when it isn't out truffling. Then you have to train it. This is the costly part of the operation in that you can only train it by feeding it your own, hard-won truffles in order for it to get such a taste for the things that it becomes keen to go out and dig up more. You also have to transport the pig to wherever you suspect that truffles might be found. Small family hatchbacks are not suitable for this, it would seem. Most importantly, in the unlikely event that you were to decide to go looking for truffles on someone else's land, and forget to inform them of this, it is hard to find a plausible alternative explanation if the landowner catches you wandering about under their oak trees with a trowel in your hand in the company of a busily snuffling pig.

Thus, people turned to truffle hounds – dogs trained to sniff out truffles. Dogs clearly don't suffer from most of these disadvantages. They can also do useful things like guarding your house or fetching your slippers when not out unearthing fungi. However, when I suggested that a large, loudly sniffing hound might be almost as conspicuous as a medium-sized pig, Régis smiled knowingly and produced Lascaux, his Yorkshire terrier, a tiny animal to which he referred as 'Mon York'. He also produced his voluminous, multi-pocketed jacket. Once he had put it on, Régis pretended to see someone coming, swept up Lascaux and plunged him in an instant into some inner recess of the jacket. 'Chien? Quel chien?' – dog? What dog? – he inquired with an innocent grin. As well as concealing a dog, the jacket could also accommodate a fair-sized trowel or two as well, of course, as any truffles that Lascaux might sniff out.

All this was explained in a fairly straightforward manner, despite the fact of my being not only English but also from *la région parisienne*, two factors which, taken collectively, might well justify a spot of harmless teasing by any countryman. So when Régis moved on to what he claimed was a third way of finding truffles, I instantly assumed that he had finally decided to indulge in a bit of 'mocking the bloke from Paris with the silly English accent'. 'On peut aussi utiliser des mouches,' he announced, a sly grin firmly in place. Use flies to find truffles? Come on! Do I look like I was born yesterday?

'Si, si,' Régis assured me, 'des mouches.'

We were well into our second *apéro* by then, and Régis had served them strong, so I initially got the wrong end of the stick. When he started enthusing about *mouches à la robe cuivrée* – copper-coloured flies – that like to lay their eggs in truffles, I somehow got the idea that Régis set out truffling with a box containing one or more carefully trained flies that, on being released, would zoom off dutifully and land on a spot just above a hidden truffle in an 'X marks the spot' sort of way. It took several deeply sceptical questions and another *apéro* to establish that it wasn't like that at all. In fact, Régis just likes to wander a potentially truffle-filled area with a long stick in his hand, sweeping it lightly through the leaves and undergrowth. If he disturbs a *mouche à la robe cuivrée* at any point, he pauses briefly to dig at the spot where it had been sitting and conjure up a truffle.

No flies on him, then.

8

Strolling down the main street of Gommeville, just down from Châtillon, leaves you with the impression that it is rather a sad village; many of the fine old stone houses which line the main road have been abandoned and left to rot. The houses have the potential to be wonderful; they have formal stone stairs leading up to the front door and coach arches that lead through into yards at the back. In this Gommeville is like increasingly large numbers of French rural villages. However, while the old houses in the centre of such villages are decaying, the villages themselves are not actually dying. Clearly, people are still not living in the old houses in the centre. So where are they? All is revealed when you get to the outskirts of such villages, for there, scattered about, are brand-new *pavillons* – modern, relatively characterless, new houses.

The *pavillons* are typically grouped together in *lotissements* – development estates – containing anything from three to a dozen new houses. Developers either buy the land and build the houses for resale or sell plots of land to people who want to *faire construire* – build their own houses. Of course, there is nothing wrong with building new houses: the problem lies in building them on the outskirts of a village. The centre of the village tends to become increasingly abandoned and loses its heart, while there seems to be no real sense of community in the spaced-apart, modern houses on the outskirts. And all because people don't want to do up old houses: they want to live in nice new clean ones.

We were passing through Gommeville as part of our exploration of the stretch of the river that leads on to Troyes, hoping above all to be able to launch the boat for its first proper voyage. Things were starting to look far more hopeful as, along this part, the Seine reaches over five metres wide for the first time. Unfortunately, it still doesn't go out of its way to welcome rowers. After Gommeville there are stretches which are more than broad enough to row about on but they are just that bit too shallow, or have rapids, or are obstructed by large rocks.

Thankfully, a kilometre or so further on we at last came to a bit of the river that seemed to have everything: the riverbank was near the road and the water was a good five metres wide and deep enough to row on. With a great sense of starting the adventure for real at last, we launched the boat for the first time on the trip.

As I slid it into the water I was suddenly struck by the fact that the boat didn't actually have a name. While I was building it I had considered all sorts of potential names, some nostalgic, some vaguely amusing and some, when things were going badly in the garage, far from flattering. In the end, I decided that the boat didn't really seem to need a name. It was just the boat. That's who it was: 'the boat'. In this, I resemble a dog owner who simply refers to their pet as 'the dog'. Indeed, when anyone who met it spoke about it in English, they seemed to refer to it in the same way I did. In most of my conversations with French people, however, it seemed to be known not as '*le* bateau' but more personally, and probably less flatteringly, as '*ton* bateau' – *your* boat.

Not only did the boat not have a proper name, I never got into the nautical habit of calling it 'she'. It was The Boat and the boat was It.

Once aboard, I rowed up and down in front of Inès to get the feel of things, because I hadn't actually taken it on the water since the day of the launching ceremony back in Port Marly. The boat handled brilliantly: it was nicely balanced, easy to row, accelerated rapidly and could turn on a sixpence with a mere flick of an oar. Under the seats were built-in buoyancy chambers that were closed with large screwed plugs. As well as providing buoyancy, you could unscrew the plugs and use the chambers for storing things. Prior to setting off I had stashed away some bottles of water and some digestive biscuits as well as a waterproof jacket and some sunscreen. With all that I reckoned that I was ready for anything the Seine could throw at me.

At last the warm-up period was over and it was time to set off in earnest. So, with many encouraging cries of 'Bon voyage!' from Inès, I took my first purposeful strokes towards the English Channel.

I didn't get far. Just around the first bend, all forward progress was interrupted by a herd of cows which were standing in the river having a drink. They were nice Charolais – or, as our friend Peter insists on calling them, Chevrolet – cows with kind, somewhat vacant faces. It was clear that none of them had encountered anything quite as exciting as an unexpected rowing boat before: their capacity for staring at me, while staying completely immobile, appeared limitless. I had (and, oddly enough, still have) no idea of how you say 'Come oop there!' or 'Get along now!' to a cow in French. I tried various things, increasingly loud, but to no avail. Not one of them moved; indeed none of them gave any sign of planning on moving that day. It was all a bit humiliating: I had no choice but to turn the boat around and head back to the car. But at least the boat had been in the water for the first time.

We travelled further along the river, but things were just as irritating. There were stretches of the river that were positively idyllic: wide enough and deep enough for a rowing boat to travel on comfortably and flowing gently past attractive fields and houses. Unfortunately, we couldn't reach them. Great swathes of the river were either fenced off with barbed wire or were so far from the road as to be inaccessible. Tracks leading down towards the distant river were closed off and had signs saying 'Baignade interdite' – no swimming. If swimming was forbidden, I dreaded to imagine how an uninvited boat launch would be viewed, though I suspected it would involve someone setting their dogs on us. I have never been driven off by dogs while carrying a small rowing boat but I can't imagine that it would be very dignified.

Thankfully, at several spots a bit further on towards Troyes, things got a lot better. We at last managed to find a series of launching sites that had everything a potential rower could possibly ask for: a shady place to park, easy access to the water and a good place downriver to get the boat out again afterwards. The only minor problem was that the access to such spots often seemed to involve going all the way down someone's drive or taking a path which ran close by their house. On such occasions, local residents, especially those who lived in the house that we were carrying the boat past, often came out to see what on earth we were up to.

Faced with locals who looked as though they were going to protest in some way at putative, uninvited boat launching, Inès came up with a simple but surprisingly effective ploy. She just said, 'Excusez-nous: mon mari est anglais' – do excuse us: my husband is English. This is a wonderful sentence. It conveys a very complex message in a very simple way. It calls for understanding and tolerance, but it is also hoping for a certain degree of pity, all while using a minimum of words. In just six words, Inès managed to express something that might otherwise have required at least forty-two: 'Yes, we look as though we are up to something suspicious, but we aren't really. It honestly isn't my fault. It's all my husband's idea: he's got it into his head that he wants to explore the river in a rowing boat. Mad, I agree, but what do you expect me to do?'

In most cases the person would regard her with deep sorrow and, in the tone of one sympathizing with a bereavement or other personal drama, would say something like: 'Ah, ma pauvre dame, ça ne doit pas être facile tous les jours' – you poor thing: that can't be easy every day. They didn't generally say anything to me at all, they would just back away a few steps, smiling sadly, shaking their heads a bit and doing that despondent sucking-air-through-the-teeth thing that often seems to accompany moments of sympathy or regret in France.

And what of the Seine itself? This whole stretch is easy to sum up: it is seven or eight metres wide, and flows slowly past banks set with shady trees and backed by fields of wheat, maize and barley. Rowing along this part of the river was perfectly pleasant but, at the same time, somewhat undemanding. In fact, at one point, things got so undemanding that I suddenly decided that we really had to go off and taste some cheese.

With that, we abandoned the river for the day and set off for Epoisses, a village that lies to the south-west of Châtillon-sur-Seine. The place is home to a fortified château and some very pretty houses, but what inspired us to go was the local cheese, a cheese that is famous throughout France. And it is famous for just one thing. Epoisses cheese is smelly. It is really, really very smelly. It is so smelly that it is apparently forbidden to take it on public transport anywhere in France. That's how smelly it is. It is easy to spot any cheese shop brave enough to stock it because they generally have two counters: one normal one which is open to the air and contains the usual selection of cheeses and one entirely separate counter for the Epoisses. This second counter more often resembles a bomb shelter crossed with a superior sort of fume cupboard. Tightly fitting, heavy glass lids generally feature strongly in its construction. There may well even be rubber gloves and masks for the staff, though I may have got that bit wrong. The cheese is sold in round wooden boxes that look deceptively like Camembert boxes. But do not fall into the trap: Epoisses and Camembert are *not* the same thing at all. In some cheese shops, the staff apparently have strict instructions to warn bystanders before they are allowed to even approach the Epoisses enclosure, let alone open it. Apparently, keener employees can go so far as to advise those of a fragile disposition to step outside the shop for a few minutes while an Epoisses purchaser is served. I have heard people claim that they have seen cheese shops being cleared in seconds at the mere mention of the name. Part of the reason Epoisses smells so strongly comes from the fact that it is a washed-rind cheese, where the partly finished cheese is rinsed in Marc de Bourgogne – the local strong alcohol which is distilled from grapes. It is then left to mature for some considerable time. When ready for eating, it is a reddish-orange colour. Napoleon, by the way, is reputed to have loved it.

Wanting to discover the cheese on its home territory, we drove to the village and asked at a bar where we might be able to taste some. The man behind the counter looked at his watch and said that if we wanted to do any tasting we should get to Berthaut's *fromagerie* as soon as possible, because they would be shutting. We raced around the corner into a pleasant square and discovered that we were too late: the *fromagerie* had just closed. Heading despondently back to the main street, we passed a butcher's which looked as though it had a cheese counter, so we went in and asked if he had any Epoisses. Unfortunately, he had just sold the last one. In reply to our howls of despair the butcher kindly pointed us towards the bar next door, saying that, as it was also a restaurant, they would surely have some cheese they could sell us.

They did! Not only did the barman sell us some, he also introduced us to the cook, who, while we were enjoying some much-needed beer, explained some of his favourite Epoisses-based recipes. The cook surprised us by claiming that, despite the ferociousness of the smell, the taste of the cheese when cooked was apparently far milder and more pleasant than might be expected.

An Epoisses recipe: pork fillets in Epoisses sauce

Ingredients

  2 pork fillets
  10 cl of dry white wine
  1 onion
  50 cl of fresh cream
  250 g Epoisses cheese

Preparation

Chop the onions finely, then fry in a casserole dish until golden brown. Add the pork fillets and brown them. Add the white wine and salt and pepper, cover then cook for twenty minutes. Cut the cheese into small pieces, taking any necessary olfactory precautions while you do so, mix in the cream then add to the pan. Stand well back. Serve once the sauce has fully melted.

But what exactly does Epoisses smell like? This is a hard question to answer. The best way to convey what the smell is like is to tell you about a cricket match. It was a house cricket match at school when I was about sixteen or so. The game was a desultory affair, in which nothing much happened for almost all of the time. Fielders in distant, undemanding positions such as mine had the choice between three principal activities: taking an active interest in the game; gazing at the dreaming spires, of which the sports field afforded fabulous views; or watching the punts on either side of the field as they eased down the Cherwell on their way to the Thames. Watching the punts, especially when they were being punted by attractive tourists, usually won hands down. So there I was on a sunny afternoon, my back to the distant pitch, staring at some very attractive passing tourists who were trying unsuccessfully not to bump into each other's punts. Engrossed in the punts and their comely occupants I was vaguely aware of a sudden increase of noise coming from the pitch behind me: my fellow players were clearly excited about something. Too apathetic to turn round I was shocked out of my reverie by the cricket ball, which struck me soundly on the back of my head.

The blow produced a number of simultaneous effects: regret at foolishly allowing myself to become a victim of such an assault; the unwelcome discovery that, at such times, you really do see stars, just like in the cartoons; a period of incoherent dizziness; and the partial loss of control of my limbs, which caused me to stagger drunkenly.

Getting your nose right up close and having a good sniff of top-quality Epoisses is exactly like that, except, I suppose, at least with the cheese you don't get a bruise on the back of your head.

Something remarkable happened the following morning as I was rowing tranquilly down the river several kilometres beyond Châtillon. Just before the village of Mussy-sur-Seine I crossed an invisible line and passed simultaneously, and, it must be said, without actually noticing it, both from the Côte d'Or *département* to that of Aube but also from the Burgundy region to that of Champagne-Ardenne.

Metropolitan France is made up of twenty-two *régions*, which in turn are made up of a total of ninety-six *départements*. The region of Burgundy, for example, is made up of four *départements*, namely Côte d'Or, where the source of the river was, Nièvre, Saône-et-Loire and Yonne. All these *départements* are named after the rivers that flow through them, something that is true of most French *départements*. The Var is an exception: there is a Var river, but it hasn't flowed through the county of the same name since 1860, when they moved the county boundary. That year, the Var lost a fair bit of its territory to Alpes-Maritimes, a new *département* which was created following the annexation of Nice by France. The river Var now spends most of its time in Alpes-Maritimes. And who can blame it? If I had the chance, I would too.

One clue that you have changed from one *département* to another comes from the fact that the local roads change their reference number, though, of course, you can't see that from the river. Minor 'D' roads – *départementales* – have a number given according to the local numbering system. Once a road crosses a boundary into another *département*, it still looks pretty much the same but thereafter it revels in a new number given to it by its new owners. Thus, the little road a short way to the west of the river which had been called the D953 in Côte d'Or suddenly becomes the D453 once it comes under the auspices of Aube. Even main roads sometimes do it: the N71, which had brought us back from Source-Seine, changes its skin and becomes the D671 as it enters Champagne-Ardenne. But it is still the same road. All this must drive GPS systems to distraction.

Despite the fact that we had crossed into the Champagne-Ardenne region of France it didn't occur to me for a minute that we would see any actual Champagne. The principal Champagne towns, Epernay and Reims, both lie a good 150 kilometres to the north of Mussy-sur-Seine. Had we had the time to go, that wouldn't have been a problem, because Epernay is worth at least a 150-kilometre drive from anywhere you care to choose. This is because the town is home to the most mouth-watering, intoxicating, though least imaginatively named avenue of any town in the world. The avenue in question is the Avenue de Champagne and it extends most of the way through the centre of Epernay. Along its length it is lined by a quite simply overwhelming series of Champagne houses. These buildings, many of which bring to mind magnificent châteaux set in fine, walled yards, can be seen and admired from the road as you drive past. They are all open to visitors and offer guided tours of the cellars backed up with wine-tasting sessions – though they do expect you to pay. One of these days I shall spend a week in Epernay – or possibly two – spending every day on the Avenue de Champagne, just drifting contentedly from Mercier to Pol Roger or from Moët et Chandon to Deutz and, with luck, back again. What more could anyone ask? By the way, can I just mention in passing that the French pronounce the 't' at the end of Moët? It really *isn't* '*Mo-ay* et Chandon'.

Reaching the village of Courteron came as something of a surprise because, not only did it appear noticeably more prosperous than the villages I had just passed through, there were several Champagne warehouses standing at intervals down the main road, and this despite it being so far away from the heart of the region. It seemed reasonable to assume that the prosperity of the village and the presence of the Champagne houses must, in some way, be connected. The houses bore the names of local producers rather than those of the famous ones of Epernay.

A short way downstream, in Gyé-sur-Seine, there was the same air of prosperity. There were also more Champagne houses, some of them near the river. Noticing this, I was struck by the idea that the ultimate way to taste Champagne must surely be to arrive by boat, moor beside the producer's buildings, taste the wine and row away with a case or two in the boat. Rowing under the influence of Champagne was something I was very keen to try. Unfortunately, travelling through the village revealed that none of the Champagne houses had anticipated my idea: they all conspicuously turn their backs on the river. We therefore had to resort to finding somewhere to taste Champagne in the car.

When it comes to choosing Champagne, the most important thing to do is read the small print on the label. If you look closely, you will generally spot, down near the producer's name, a couple of tiny capital letters. Typically, these will be RM, NM, RC or possibly CM. Deciphering these letters can tell you a lot about the Champagne, how it was produced and by whom.

For example, the letters RM on a label are generally accepted to indicate the best-quality Champagne because they stand for *Récoltant–Manipulateur*. The *récoltant* is the chap who actually harvests the grapes, while the *manipulateur* transforms the grapes into wine. In the case of an RM label it means that the wine has been produced by the same person as harvested the grapes in the first place. Champagne producers who use their own grapes to prepare their own wine are generally assumed to take the most trouble over it and generally adapt the vinification process to best suit the sort of grapes they produce. Then there is NM – *Négociant–Manipulateur*. The *négociant* buys in grapes from other vineyards, often in addition to the ones he produces himself, and then takes all the grapes and transforms them into Champagne using his own particular winemaking technique. NM is probably the most common of labels and is used by most of the big names, many of whom don't own enough vineyards themselves to make all the wine

they need and so have to buy in extra grapes from other growers. *Coopératives* – farming co-ops – are quite common in
France, whether in general agriculture or wine making. The
huge grain silos that you see scattered around rural France are
often owned by cereal cooperatives that gather together grain
from all the neighbouring farmers. In Champagne production
a CM – *Coopérative Manipulante* – brings together grapes harvested by a number of local vineyards and produces a blended
wine that is then sold by the co-op under its own label.

We drove slowly through Gyé-sur-Seine, looking at the various Champagne houses that flank the road, and ended up
picking a cellar more or less at random on the grounds that it
didn't seem too prosperous and expensive but just looked simple and friendly. Having selected it, we parked the car and
walked into the reception area. We were greeted by the proprietor but had barely started chatting to him before a large blue
coach drove into the yard outside and parked beside our car.
'Oh! Merde! Les Anglais!' cried the man at the sight of it. Looking at the coach again, I could see that the driver was indeed
sitting on the right-hand side. That the coach really was English was confirmed by the name of the travel company
emblazoned down the side. When we asked whether he was
expecting a visit, the man replied that an English choir which
was touring in the region had made an appointment for a wine
tasting. Unfortunately, he had completely forgotten that they
were coming that day and he had failed to warn his son to be
there. His son was the only person in the family who spoke
English well enough to do a proper guided tour.

At that moment, the door opened and the members of

the choir started streaming in. There were about twenty of them, all wearing identical blue sweatshirts with the name of their choir stencilled across the front. The proprietor rushed to greet them and could be heard asking in fairly halting English whether any member of the choir could speak French well enough to help out with a tour of the cellars. It was clear from the way his shoulders slumped that there wasn't. I wandered over and tentatively suggested that if we could come and see the cellars too, I would happily translate whatever he had to say, provided that he kept his sentences nice and short. The proprietor, who declared himself, somewhat improbably, to be called Monsieur Joséphine, was delighted at this, as was the choir master, a pleasant-looking chap with a remarkable resemblance to Elton John, though without the diamond earring. As soon as everyone was ready, Monsieur Joséphine led us all through a heavy wooden door down into a large cellar.

The tour was fascinating, although I did end up feeling that I had done it twice: once in French and once in English. At several points in the visit, Monsieur Joséphine would gather everyone round him and explain in French what he wanted us to look at. Once he had finished his explanation, I would do my best to repeat what he had just said in English. Luckily, he had taken note of my request that he keep his sentences nice and short.

The only time I got badly out of my depth was when he started talking about the way you clear the sediment out of the bottle at the end of the fermentation process. The first problem was the word he used, which I heard as *égorger*. *Egorger* means to slit someone's throat, a term which, even to someone who isn't a Champagne specialist, didn't seem to fit with the rest of what he was saying. In fact he had actually said *dégorger*, which is the proper term for removing the sediment from the bottles.*

Even once I had realized what Monsieur Joséphine was really talking about, things remained a little confused. The sediment-removal process seemed to involve turning the bottles upside down, freezing the necks by some means or other and then shooting out a plug of sediment. Monsieur Joséphine got a bit carried away when describing this bit and forgot all about the need for short, simple sentences. Things thus ended up getting a bit hazy. He may well have been describing how they used to do it in the old days and explaining that nowadays they do it by some other means: I really couldn't tell you. And I certainly couldn't tell the choir either, though I did manage to tell them something or other. Thankfully, no one seemed to notice that I had made that whole bit up.

Having finished the tour, we emerged back into the reception room, whereupon Monsieur Joséphine asked if everyone would like to taste some of his produce. To no one's surprise, everyone accepted enthusiastically. He produced a selection of bottles from a fridge under the counter and set about pouring small quantities into twenty glasses. As the tasting session went on it became clear that Monsieur Joséphine's strategy was

---

* In my defence, even French people occasionally get confused by the word *dégorger*, a word which also applies to the act of soaking snails prior to cooking them. My sister-in-law Nathalie, upon hearing that someone was planning on getting some snails ready for the pot, also heard the word as *égorger* and became very upset at the idea of the poor snails having their throats cut. Soaking is in fact carried out by covering the snails – which have been kept without food for at least five days – in salt. The salt causes the snails to *baver*, a word which usually means 'drool'. Once all the liquid has been drawn off, the snails are washed and then cooked. Watery vegetables such as aubergines and courgettes can also be *dégorgés*.

based on the principle of the more you order, the more you get to taste. As the choir was busy ordering cases of the stuff, the quantities poured into the various glasses increased fairly rapidly, as did the quality being offered.

The only slightly frustrating aspect of the tasting session was that, what with all the translating and explaining that I was still doing, I didn't get a chance to try out my recently acquired wine vocabulary on him. One evening a month the twenty members of my firm's *club d'oenologie* – wine club – and I gather round a long table set out with three glasses per person, wicker baskets filled with chunks of *baguette*, plates of bits of Emmenthal and Comté cheese to nibble with the bread, some bottles of mineral water (for rinsing your glasses, or even, in some rare cases, actually drinking) and a number of red plastic washing-up bowls. The bowls are for emptying the remains of your wine into, but also for spitting in. The most important lesson, and one which I first learned just fractionally too late on my first evening, is that, when it comes to clearing up at the end, it is imperative to seize the cheese plates and make off with them, rather than find yourself stuck with any of the unspeakably revolting red bowls.

Each month an expert will present wines from a given region, usually giving us six or seven different ones to taste. Once everyone has their sample of wine, the sniffing and tasting can begin, whereupon some astonishing vocabulary starts to flow. The experienced club members see colours, find smells and spot tastes that I never previously would have imagined. They describe wines to each other using terms like *droit* – straight, *anguleux* – bendy, and *aérien* – airy, none of which, at first sight, seem to apply to wines, though the members do seem to know what they mean. One handy phrase which can be used to great effect when you can't think of anything else to say, is: 'Il n'est pas à exclure' – it shouldn't be dismissed or discounted. This works particularly well if you say it knowledgeably, nodding your head slightly with just the hint of a frown. If you get the tone and the frown just right you can be sure that at least two other people will start nodding and frowning too and repeating 'Oui, il n'est pas à exclure'. It has got me out of many a tight oenological spot.

I generally start off writing my tasting notes in careful French, doing my best to use the language of the experts – 'Belle attaque; fruits confits' – but, doubtless due to the fact that I swallow more and spit less than perhaps I should, around the seventh glass my notes end up descending into scrawled, occasionally incoherent English – 'Stingy and horrid . . . bloody amazing . . . buy . . . must some of this cos it's so . . .'

When at last everyone seemed to have finished tasting and ordering, Monsieur and Madame Joséphine put away the bottles and calmly set about washing up all the glasses. The choir seemed to have other plans. 'We really should thank them for the visit,' said a blonde woman who was clearly the head singer. 'It would be kind,' agreed another. Their thank-you certainly took the Joséphines by surprise. There they were, chatting together quietly behind the counter, drying up the glasses and putting them away when, in response to a brief command from the choir master, twenty singers launched, in perfect unison, into an *a capella* version of 'Let's Do It, Let's Fall in Love'.

When they had finished singing it seemed that someone really ought to clap, so, with the spontaneous support of the coach driver, we did so. After a few seconds, the Joséphines managed to shake themselves out of their bemused state and joined in the applause politely, though somewhat hesitantly, clearly unsure how best to react. They seemed not to have understood that the singing had been intended as a thank-you but rather to have assumed that it was the exuberance of a choir who had just drunk rather too much Champagne.

Once the choir was safely back on their coach, everything ended on a very positive note, because Monsieur Joséphine came over to our car to give me a bottle of Champagne 'pour la traduction' – for the translation.

Incidentally, you may well be imagining that one of the few advantages of being a married couple called Joséphine is that they could amuse each other throughout their entire married life by saying: 'Not tonight, Joséphine,' or, possibly, on happier occasions: 'Tonight's the night, Joséphine!' Unfortunately, while the expression in question is very common in the UK, it is quite unknown in France. Perhaps I should have told the poor Joséphines what they were missing.

9

Where the Seine passes through the villages between Châtillon and Troyes it tends to go past the backs of the houses rather than the fronts. But while the river constantly passes people's houses, or delimits the ends of their gardens, none of the residents appears to make much use of it. From the source almost to Troyes I didn't see a single other boat on the water. Occasionally, houses had steps leading down from a yard or garden to the river, but they seemed to be there just for collecting water rather than letting someone get in or out of a boat. Because none of the locals seem to travel on the river there appears to be very little expectation on the part of residents of seeing anyone else actually do so. What's more, there are very rarely walls or fences to preserve people's privacy: clearly, if you have a view of a river, you want to make the most of it. Travelling through a village on a boat thus provides a rolling view of yards, gardens and vegetable patches and also gives unexpected insights into people's lives.

The main thing about rowing a small boat with the current is that it is a fairly quiet way of travelling. If you actually stop rowing altogether to give yourself time to gaze at the view, you drift along making no noise whatsoever. Travelling silently like that means that, from the point of view of the local residents whose houses you are drifting past, you appear completely out of the blue and burst briefly, and unexpectedly, into their lives. Small children playing outside on a sunny afternoon would stop at the sight of the boat and run to the end of their garden to wave and call out a friendly 'Bonjour'. Women hanging out washing stood and stared, the clothes caught midway to the line. In one village I was treated to the sight of a man peeing on his compost heap – doubtless to improve the mix rather than due to a lack of inside amenities – and memorably surprised a couple of sunbathers. Later on, I interrupted a quite heated argument about whose turn it was to mow the lawn (his, obviously, because she had done it last Friday), witnessed parental goalscoring celebrations and distracted a couple of artists from their easels. In every case it was the same: I would appear, be noticed, provoke some kind of reaction and drift out of view, all in a few, brief seconds. It was surprisingly entertaining: hopefully many of them are still talking about me now.

The only aspect of this part of the trip that fell short of expectations was the question of passengers. The boat is quite small, and, on the occasions where Inès travelled some of the way with me, we found it a bit cramped, even though we know each other quite well. Despite the lack of space I had somehow assumed that the opportunity might arise to pick up a passenger at some point. I thought, for example, I might be called upon by an old countryman to ferry him across the river and then be thanked with an invitation to taste his homemade Marc de Bourgogne in his charming old cottage. But, assuming such a chap still exists, he wasn't trying to get across the river when I was rowing past his cottage.

In short, the Seine was hardly more stimulating along this stretch than it had been some way further up, when the lack of excitement had made us dash off and taste some cheese. It wasn't that the river was in any way unpleasant; it was just a bit 'same old, same old'. So much so that, when, the next morning, we came to a village called Bellevue and spotted a sign to somewhere called Essoyes, which was apparently the birthplace and home of Auguste Renoir, we instantly turned our back on the river and set off to have a look.

The road to Essoyes took us up a hill through woods and then out into a series of vineyards. It was months too early for grapes, but in each field we passed there were men at work. They all had overalls and gloves on and carried tanks of liquid on their backs and could be seen, bent over, progressing steadily along the lines of vines. One man was quite near the road, so we stopped the car, and I went to ask him what they were doing. Late April is the time of year when all the pruning is finished and the first new shoots are starting to appear. The man said that they were doing *sulfitage*, which apparently involves spraying the shoots with a sulphur-based pesticide from the tank on his back. From the way he spoke about it, he seemed somewhat less than proud about what he was doing. When I pressed him he said that other, more eco-friendly vineyards frown on what they consider as a too-generous use of pesticides, which they believe do nothing for the soil, even less the local flora and fauna.

Further along the road we spotted our first *cadole*. This is a traditional vineyard worker's hut built out of stones. It looks more like a dry-stone igloo than a typical rectangular hut and has a simple doorway, a tapering conical roof and no windows. It isn't clear whether *cadoles* were used just as a handy place for a worker to shelter from the elements and eat his sandwiches or whether he – singular, for there doesn't seem to be enough room for two – actually had to spend the night there. Most *cadoles* seem to be walking distance from a village, so it seems likely that whoever used them went home to a proper bed for the night. *Cadoles* are one of the icons of this part of the Champagne region and tend to appear on a broad selection of postcards and posters. You can even spot miniature ones in public squares or, occasionally, in people's gardens. What people do with the ones in their gardens isn't clear. The only thing I can come up with is that they could make a useful home for a pet, provided that it wasn't too claustrophobic.

There is no doubt that Essoyes was Renoir's home because the first thing you see when you drive into the village is a huge canvas stretched across the wall of a house and bearing the image of one of his paintings of a mother and her baby. Canvases of varying sizes appear throughout the village, each showing one of his major works. There are also easels dotted about the place with pictures or information about the great man. We thought we would look for his house – unsurprisingly, in Rue Auguste Renoir – but it is just an ordinary-looking nineteenth-century house with no outward sign that he had lived there. There is no equivalent in France of the standard blue plaque used in the UK to mark the homes of eminent people. The family that now lives there appears to want nothing to do with the previous owner, and our cheery 'Bonjour' went unanswered. Round the corner from the house was the Atelier Renoir: this looked much more promising. Unfortunately, like the museum in Châtillon, it was shut for renovation.

The area near Renoir's house is sadly run down: there are several houses that are empty and clearly abandoned, and at least two with smashed windows. There is a single, lonely *boulangerie* and a sad-looking church. Renoir would very probably be keen to move if he saw the place now. But when we went in search of a café we found ourselves in a completely different, and far more attractive, part of the village. This is centred round a market place, with some shops, a café and, would you believe it, another river, this one called the Ource. There was no question of putting the boat in the water, though, because the Ource was infested with sharp-looking rocks and was also very fast-flowing. Much more importantly, there was a group of fishermen upstream of us who spent their whole time spitting in it in the most disgusting way.

The name of the river – Ource – sounds like the word for bear – *ours*. Sitting a few minutes later on the café terrace overlooking the river, we amused ourselves for quite a while just by making silly jokes based on a famous French saying, 'l'homme qui a vu l'homme qui a vu l'ours'. This literally means: 'the man who saw the man who saw the bear'. It generally applies to a story or a situation which is described by someone who wasn't actually there at the time but who is trying to make him- or herself look important through some sort of reflected glory, though it isn't really justified by the true facts.

The café proved to have an unusually confusing loo. This came to light when I found myself standing in front of a wash basin, soapy-handed, looking for a source of water to rinse it off. The basin was clearly a basin – I can generally be relied upon to recognize a basin because I have seen one or two in my time and, frankly, there's not that much variation possible when it comes to such things. There was also a neck of a tap sticking out in a potentially useful way, but where was the tap part? How were you supposed to turn the water on? A long stare at the neck revealed that there were no mechanical taps of any description. There was just the basin and a spout; nothing more. As many regions of France have at last reached the twenty-first century when it comes to plumbing, I waved my hands under the spout, thinking that there might be some kind of proximity sensor. Nothing happened. I even bent over to look underneath the tap in case there was a sensor that had bust, but there didn't seem to be anything. Showing surprising lucidity for one with soapy hands, I then had a look at the floor, wondering whether there might be one of those foot-operated, squishy buttons like you get in the loos of TGVs. Other than relatively clean, grey tiles, there didn't seem to be anything on the floor at all. However, while staring downwards, soapy hands in the air and a frustrated frown on my face, I noticed there appeared to be some kind of stick-like thing pointing out from under the basin at about the level of my knees. I poked at it tentatively for no real reason, and, to my surprise, the stick thing moved sideways, whereupon water sprayed from the tap. A knee-operated tap! What will they think of next? In fact, it is actually a pretty clever idea because people's knees are usually a fair bit less grubby than the rest of them and, what's more, are generally protected from bugs by their clothes. There is thus much less of a health risk than you get with manual taps, which have usually just been grasped by someone with considerably dirtier hands than you.

Back on the river that afternoon I realized a childhood ambition at long last. When I was about twelve I read a book called *The Islanders*, which described how three boys were let loose on a country estate in Devon, where they spent the entire summer holidays having incredible adventures. At one point in the story, one of the boys wants to find something that has fallen into the river. After thinking about it for a bit, he finds a length of pipe, sticks it in the water and peers down it into the depths of the river. Looking down the pipe, he can see the bottom of the river without being dazzled by the reflections on the surface. He was so pleased with his idea that he called it a 'Seethebottom o'scope'. The previous evening, I had spotted a short length of plastic drainpipe that someone had dumped by their dustbin. Dashing to grab it, I waved it triumphantly above my head, crying, 'This will make a perfect "Seethebottom o'scope" for tomorrow!' to Inès's understandable alarm. In response to her questions I launched into a detailed explanation of the plot of *The Islanders*. 'Oh!' cried Inès, interrupting me before I could get to the really interesting bit. 'Another one of your beloved *Swallows and Amazons* books. Why do English children only ever read books about rivers?'

According to Inès, while English literature is crammed with books that are at least partially centred on rivers or lakes – *Swallows and Amazons*, *Three Men in a Boat* and *The Wind in the Willows* to name but three – French children seem to grow up reading about other things altogether. On our walk back from the restaurant, Inès failed to come up with any French children's book that included a river or a lake as a key feature of its plot. Since then, I have tried asking loads of French people the same question, but no one seems to be able to think of a single one.

This difference in childhood reading matter seems to be the result of one of the fundamental differences between France and England. England is essentially an urban society. Ask all your friends where their grandparents lived and very probably most of them will say that they lived in cities or towns. Relatively few of them will have grandparents who lived in a rural environment. This may well explain why children's books are often based on some kind of escape from the city to the country. This, coupled with the fact that Britain is a country with a strong naval tradition, appears to explain the number of water-centred books that are read there.

France, on the other hand, is a country with a much stronger rural character, probably due to the fact that there is an awful lot of rural France spread about the place. This means that, if you ask French people where *their* grandparents lived, many of them will say that they lived somewhere rural. Feeling closer to their rural roots like that means that French kids feel less of a need for some kind of rural escapism in the books they read. Thus, if the plots aren't centred somewhere rural, there is less likelihood of rivers and lakes figuring in them.

I had a fair bit of fun with my 'Seethebottom o'scope'. Having rowed out into the middle of the river, I shipped the oars, stuck the pipe over the side and looked down it. The water was so clear that without the reflections on the surface I could see right to the bottom of the river.

Unsurprisingly, the thing I saw most of was water weed – long lengths of green weed swaying idly in the current. But there were also fish, quite a lot of them, though not particularly big ones. Nevertheless, watching any sort of fish through a plastic pipe is vastly more entertaining, even though you can't see them nearly so well, than it would be watching them in an aquarium. What's more, the pleasure of seeing them was in no way diminished by the fact that I had no idea what sort of fish they actually were. They were fish, and I could see them, while other people couldn't: that in itself was satisfaction enough.

10

Arriving by water at Bar-sur-Seine, the first small town on the river in the forty or so rural and winding kilometres since Châtillon, is somewhat alarming, because the first thing you see is a huge ruin of a mill. From a distance, the mill seems to straddle the river most impressively. Once you get a bit closer, you realize that great sections of its walls have fallen down, revealing most of its inner wooden structure. It looked so precarious that I stayed well away in case it chose that precise moment to finally collapse into the river. If you ever see it from a small boat you will understand how I felt.

Apart from its intimidating mill ruin, Bar-sur-Seine seemed a good place to stop for lunch. The town is essentially made up of one very long street that runs parallel to the river. This leads you into the town centre, where there is a square where we spotted some promising-looking tables set out under an awning. These turned out to be part of a restaurant which stands on the other side of the road to the square. Thanks to this arrangement, lunch there proved to be more entertaining than usual because we spent most of it watching the waitresses racing backwards and forwards with trays held high, desperately dodging in and out of the passing traffic.

On one of her dashes across the road, our waitress brought us a jug of water. This she referred to, not as a *carafe* or a *broc*, both of which are common 'jug' words, but as a *cruche*. All three words refer roughly to the same sort of water carrier but noticing her choice of words made me realize that a surprising number of French words for things that hold water can also be unflattering slang descriptions for women. As well as being a jug or a pitcher, *cruche* can describe someone who you think is a bit gormless or idiotic. A friend whose pretty wife is not known for her outstanding intelligence was given a splendid antique jug for his birthday. 'Oh!' he exclaimed. 'Quelle belle cruche!' Whereupon one of the guests cheekily observed 'Maintenant, tu en as deux' – now you have got *two* beautiful *cruches*. Or how about *gourde*, which is a flask of the kind that you attach to your belt or your rucksack but which can also be used to describe a girl who is a bit of a twit. 'Oh! Quelle gourde,' can be heard being muttered in exasperated tones either by a female speaker of themselves in reproach for some minor mistake they have just made or, of course, about some other idiot. But my favourite unflattering water-container term is *potiche*. This is a large, ornamental vase, the sort of vase that is put somewhere in a living room just to look nice, but isn't actually used for any real purpose. From this, the word has come to be used for a pretty girl who features on something like a TV game show or in an office reception area, where all she has to do is sit there, look pretty but not say anything.

I outlined this theory to Inès while we were having our coffee. She thought about it for a while then pointed out that, if water words applied to women, then perhaps fruit and vegetable words could be said to suit men. Pressed for examples, Inès offered *cornichon*, *banane* and *patate* – respectively gherkin, banana and potato. Of the three, you can't really use the word *cornichon* just on its own: it needs an *espèce de* – type or species of – to support it. You thus call someone – a bloke you think is a bit of an idiot – an *espèce de cornichon*! Don't ask me why a species of gherkin is more suited as an insult than a gherkin on its own: it just is. *Banane*, on the other hand, can be used all by itself as a word for an idiot, but is also often heard in the reproach *Tais-toi, banane!* – shut up, idiot. When it comes to potatoes, French ones don't spend their time on couches; they are mainly used as an insult for someone who is being a bit gormless. Used on its own, *patate* works quite well – *Eh! Patate!* but can be made a bit more wounding by adding *grosse* at the beginning to give *Grosse patate!*, even for someone who isn't noticeably fat. Interestingly, even though the words *patate* and *banane* are feminine, they apply perfectly well to males. What's more, I am assured, they are particularly pleasing to use because of the plosive *pa* or *ba* at the beginning.

After lunch, Inès decided to come in the boat with me for part of the way. As I rowed along, Inès dreaming contentedly in the stern, I noticed, away to my left on the towpath, an elderly couple and what appeared to be their young granddaughter. As we got level with them, the woman raised her arm in a brief but friendly greeting, the sort of gesture we had seen dozens of times along the way. Inès turned towards them and raised her arm in reply while I called out my usual cheery 'Bonjour!' Nothing much happened for a few seconds. Then, while we were still very close by, the woman turned to the others and in a very aggrieved tone said 'Ils auraient pu répondre!' – they might at least have replied. The little girl vaguely pointed out that she had seen us wave and thought she had heard a 'Bonjour'. But the grandmother was having none of it. She launched into a furious tirade about ill-mannered idiots who couldn't be bothered to acknowledge even a simple friendly greeting. To her credit the little girl stuck to her guns, insisting that Inès at least had waved: 'Mais, Mamie. J'ai vu la dame: elle t'a fait signe.'

Her grandmother admitted grudgingly that perhaps the woman had made a feeble gesture, 'Mais, l'imbécile avec la casquette bleue et son regard de con: lui n'a rien dit du tout.'

Whatever was she talking about? Which idiot with the blue cap and the moronic expression had said nothing? 'She means you,' Inès explained helpfully.

'Mais je vous ai dit "Bonjour"!' – but I said 'Bonjour' – I yelled, much wounded by both the description and the unjust accusation. Getting no reply, I yelled it again, much louder. The grandmother made no sign of having heard me and just carried on grumbling about the ill-mannered yobs you got on the river nowadays. It hadn't been like that when she was a girl, oh no.

Trivial as it was, the situation was so irritating that Inès and I ended up somewhat losing our cool. We launched into a torrent of *Bonjours*, each louder and more forceful than the previous one, with Inès varying both the pitch and the accent of hers to great effect – Canadian *Bonjours*, Belgian *Bonjours*, even a fairly convincing Cameroon *Bonjour*. But she got no response. We also did a fair bit of pantomime waving, accompanied by loud 'Yoo hoos' and the occasional 'Coucou, madame!' to such a degree that I thought we were both going to fall out of the boat.

But there was no reply. Still muttering angrily to herself – 'Je leur ai fait un geste amical et . . . rien. Rien du tout. C'est honteux' – I waved nicely, but nothing. Nothing at all. It's shameful – the three of them walked away up the towpath and were lost to view.

I have often wondered what I am going to do when I retire. Thanks to the grandmother I now know exactly how I'll spend my free afternoons: I shall lurk on a riverbank, greet passing boatmen and then drive them to distraction by accusing them of not replying. I am looking forward to it already.

I was keen to visit Troyes, the first place since leaving the source that is considered by the Michelin Green Guide to be 'worth a detour.' Despite this endorsement, the fact that the city doesn't lie on any tourist route to or from anywhere in particular means that many visitors to France haven't actually heard of it. What's more, a fair number of French people don't seem to have been there either. This is a pity for all concerned, because Troyes is quite simply a splendid place and well deserving of both its stars. For a start it is big enough to have a good selection of everything that you want in a town – a cathedral, some delightful pedestrian streets to explore, a selection of interesting shops and a good number of bars and restaurants to revive you once you have finished exploring – while being small enough to discover comfortably on foot. And, even better, it lies on the Seine.

As you wander through the pedestrian centre, the first thing that strikes you is the large number of half-timbered buildings that line the narrow streets. These buildings – known as *pan de bois* – are key to Troyes' charm. The old city centre is a veritable maze of narrow streets that all seem to be interlinked by even narrower, mysterious dark lanes. The way the streets are set out means that you can have great fun diving down a narrow lane at random because, whichever one you pick, it will very probably lead you out into another lane at least as interesting as the one you have just left. Troyes is obviously a watery place: there are a surprising number of wells dotted about the place.

As well as a decent cathedral and several pretty churches Troyes boasts a light and airy covered market and a large number of nice shops. It may be that we went on the day when everyone was in a good mood, but everywhere we went we were struck by the friendliness of the locals and by the generally pleasant atmosphere that pervaded the town. At one point a minor change in the wind direction showed that one of the nearby shops was a *torréfacteur*, an on-the-spot coffee-roasting establishment. From outside they appear wonderful places: different sorts of coffee are roasted all day long, filling even quite distant streets with the enticing smell of fresh coffee. There was a *torréfacteur* near the building where I used to work in Paris, and if the wind was in the right direction I could even smell the roasting coffee in my office. At the time, one of the secretaries used to make coffee twice a day in her room, and her colleagues were allowed to share it provided we contributed a packet of coffee now and again. As it was on the way to the Métro station, we all passed the *torréfacteur* twice a day and so had no excuse for forgetting to go and buy a packet.

As soon as you set foot inside a *torréfacteur*, its special magic starts to take hold. There, surrounded by the wonderful smells of roasting coffee, you happily believe the man with the soft voice and the strangely staring eyes as he explains the subtle differences between the various sorts of beans; why you should choose this particular Arabica in preference to that fractionally less satisfying (and cheaper) Colombian. Without really understanding how you come to do so, you willingly accept that it is worth spending a fair bit extra just to have an especially fragrant blend of coffee which, that soft voice soothingly assures you, is guaranteed to delight your taste buds but especially those of your colleagues. 'Buy this coffee,' the man seems to say, 'and your colleagues will love and admire you for ever.' And so, of course, you do. And you smile as you do so.

Unfortunately, once the beans have been removed from the magical shop and have been turned into coffee in the office, the resulting drink turns out to taste pretty much exactly like any other sort of coffee you have ever drunk in your life. Feelings of disappointment and frustration then set in and you resolve that, next time you will avoid the *torréfacteur* altogether and just buy the stuff in a supermarket. You can make all the resolutions that you like because, of course, you will never even make it to the supermarket. The magic of the *torréfacteur* is all powerful.

But despite all these wonders, surely Troyes must have some shortcomings? It does: there are two of them, and they are quite serious ones. The first is a frankly quite unhealthy obsession with my pet culinary hate – *andouillette*. This cross between a sausage and tripe, a dish made from bits of a pig's small intestine stuffed into a length of its large intestine (and then cooked, of course), is probably what Troyes is best known for. It is the headline dish of seemingly every restaurant in Troyes, even in the *crêperies* and Chinese restaurants and very probably in the local fast-food outlets, though I didn't visit any to check. *Andouillette* in Troyes is quite simply everywhere.

A menu for serious *andouillette* fans

Andouillette: a guide for aficionados

If you look on menus and in butchers' shops for *andouillette* (not that I am in any way urging you to do so, of course) you will often spot the letters AAAAA. This is not an attempt to imitate the sigh of pleasure that an enthusiast might make when seeing it, or possibly the one I would make on hearing that they have run out of the stuff, but an abbreviation. It stands for Association amicale des amateurs d'andouillette authentique – the Amicable Association of Authentic Andouillette Enthusiasts. This is an association which checks the quality of local produce and gives its label of approval to the ones it judges to be the best. True *andouillette* enthusiasts will actively seek out AAAAA-approved products and may well eschew anything inferior.

Typical *andouillette* recipes include: *Andouillette de Troyes*, *andouillette* served in a sauce made from white wine, mustard and shallots; *Andouillette à la crème*, *andouillette* in a cream and cider sauce; and *Andouillette au vin rouge*, *andouillette* in a red wine sauce with butter and shallots. In each case, I'm sure, the sauces would taste a whole lot better if you just forgot to put in the *andouillette*.

The second problem with Troyes stems from its name. The name of the town sounds just like *trois* – the word for three – as well as Troie, the French name for the town of Troy. As you wander the streets you spot numerous, semi-humorous references to the similarity of these names in shop windows. In a toyshop window there were some toy pigs for sale with a little label that referred to the rules of a well-known game of the three little pigs. This read 'Le jeu des trois petits cochonnets est un jeu qui se joue à trois . . . Non pas Troie en Asie mineure, ni Troyes en Champagne, mais trois 1 2 3 . . .' Further along, in a sweetshop window, there were some chocolate horses, some single ones labelled 'Cheval de Troyes' – a play on the wooden horse of Troy – and some in groups of three labelled 'Chevaux de 3'.

If you are prepared to overlook these faults, Troyes really is a very nice place indeed.

While doing my best not to get too close to any *andouillete*, I didn't forget the river. A brief and evidently too cursory look at the map of Troyes city centre had appeared to show that the Seine made a loop around the cathedral. Not pausing to wonder at how this should be possible – rivers don't often flow in circles after all – I declared my intention to Inès of rowing right round the cathedral, fond in the belief that this would be something that few people had ever accomplished. Indeed, I was quick to convince myself long before we actually got to the town that I would be the very first Englishman ever to accomplish such a feat in a homemade boat.

Unfortunately, when I actually came to see it in the flesh, it became clear that what looked like a welcoming loop on the map was in fact a series of stretches of water, none of which did anything to accommodate visiting rowers. There was a long straight length of canal by the cathedral which was crisscrossed by very low bridges, too low for a rowing boat to get under, followed by a distinctly grubby bit of the Seine which was fast-flowing and full of obstacles. Round the corner was some other, nameless stretch of water that raced along in the opposite direction then met up with the Seine somewhere behind the cathedral in an unfriendly turbulent swirl before they hurtled off together into the distance. Clearly, Troyes cathedral will have to wait a while longer to be circumnavigated, by an errant English rower and very probably by anyone else.

II

The next morning got off to a tremendous start: maximum points were scored, and I hadn't even been trying. For years, one of my favourite tests of how rural an area of France really is has involved spotting a Citroën Ami 6. These splendid vehicles used to be the car of choice for *paysans* – peasants. It is interesting by the way that calling someone a peasant in French is considerably less insulting than it would be in English. It is not actually a compliment, of course, but the chances of saying it without the person concerned setting his dogs on you are noticeably higher in France than in England. Indeed, my sister-in-law Nathalie – she who worried about unnecessary cruelty to snails – was once married to a member of a family of farmers near Grenoble who freely used the term *paysans* to describe themselves.

As *paysans* no longer exclusively travel in Ami 6, these cars are becoming increasingly rare. The fact that the last one was produced forty years ago may also be a contributing factor. However, if you are lucky, you can still spot them lurking in deeply rural areas of France such as Creuse or Auvergne. The area of Champagne which we were then travelling through is several steps up the rural ladder from places like Creuse, which explains why I hadn't been actively seeking out ageing Citroëns. In my system you score maximum points for seeing either of two specific vehicles: a light-blue Ami 6 saloon or a beige estate version. The Ami 6 saloon is my favourite with its re-entrant rear windscreen and its drooping, dented bonnet that looks as though the driver has just driven into the backside of an unanticipated elephant. The steering wheel is good too: it has just one curving arm connecting the rim to the steering column, while the gear lever is one of the umbrella-handle sort that sticks out of the dashboard. Sadly, you don't get that sort of equipment on Citroëns nowadays. The squishy Citroën suspension system gives the car very good ride characteristics, but these are never used to the full, because no Ami 6 owner has ever been known to exceed seventy kilometres per hour. Of course, Ami 6 come in colours other than light-blue or beige, but these seem to be the colours preferred by the true *paysan*.

In an ideal sighting situation such as the one that occurred that morning, the car has to be driven by a gentleman who must be over sixty, comfortably overweight, be attired in a *bleu de travail* – the traditional blue one-piece overall – wearing a flat cap (*not* a béret), poorly shaven and, most importantly, having ears that stick out so sharply they are clearly visible from the car following behind. If you want absolute perfection, the *paysan* has to have a red face and be smoking a filterless cigarette.

It has always puzzled me what exactly happens in a young Frenchman's life that causes him to end up, thirty years later, clad in a *bleu de travail* at the wheel of an Ami 6. Is it written in his genes? Or is it perhaps a result of some deficiency in his diet? If you were shown a photo of the members of a junior-school class taken fifty years ago, could you look at all the children and say, 'That little chap there, second from the left in the back row, will end up fifty years later in a flat cap at the wheel of a pale-blue Citroën'?

The morning's sighting – a pale blue saloon with a white roof – had everything except the cigarette. There was even an elderly black and white dog sitting on the passenger seat with its head sticking out of the sliding window. I felt cheered for the rest of the day.

Une voiture sans permis

Apart from the classic Ami 6, another sort of car is also popular with French rural dwellers. This is *une voiture sans permis*. This is a specific sort of small car that, as its name suggests, is intended to be driven by someone who hasn't passed his driving test. The original idea was quite commendable: devise a small car with an equally small engine, fit the minimum of controls and bodywork and allow those unfortunates who haven't been able to pass their test to drive it with no formal training whatsoever. This sort of car was primarily intended for isolated rural residents to allow them to get from their farm to the local market. In this, the idea was a great success. It is now common in *la France profonde* to encounter these tiny vehicles – they are even smaller than a Smart – tootling along a country road filled with country dwellers and their baskets of produce. Where the idea falls down is when such cars encounter other road users. For *voitures sans permis* are limited, by law but more importantly by the power of their engine, to a maximum top speed of forty-five kilometres per hour. This is very slow indeed. They also have the acceleration characteristics of a despondent sloth.

Spotting a *voiture sans permis* – or *voiturette* – is generally very easy: all you have to do is look for the car which is at the head of a line of very impatient, very slow-moving other cars on a French country road.

The day may have got off to a splendid start, but things declined considerably once I put the boat on the water. It was turning into one of those overcast, grey, damp mornings with not much wind, the sort of morning where you have to put up with the same dreary weather for several hours. Nevertheless, determined as ever and, more importantly, equipped with my waterproof jacket, I launched the boat and headed off downstream. At the precise point where I was exactly too far from the car for it no longer to be practical to turn round and row back, it started to drizzle. But the term 'drizzle' can't properly convey the nature of the constant, fine, chill spray that had started to fall slowly from the clouds. What's more, it managed to fall just slowly enough to make sure that none of it missed me on its way down. It was quite simply the most demoralizing sort of rain: not quite strong enough to justify taking shelter under a tree, assuming I could find one, but sufficiently persistent to make sure that every part of me not covered by the waterproof got cold and wet and clammy.

The clouds were so low, and the rain so fine, it was like rowing in a fog. As well as the rain, the repetitive to and fro movement caused by rowing produced a mind-numbing rustle from the sleeves and hood of the jacket. Swish – rustle – swish. Worse, the hood fabric revealed itself to be the cowardly sort that clings to your ears and so amplifies each rustle. Even in the best of conditions rowing can become tedious, because you can't see where you are going. Rowing in a cold drizzle, in a fog, where the movement each time you turn round to see where you are going opens up your jacket hood at exactly the angle that lets rain drip down the side of your neck, becomes soul destroying. And of course, where there were trees they were set just far back enough along the bank that they didn't provide any shelter at all.

A further effect of the low clouds and the rain was to somehow deaden all other sounds. There was nothing to distract me from the endless rustling of my jacket: no birdsong, no quacking of ducks and especially no voices, because everyone else had had the sense to go inside out of the rain. And so I rowed on, under grey clouds, through grey drizzle, on a grey river down to a rendezvous point with a grey car.

Once I was warm and dry again, Inès and I had an emergency meeting. Not only was the rain showing no sign of letting up but, more importantly the Seine seemed to have got itself stuck in something of a rut. It had grown into a small, but very rural river, idly winding its way – and when the Seine sets about winding its way, it can really wind – past a series of similar-looking villages. Worse, the river seemed somehow pleased with its lot and didn't look as though it was planning on changing much in the near future. Even if it hadn't been raining, there was a distinct feeling about this part of the river that if you had seen one rural bend and one pleasant village along its bank, then you had seen them all.

No further discussion was needed: it was time to drive on towards Romilly-sur-Seine to look for a bar. Exploring a river is thirsty work, and can also work up a bit of an appetite. If you are like me and prefer instant gratification, you will find yourself over time walking into all sorts of establishments. This experience of the bars along the Seine has led me to develop a theory which says that, the rougher the bar, the more entertaining the signs that you can see posted on the walls.

In my youth, the height of humour in an English pub was probably a fake car number plate hung over the fireplace which read 'RU 18' – a supposedly amusing means of checking whether you really were old enough to drink in there. Things seem to have moved on a bit since I was young. On a recent trip back to the UK I spotted a sign over a bar which read: 'We are sorry to announce the death of Mr Credit.' Some time earlier, in the gents of another bar, I had been faced with a charming sign over the urinal which read: 'Don't drink water here: drink at bar.'

In an upmarket French bar, there will be little humour in evidence: the walls will probably be hung with a menu or two offering the 'plat du jour' and a selection of other dishes, the usual formal sign explaining what may be sold on the premises and to whom, and a few tasteful pictures or posters. At the other end of the scale, going into a rough, shabby bar will probably get you a simpler menu offering such basic essentials as *sandwichs* and *croque monsieurs*, some pictures cut from magazines and, if you are lucky, a jokey sign or two.

Walking into the first bar that we came to on the way to Romilly, a grubby place that was unfortunately the only one in the village, we were greeted with a blue-and-white plaque the shape and size of a street sign which proclaimed the bar to be in 'Rue de la Soif' – welcome to Thirsty Street. Then, once we were perched on a couple of tall stools, I noticed another sign hanging charmlessly between the spirit dispensers:

Le patron aime toutes les couleurs – the landlord likes all sorts
    of colours
les petits noirs – small blacks, i.e. cups of coffee
les petits blancs – small whites, i.e. glasses of white wine
les petits rouges – small reds, i.e. red wine.

From the look of the *patron*, a well-padded chap with a florid face and long straggly hair, he liked his reds and whites even more than his *petits noirs*. On the wall there was also a hand-drawn notice warning that 'La maison n'offre pas de crédit' – no credit. This is a fairly common sight, but the message isn't always proclaimed so bluntly. Some way upriver we had stopped at another memorably shabby bar, where the same message had been conveyed in a rather more subtle way: 'La maison propose du crédit, mais uniquement aux personnes âgées d'au moins 85 ans et lorsqu'elles sont accompagnées par leurs parents' – credit is available, but only for people aged eighty-five or over who are accompanied by their parents.

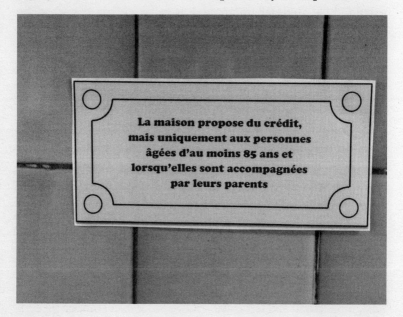

But my favourite sign was the one over the bar of a distinctly dark and dusty café in a village in that most rural of French *départements*, Cher. In a place in which everyone except us, but especially the *patron*, gave the impression that they had been three parts drunk every day since leaving school, there was a carefully drawn and lovingly hand-coloured sign which read: 'Il vaut mieux être saoul que con: au moins ça dure moins longtemps' – it is better to be drunk than bloody stupid – at least it lasts less long.

12

We headed on to the village of Marcilly-sur-Seine, where an extremely heated debate arose. For it is near Marcilly that the river Aube joins the Seine. And with that we get straight to the very nub of the debate: does it really? For there are those who would argue that map makers and historians have got it all wrong and that, in fact, it is the Seine that joins the Aube rather than the other way round. This is not just a question of proto-col – along the lines of who goes before whom at a social event – it is a question of the subsequent river's whole identity. For, if it is the Seine that joins the Aube, then the resulting bigger river that flows on downstream should properly be called the Aube.

It seemed a good idea to start by checking out the two con-tenders. If you stand near the confluence you can see a fairly broad stretch of water flowing from the north-east to the south-west, with a smaller piece of water joining it from the east. The broad stretch is the Aube, while the smaller piece is the Seine. At first sight, the Aube clan do seem to have a point.

If you want to actively support the 'The Seine is a tributary of the Aube' theory, just weighing up the two rivers from the bank won't cut much ice. If you are going to get anywhere, you have to start talking about the relative mass flows of the two rivers. To do this, you first determine the volumetric flow rate of the Seine at Méry-sur-Seine, a village a short way upstream of Marcilly.

Apparently, there are people who have spent time measuring this sort of thing, and, according to them, the average flow at this spot over a fifty-year period is 32.8 cubic metres of water per second. The next step is to go downstream of the confluence and measure the volumetric flow rate there. This, I am reliably advised, averages out over a thirty-year period to 77.1 cubic metres per second. This is the sort of flow that would fill a decent-sized swimming pool in just a couple of seconds. The difference between the two flow rates logically has to come from the water brought to the table by the Aube (assuming you discount one or two little streams that also join the party nearby). This difference is 44.3 cubic metres of water per second. This leads the Aube supporters to argue that their river brings a whole load more water to the table than does the Seine (44.3 as compared to 32.8 cubic metres per second).

The Aube clan, who have obviously gone to a lot of trouble over this, also point out that the catchment area for the Aube is far bigger than that of the Seine (4,660 km² as opposed to 3,960 km²), and thus, given that the rainfall characteristics are closely similar, a whole lot more rain must flow into the Aube than into the Seine.

As it is always the bigger of two rivers that keeps its name after the confluence, this, say the Aube lot, means the river leaving Marcilly must be the Aube.

If it really is the Aube which flows on downstream and not the Seine, how on earth did such a mistake occur? The explanation probably lies in the mapping of France, or rather in the lack of it. Right up to the mid eighteenth century there were not only no reliable maps of the country, no one even had any idea how

many villages and hamlets there actually were. This was understandable because, France being so big and so rural, an awful
lot of the country was well off the beaten track. Rudimentary
maps existed, but the location of the places shown was generally unreliable. At this time much of the area along the Seine
upstream of Paris would have been almost completely isolated
with practically no roads and absolutely no question of public
transport. The region was known only to its immediate inhabitants and most of them were too busy just trying to survive to
worry whether the water flowing off down to Paris came
properly from the right branch or the left at a confluence.

Given that the source of the Seine had been well known for
its magic properties at least since the time of the Gauls, early
inhabitants, having sampled the spring, must have followed the
stream to see where it led. If you do that, of course you end up
in Paris. But this is true if you start from any tributary, for
example one of the Aube's, and follow that downstream.
Whichever minor tributary you pick you will eventually find
yourself at the capital. It can only be the relative fame of the
source of the Seine – and, of course, Sequana's magic – that
led people to follow the water downstream from St-Germain-
Source-Seine and give her name to every length of river into
which the water branched, regardless of the merits of the
other pretenders. Of course, if one was starting afresh with a
blank map and seeking to name the rivers correctly, one would
work in the opposite direction, heading upstream from the sea.
At each confluence a decision would be made as to which was
the bigger player, and so on right back to the correct, individual source. This type of map making wasn't undertaken until
much later, long after everyone had accepted that the river
flowing through Paris was the Seine.

In around 1750, Louis XV charged the Cassini father-and-son

team to prepare proper maps of the kingdom. They were specifically asked to determine the location of all habitations, measure the distances between them and generally show everything that was unchanging in the landscape. Cassini's teams set off to map the country with an enthusiasm which wasn't always shared by the inhabitants of the villages they visited. Many of the smaller hamlets were so totally isolated that the residents were familiar with only those places they could reach in a day's journey on foot. And they didn't visit those very often. When such rural people were confronted by foreigners who turned up dressed in strange clothes and, more importantly, brandishing mysterious devices, their understandable reaction was to drive them away. If the strange visitors persisted with their activities, they were sometimes killed.

Despite the difficulties they faced, the Cassini teams persevered and completed the project. They even came up with something called the Cassini projection, a distorted and less satisfactory precursor to Mercator's later idea. Like most things, Cassini's beautifully drawn maps are now available online. If you look at his view of Marcilly, it shows castles, churches, marshes and woods as well as the Seine and the Aube. The map shows that he clearly realized that the Aube was the larger river: it is shown noticeably wider. I still wonder why he didn't say something. Nevertheless, whether it properly is the Seine or the Aube which flows on downstream, it may all become rather academic when the Yonne joins the party a bit later on. But more of that later.

Regardless of what it should properly be called, it was along this part of the river that I first began to wonder whether I should have a go at living off the land, or rather, out of the water. For the previous few days I had been travelling along a river that, at least theoretically, could provide the makings of a decent meal. There was no shortage of firewood about the place, so building a fire to cook on shouldn't have presented too much of a problem. What's more, the river banks seemed to offer an endless selection of suitable secluded places. The only problem was finding something to cook.

I was pretty sure that I could make a camp fire and that, given a decent bit of fish, I could very probably set about cooking it. On the other hand, I was a whole lot less happy about the part of the food chain which involved getting the fish out of the river and into a state where it could actually be cooked. If asked, I am quite willing to bait a hook and will even sit quite contentedly on a riverbank or in a boat, holding a fishing rod until a fish is caught. The bit of the process that I'm not so keen on is the getting-the-fish-off-the-hook part. There is also the getting-the-fish-ready-to-be-cooked-once-you-have-got-it-off-the-hook part that has to be coped with too.

My lack of enthusiasm for grabbing hold of a wriggling, newly caught fish undoubtedly dates back to the Great Wriggling Fish Roundup, which marked me for ever when I was thirteen. For reasons which never became clear, my school had selected four likely candidates, one of whom being me, for a free weekend vaguely centred on boats somewhere near Littlehampton. It sounded great – further proof of my long-term liking for boats – so I signed up straight away. We all spent the first evening having a camp-fire meal on the beach, a meal that we would have called a barbecue had we known the word at the time. It had got dark by the time we had finished eating, but, rather than head home to bed, our host Clive announced that it was time for us all to help catch something for the following day's lunch. At this, he drove his Land Rover down on to the beach and produced an incredibly long net from inside it. Spacing the boys and adults who were present along the length of the net he told us to walk out into the sea in a huge loop, while holding up the net between the sea bottom and the surface. 'Don't go in over your depth,' he advised us helpfully.

The problem with being thirteen is that you don't have to wade out very far on a steeply sloping beach before you get spectacularly out of your depth. This is even more memorable when you do it in the dark, when both hands are being used to hold up a net, and with nothing but the lights of a distant Land Rover to guide you. At least I thought to keep my sandals on, so I only had to concentrate on not drowning rather than worrying about stepping on anything unpleasant while I was doing it.

Once the net had been walked out into a big loop, we were allowed to struggle back to the beach in time to see Clive attach both ends of the net to the bumper of the Land Rover and then back it up the beach. Pulling in the net revealed what we had caught in startling detail in the headlights. There were dozens of fish of all shapes and sizes, all leaping about the place, and all exceedingly displeased at having been caught. The four of us were encouraged to help pick all the fish up and bring them back to the Land Rover. This is the part that I remember most vividly: I had survived the net walk, narrowly avoiding drowning, and had shortened the life of my favourite sandals by soaking them in sea water, all without a murmur. But having to grab hold of a load of flappy, wriggly fish at midnight seems to have scarred me for life. I haven't grasped another wriggling fish to this day.

Despite these deep emotional scars, I really did like the idea of cooking a piece of freshly caught fish on the riverbank. All I needed was to find a friendly fisherman who had some that he was willing to share with me. Unfortunately I failed to find a fisherman of any kind, whether friendly or not. So we went and bought some nice pieces of salmon and a small, cheap frying pan at Marcilly market instead.

Back on the riverbank, in the evening sunshine, it was the work of only a few minutes to gather some armfuls of dry wood and build a fireplace with stones from the riverbank, just like they had done in the *Swallows and Amazons* books, though I can't claim to have got the fire going with a single match. The fish, the new frying pan and a bit of butter, when all brought together over the camp fire, resulted in some wonderfully appetizing sizzling, and, when that was combined with some fresh bread, the best part of a bottle of wine and a selection of cheeses for afterwards, it produced one of the most satisfying meals I had had in a long time.

Sitting on the bank, contentedly watching the sunset and feeling justifiably pleased with ourselves, we could suddenly hear singing coming from a short way down the towpath. Inès thought she could recognize the song, so we abandoned our camp fire and went to check if she was right. Following the music, we came upon a group of teenagers clustered around a camp fire who were all listening to a soulful-looking lad playing a guitar. As Inès had suspected, he was singing 'La Chanson de Prévert', a song written by a very young Serge Gainsbourg. There are those who say that it is the best song Gainsbourg ever wrote; at the very least it is the most moving. The young people certainly seemed to think so. Each time the earnest-looking lad got to the chorus, they all joined in, swaying to the rhythm, some of them actually crying from the emotion of it all.

But what is it about French people and songs? Or rather, what is it about French individual singers and their music? If you ask anyone, even some French people, to name three French rock groups, they will be hard put to do so. Off the top of my head I can come up with two –Téléphone and Indochine. Try asking the same people to name three individual French singers and there will be no stopping them: Gainsbourg, Brassens, Brel, Montand, Moustaki (OK, he was Greek, but what the heck, the French love him) . . . Conversely, if you ask British people the same two questions, the results will be reversed: they will come up with a whole load of names of British groups and relatively few individual singers of ballads.

Part of the explanation must lie in the shape and the rhythm of the words in the two languages. English seems to lend itself to rock songs, while French quite definitely doesn't. You only have to listen to one French rock song to see the truth of that. The words just don't seem to fit. This is true even if you take a successful English rock song and translate it into French, as artistes such as Johnny Hallyday or Sylvie Vartan have tried doing. Once the song has been translated, it just sounds clumsy and wrong, even to French ears. On the other hand, the simple form of English verbs and their lack of conjugation mean that it's easier to make them fit in with the beat. French seems to suit slower, more thoughtful songs.

Of course, the French character must play its part somewhere. Being individualists, they seem to appreciate songs that are the work of one person. They also like thoughtful *chansons à texte* – songs whose words sound like poetry. If you take away the music of many French songs, the words on their own remain worth reading. This isn't true of many English ones. Songs that are *frédonnable* – that you can hum along to – are also much appreciated in France. Give them both together – as in 'La Chanson de Prévert' – and they are away. As far as I can see, the French language coupled with the Latin temperament means that the French are essentially predestined to appreciate a bloke with a guitar – *un mec avec sa gratte* – and a thoughtful song or two.

13

Despite the problems in the early days of the trip of getting the boat onto the water, I did end up doing quite a bit of real rowing, notably before and after Troyes. Prolonged rowing can prove quite strenuous, but, thankfully, some uncharacteristic forward planning had led me to try and get into some kind of shape before I headed off for the river.

Prior to an important competition, top Olympic rowers average 370 kilometres a week on the water. 370 kilometres in a week means rowing more than fifty kilometres each day: an incredible distance. On top of that, they also do numerous weights sessions in the gym. Then, two or three times a week it seems that they do more intensive exercises – as if the ordinary ones weren't intensive enough – to up their heart rate even further. This means that once a week they get up to a competitive race pace of thirty-six strokes a minute. This astonishingly fast pace gets their poor beleaguered hearts beating at 170 to 180 beats a minute. To fuel them for all this effort, top rowers eat between 4,000 and 6,000 calories a day spread over several meals.

As part of the planning I thought it might be a good idea to check the kind of training regime used by real rowers to see if it could be adapted to suit my sort of rowing.

I gave the regimes used by professionals considerable thought, carefully weighing up the pros and cons, but, in the end, decided they weren't really all that suitable; for a start, I don't think I really need any more calories, thank you very much. Instead, I devised my own training programme for the weeks before setting off. Regular rowing on water didn't seem all that practical, especially as it was late winter, so I decided that, each evening when I got home from work, I would spend some time on a rowing machine in front of the television. Our machine is the sort with a sliding seat and a wooden bar that you pull which is attached to some kind of mechanism by a long cord. As you row you zoom backwards and forwards, gasping and wheezing, to the sound of the seat sliding on its rails and the mechanism whooshing round and round. I found that a rate of thirty strokes a minute was far more my kind of thing than thirty-six. Looking for something to pass the time, I quickly discovered that whizzing noisily backwards and forwards is not the best of conditions in which to watch any TV programme with a complex plot and lots of dialogue. Instead, I used to row in front of LCI – La Chaîne des Infos – the French rolling-news channel. This is perfectly suited to being watched in a noisy environment because you can just look at the images of whatever is being discussed on the news and amuse yourself by trying to figure out what the story actually is. This helps to pass the time no end. What's more, with LCI, if you get fed up with trying to guess what's going on, you can always read the general news text that scrolls across the bottom of the screen. The only minor problem with watching while rowing is that the newsreader's face zooms larger and smaller with each stroke, which, with some newsreaders, can be quite disconcerting.

*

That morning's rowing took me down to the village of Marnay-sur-Seine, where I stopped to stretch my legs. Walking down a quiet street took me away from the river and past several pleasant houses, some of which had *marquises* – old-fashioned glass awnings set in wrought iron frames above their front doors. Some way further on a house announced the presence of a dentist's surgery with a sign made up of a large tooth and an attendant toothbrush. While, in France, dentists don't generally advertise their presence with images of teeth, a surprising number of professions still use traditional signs.

Probably the most common one is for a tobacconist. A *tabac* advertises itself with a red lozenge-shaped sign with the words 'Tabac' on it in white letters. Such signs are known as *carottes*, because they used to be made up of two orangey red cones mounted back to back. While dull, lozenge-shaped signs are now everywhere, you can still occasionally spot a proper old-fashioned carrot-shaped one. A newsagent, or *maison de la presse*, lets you know it's there by a diamond-shaped yellow sign with a red quill drawn on it and the word 'Presse' in black letters. Both of these signs set out to be as helpful as possible by including the name of the shop on them just in case you need a bit of help in recognizing them. Not all *enseignes* do this. One that doesn't really provide a proper clue as to what it is for is the sign for a *notaire*, which is essentially the French equivalent of a solicitor. *Notaires* proclaim their presence by mounting a gold plaque shaped like a large, oval medallion outside their *cabinet* – offices. The plaque shows a seated figure, presumably that of Justice, with a sheaf of wheat to one side and the words 'République Française' underneath. If you hadn't seen the sign before, you might guess from the words 'République Française' that it was for something official but, unless you recognized the seated Justice figure, you would very probably be stuck as to exactly what it might be.

These kinds of signs are essentially passive; they just sit there quietly up on their wall and leave it up to you whether you want to look at them or not. They don't jump out at you and make a fuss. The same cannot be said for *pharmacie* signs. French *pharmacies* – chemists – advertise themselves with a green cross. Up until the 1920s they had been free to use a traditional medical red cross but, when this became the exclusive right of the International Red Cross, they slowly switched to using a green one. If only they just used a plain green cross, there wouldn't be any problem. Unfortunately, pharmacies seem to believe that sick people will only be able to find their way to them if there is a brightly illuminated, flashing sign outside the shop for them to follow. It used to be that the cross was lit up when the shop was open and switched off when it was closed. Progress being what it is, *pharmacie* signs are not only left on all the time but are often made up of light and dark green patterns that are arranged to flash separately and very brightly, often in irritating cycles.

We once inadvertently found ourselves trying to sleep in a hotel bedroom opposite a *pharmacie*. The sickly green disco light patterns that the flashing sign cast on the ceiling were so annoying that by 2 a.m. Inès had to restrain me from going and borrowing an axe from the manager to chop through the sign's power cable.

A short way downstream from Marnay-sur-Seine I found myself enmeshed in a new version of a familiar argument. About twenty kilometres above Fontainbleau, in the small town of Montereau-Fault-Yonne, the whole which-river-is-it-really debate starts all over again. For it is in Montereau that the Yonne flows into the Seine. Alternatively, should you subscribe to the local view, it is here that the Seine flows into the Yonne. The campaigning here is even more heated than it was back in Marcilly. Montereau is the last place before it reaches the sea that a serious contender joins the Seine. More importantly, the winner of the tributary debate at Montereau wins the ultimate prize: the honour of flowing through Paris. And the argument is still quite definitely *d'actualité* – of current interest. When I paused for a coffee it took only the briefest of mentions of the Seine to get the *patron* and two of the regulars to start grumbling heatedly about the harsh treatment of the Yonne and the favouritism shown to the Seine by 'ces Parisiens qui n'y connaissent rien' – those Parisians who know nothing about anything.

The basic premise of the argument in favour of the Yonne is exactly the same as that advanced in support of the Aube. Rather than go through it all again, I will just give you the scores: the Seine – 80 cubic metres per second; the Yonne – 93 cubic metres per second. You have to admit that the Yonne supporters have got a point: their river does bring a whole lot more water to the equation than the Seine. Nevertheless, whichever way the debate goes at Montereau, it is bad news for our friends from the Aube fan club who presented their argument a while back. For, if they were to win the debate at Marcilly on the basis of their volumetric arguments, their success would be short-lived, because they would lose at Montereau on precisely the same reasoning. In any case, it is tough luck for both of the Aube and the Yonne because, no doubt thanks to Sequana, the Seine wins both times. And it is much too late to change anything now.

Later that afternoon we nearly lost the boat. We also nearly lost our friend Siggi – he who came to help with part of the boat-building process – though really that would have been his own fault. The wonder of mobile phones means that it is remarkably easy to meet up with people on a riverbank in the middle of nowhere. We thus found ourselves sitting on the grass enjoying an unexpected beer with Siggi and Christine. As the spokesperson who threw down the gauntlet of the quest in the first place, Christine was keen to find out how likely it was looking that she would have to drink warm beer on a double-decker bus surrounded by bowler-hatted businessmen or whatever peculiarly British experience I was planning. After we had caught up, Christine asked whether she could go for a row. The ease with which she slipped aboard and fitted the oars into their rowlocks clearly showed that she knew one end of a boat from the other. I thus sat back with Inès and Siggi, enjoying our beer, and watched her happily pootle up and down the river.

But Christine's nautical professionalism lulled me into a false sense of security. Somehow I assumed that, if a woman was a skilled rower, her husband must be fairly capable too. So when Christine came back to the bank and offered to let Siggi take her place, I just sat there and let him get on with it. Siggi's first movement towards the boat revealed his lack of experience with blatant clarity. Unfortunately, by then, it was far too late to do anything about it. For, instead of crouching down and slipping into the boat, placing his feet near the middle and sitting down quickly, Siggi revealed his Germanic origins by attempting to march his way onto a small rowing boat. From standing rigidly upright on the bank, he took one long stride out over the boat, his arms swinging with military precision. Rather than reaching the middle of the boat, Siggi's leading foot landed on the far side, at the exact spot where it would produce the most spectacular effect. Still ramrod straight, Siggi found himself briefly balanced with one foot on the floor of the boat while his other foot left the safety and support of dry land. This situation did not last long. Under the impact of an off-centre and sizeable

German, the poor boat did not so much rock from side to side as spin about its axis. The boat spun; Siggi lurched. The boat appeared to fly into the air, keel upwards, and, with a huge, Teutonic splash, Siggi vanished underwater.

This short, but intense period of drama was followed by a much longer moment of inactivity. The three of us stood rooted to the bank gazing at the partly submerged, upturned rowing boat and a pair of drifting oars. A fisherman, sitting quietly a short way along the bank, took stock of the situation and observed, most helpfully, 'Il est tombé dans l'eau' – he's fallen in the water – but made no move to assist us in any way. But of Siggi there was no sign. The three of us reacted in different ways: Christine, seemingly unalarmed by the disappearance of her husband, dug her camera out of her bag to record the event (though she unfortunately forgot to take the lens cap off), while I, a proud holder of a French lifeguard certificate, railed briefly, but with considerable feeling, about the state of my poor boat – 'I built that boat with my own hands!' – before starting to grumble at greater length at the idea of having to jump into the water to look for Siggi. Of the three of us, Inès reacted the most creditably by immediately setting off in search of a fallen tree branch.

Long seconds passed: still no Siggi. I started, quite reluctantly, to pull off my shoes and take my wallet out of my pocket with a view to launching a rescue bid, when, with the air of a benevolent and contented walrus surfacing after a long and fruitful dive, Siggi's head reappeared near the boat. This moment coincided quite neatly with Inès's return to the bank carrying a long branch. She stretched it out over the water towards Siggi, who was able to grasp the end with one hand and somehow gather the oars and the boat with the other before being pulled to the side.

Once boat, oars and Siggi were all safely on the bank, Siggi, apparently none the worse for his dip, squelched off to their car to find some dry clothes. While he was doing that, I rubbed the boat down and sorted out the inside as best I could.

This might be a good point to pause and reflect. Given the fact that the Germans have spent much of the previous couple of centuries vigorously invading France while the English and French haven't had a decent war since 1815, relations between the French and the Germans might reasonably be assumed to be more strained than those with the English. Oddly enough, this isn't really the case. A clear distinction is made in French minds between modern-day Germans – *les Allemands* – and the invader-occupiers of the Second World War– *les Nazis*. This doesn't mean that the events of 1940–45 (and not 1939–45, as it is seen from a British point of view) are forgiven and forgotten. Far from it: plaques commemorating various events and atrocities suffered in the war continue to be put up on walls in Paris, most recently in the major railway stations, from which the mass deportations took place.

While films set in wartime are shown regularly on TV and, in the case of classics such as *La Grande Vadrouille*, are still hugely popular, there is probably less chance of coming across lines such as 'Don't mention the war!' in a modern TV programme than there is in the UK. France has moved on. Modern-day *Allemands* are friends. You only have to watch French news once to see that Germany is France's economic ally and role model.

Another example may be peculiar to our village, but I would like to think that it also provides an indication of how Franco-German relations have moved on. On 11 November – Armistice Day – each year there is a small service in front of the village war memorial. Elderly servicemen, either in uniform or in suits, with medals proudly displayed, gather round Monsieur le Maire, other local dignitaries and one or two senior military personnel. There are usually also about thirty villagers who have gathered round to watch and to remember. The ceremony begins with an elderly soldier reading out the twenty-four names on the village memorial (at the time of the First World War the population was just a few hundred) in groups of four. After each group has been read aloud, the soldier intones: 'Morts pour la France' – they gave their lives for France. It is all very simple but surprisingly moving. The reading-out of the names is generally followed by a medal ceremony with *anciens combatants* – old soldiers – receiving medals for long service or for the anniversary of some notable battle or campaign in which they took part.

Last year I took Siggi along, somewhat reluctantly on his part, because he felt his presence might not be appreciated given that, in our small village, his German nationality is well known. In fact he was warmly welcomed by all those who recognized him. Indeed, after the ceremony Monsieur le Maire himself came over and declared that Siggi's attendance was symbolic of modern Europe.

Incidentally, one of the things (the endless number of things) that confused me when I first arrived in France was when people appeared to be imitating some kind of foreigners by saying 'Ah . . . so'. For me, when younger, 'Ah . . . so' was firmly believed to be typical of Asians, more particularly Japanese, people. But the French people I heard saying it didn't seem to be talking about Asians at all. Much later I discovered that they were actually saying 'Ach, so' (with a *z* sound rather than a soft *s*) and were in fact imitating Germans.

★

Having managed to make everything as shipshape as possible (a few days in a boat would get anyone using nautical expressions), I was keen to get back in it to have a brief row about in much the same way that you are supposed to get straight back on a horse after a fall, even though I hadn't actually been the one who had fallen off. I particularly wanted to have one last row about on the river with Inès that afternoon, because this was to be the end of our exploration for the time being. It was time to head back home because the people carrier was expected back at work the following day, as, indeed, was I. What they were going to make of the musty, riverine smell pervading their once pristine car remained to be seen.

More importantly, the confluence with the Yonne at Montereau-Fault-Yonne changes the entire character of the river. From the source as far as Montereau, the Seine had been in its infancy, something which is reflected in its local name – La Petite Seine. From Montereau onwards to Paris, the river enters its adolescence. From here it becomes known as La Haute Seine and is officially declared *navigable* for the first time. This means its size and depth are officially considered suitable for proper vessels. The sharply increased size of the river and the real risk of being swept aside or swamped by barges and other motor boats meant that, once downstream of Montereau, the Seine would no longer be a safe playground for irresponsible little rowing boats and their builders.

On reaching home, Inès and I carried the boat into the garage and put it in the empty space waiting for it. That the boat had had a busy time of it could be seen by the state of the inside: muddy footprints, twigs, leaves and gravel all needed cleaning out. There were also the buoyancy chambers to think of. Opening them revealed the souvenirs of several days on the water: empty plastic bottles, the wrappers from several packets of biscuits, a damp and rather smelly waterproof jacket, a brochure about Epoisses, a street map of Troyes and my much-used and much-creased Dijon–Chaumont and Troyes–St-Dizier maps. The last things to fetch from the car were the oars. These I carefully laid inside the boat, the blades to the bow, as had been drummed into us in Salcombe all those years before. We were taught to put them that way because any passengers would always travel in the stern of a boat, where there is more room, and no passenger wants to sit on a thwart that has been made all wet by dripping oar blades. Old habits die hard.

Having made the boat as comfortable as possible, I turned out the light and quietly closed the garage door, leaving it to reflect on all its adventures.

14

Travelling the next stretch of river involved going *avalant* along a *bief*. In fact, it turns out that *avalant* along a *bief* was something I had been doing a lot since setting out from the source but I just hadn't known that this was the proper term. *Avalant* means heading downstream, as opposed to *montant*, which means going upstream. *Bief* is the formal name for the stretch of river between two successive locks. It had never occurred to me that a piece of river would need its own special name just because it has a lock at each end of it, but, seemingly, it does.

I learned this new vocabulary on a pleasure-boat trip on a sunny Sunday afternoon. The boat having gone back to the garage to put its feet up, I had set about finding alternative means of travelling down the river. This would be the first opportunity since leaving the source to travel on the river while someone else was doing the driving, so I positively jumped at it. We found ourselves aboard the *Renoir*, a converted Parisian tourist boat that could carry about sixty passengers. Our captain was an enthusiastic chap called Denis. His wife, Marie, dressed in a stripy T-shirt so as to be sure that everyone would know that she was the ship's *mousaillonne*, or cabin girl, dealt with handling the mooring ropes and distributing coffee and biscuits to the passengers.

We joined the boat at Saint-Mammès, a village that lies at the confluence of the Seine and the river Loing, about eighty kilometres upstream of Paris and only a little way downstream from the site of Siggi's Montereau shipwreck. Once everyone was on board, the journey started with a brief trip up the Loing past the numerous barges that were moored along the banks. Many of these were the classic sort of barge called a Freycinet. This is the typical French metal barge with a characteristic blunt bow, a long deck and a wheelhouse at the stern. They are sizeable things. Indeed, they are so big that, in order for the barge to get under the lowest bridges, the wheelhouse has to be taken down first. There is a huge difference between a barge that is empty – which looks enormous because practically its entire hull is out of the water – and a heavily laden one. A fully loaded barge has only its gunwales out of the water and seems all thin and frail in comparison. I always find it hard to imagine the huge quantity of it that remains hidden like an iceberg below the surface. Clearly, you only need to take the wheelhouse down when going under a low bridge in an empty barge.

We left the Loing and swung into the Seine and set off, *avalant* happily in the sunshine towards Champagne-sur-Seine, a place that unfortunately has nothing to do with sparkling wine. Here the *Renoir* entered the biggest lock I have ever seen, able to hold twelve Freycinets at one time, though, as Denis, reasonably pointed out, the chances of having twelve such boats all wanting to go through the lock together are fairly small, especially nowadays. Once through the lock we continued downstream, with our boat sitting right in the middle of the river because that's where the water is deepest. Obviously, when two boats come face to face in the middle of the river, they both have to pull over to the right, otherwise problems may arise.

I had been wondering for some time now whether the river around here was clean enough to swim in and beyond the lock I got the answer to my question. In between a series of attractive houses which sat in well-kept gardens were areas of woodland, where, amongst the trees, were bathing spots. At each of them quite a few people, young and old, were taking advantage of the hot weather to go and jump in the river. The spots were obviously intended for swimmers because some had rope swings hanging from nearby trees. I got the distinct impression that the swimmers had been waiting for an audience because, as soon as they spotted our barge, they all rushed for the rope and set about throwing themselves into all sorts of wild swings and leaps into the water, some of which were really quite impressive.

During the later part of the trip Denis started offering the various young children on board the chance to take the wheel. Unsurprisingly, quite a few of them accepted. Once they had all had a go, Denis went round the children a second time in case any of them wanted another try. I know for a fact that at least one adult on board found this favouritism a bit frustrating. When, at last, the children had finished their second go and Denis was on his own at the wheel again, I was able to sidle up and ask whether taking the wheel was exclusively reserved for small children. Somewhat surprised, because he apparently doesn't get asked that very often, Denis handed me the wheel and gave me a brief rundown on the controls.

Shortly afterwards we passed close by a green buoy – as I had been instructed to do. Looking down into the water, we could see the wreck of a large barge that had just been left to rot away on the bottom. The fact that the VNF – Voies Navigables de France – who manage the waterways, had simply decided to leave the wreck there with just a marker buoy rather than get rid of it upset Denis deeply. He pointed out that each river user has to pay a licence fee to the VNF and suggested that it would be nice if some of the money went on essentials like keeping the river free of obstructions.

A few minutes later, while I was still getting the hang of things, Denis turned to me and said cheerfully 'Je vous laisse les commandes: je vais prendre un petit café' – I'm leaving you in control: I'm just off for a quick coffee. What? Surely he wasn't going to leave me alone in charge of a strange boat and a whole load of innocent, fare-paying passengers? And with a bend coming up, a bridge to pass under and, most importantly, a large number of ducks fooling about just ahead?

I got round the bend, and through the correct span of the bridge, and even persuaded the ducks to move out of the way by the simple expedient of yelling, 'Get out of the way, ducks!' from the bridge window. But then, all too soon, Denis returned, coffee cup in hand, to reclaim the wheel.

The only mildly irritating aspect of the cruise was the presence of a teenage girl who spent much of the trip calling her friends on her mobile phone to tell each one in turn that she was on a barge on the river and it was sunny and she was having a good time and her parents had bought her a Coke and she was getting brown and she had broken up with Kevin but that he had just called her to tell her that he still loved her . . . over and over again. At least we learned to recognize when a call was at last coming to an end because she ended each one with the same word – 'Bisous'.

In days gone by, French people would finish affectionate notes, postcards and phone calls with the words *Je t'embrasse* or, if they were addressing a couple or a family *Je vous embrasse*. This literally means 'I kiss you' but, like most endearments, it loses something on being translated. If you aren't convinced about this, try translating 'I send you my love' into French and then saying it to someone. Believe me, and I speak as one who knows, it will sound at least as silly to them as 'I kiss you' does to us. For some people a simple 'Je t'embrasse' isn't strong enough and they will reinforce the message by saying *Je t'embrasse très fort* or by adding some warmer endearment like *Je t'embrasse de tout mon cœur* – I kiss you with all my heart. (You can try pointing out that you don't actually kiss anyone with your heart, but see where it gets you.)

Young people, however, think that *Je t'embrasse* is old-fashioned. 'Ma tante me le dit' – my aunt says it to me – said a teenage girl of our acquaintance, and you don't get more over the hill than that. Brought up in a world of texts and emails, they use shorter words like *Bises* – kisses – to finish their messages with. If a simple *Bises* isn't strong enough, you can always resort to *Grosses bises* – big kisses. But even *Bises* seems to be falling from favour as people have moved on to *Bisous*. This is just a younger, more modern way of saying 'kisses'. Younger people seem to end any sort of communication with *Bisous* whether it's phone calls, texts (where you can use the shortened form of 'Biz' if you like) or emails. As might be expected, while young people despise *Je t'embrasse* as being the domain of fuddy-duddies, so more mature people deride *Bisous*. 'C'est vide et énervant' – it's vacuous and annoying – declared a friend of more mature years.

However, despite its detractors, *Bisous* is gaining ground. There are now people who use it to finish emails at work – something I can't see myself doing, even when writing to someone I know well. And seemingly, once you start throwing out *Bisous* here and there, it becomes hard to stop. Our daughter Sarah had to ring the Social Security to sort out some problem or other. To our astonishment she finished the call with 'Merci beaucoup. Bisous.' Then, as soon as she realized what she had done, she apologized profusely to the woman for her over-familiarity, before saying: 'Finalement, vous êtes très sympathique. Je vous dis "Bisous" quand même' – in fact you are so nice I shall stick with saying 'Bisous' to you. When we asked, Sarah described the woman as being 'Surprised . . . but pleased . . . I think.'

Following the river on the way home from Saint-Mammès, we found ourselves in the town of Melun. Much like Paris, Melun is a town which extends from one side of the Seine to the other and includes a large central island. There, unfortunately, the resemblance ends. Poor Melun is generally believed by French people to be not an especially nice place at all; indeed it is best known for being the butt of jokes and snide remarks. There is a famous comedy sketch by a duo known as Chevalier and Laspallès which describes how one of them spent their holidays in

Melun for a second year running; this year, for some unknown reason, he chose to camp in the wilds on the south side of the town. The idea of anyone choosing to spend their holidays in Melun is clearly so ridiculous as to be unimaginable, and each mention of the town's name has the audience hooting with laughter.

The best thing that I can say about Melun is that it was a whole lot nicer than I had been expecting. The stretch of the river around the island is pleasant and obviously clean because we spent an entertaining time watching some grebes catching and eating fish in it and clearly enjoying the experience. Parts of the town centre are pretty enough, with one or two nice squares set about with shops, restaurants and the occasional fine fountain. There is, however, a slight but persistent feeling that the town has either fallen on hard times or more probably that it has never known anything better. Even though I did my best to like the place, I have to admit that some of the streets were fairly uninspiring. Inès uncharacteristically took against the local architecture and raged about the lack of imagination that had been shown in designing many of the local houses. 'Look at that: it's just . . . it's just a house,' she grumbled. As, indeed, it was.

Melun is not without its oddities. For example, the bridge leading to the island seems to have more names than you might expect for a simple stone structure. The sign in the middle showed it to be called Le Pont Jeanne d'Arc (what on earth was *she* doing here?), Le Pont du Châtelet and Le Pont aux Fruits. And then there was the restaurant on one of Melun's nicer *places* where we went for supper. This was very odd indeed. It was a tea room which at meal times offered a set menu. But it was the only place I have ever been in where the starter arrived and was set on the table while I was still standing up hanging up my jacket. It was so unexpected that we worried that the plates must have been intended for another table so, for quite a while, we just sat there, not daring to touch them. In fact, at meal times, the tea room only served its set menu. As there was nothing else on offer, the mere fact that you had entered the place was interpreted as being an order for the starter.

Just before we left, Inès asked the waiter, whose name badge showed him to be called Dominique, what we should see in Melun, given that it was our first visit. 'Je n'ai aucune idée: je ne suis pas d'ici, je suis de Montereau' – No idea: I'm not from round here, I'm from Montereau (the place only a short distance upstream) – replied the waiter in the tone of one being asked to give travel advice about some rural corner of Bolivia. And yes, we checked: he had been working in Melun for a long time. In his defence, I should perhaps point out that it isn't the easiest thing in France to be called Dominique: it is a name which can cause severe emotional scarring. This is thanks to a well-meant, but unfortunate song by a nun with the wonderful name of Soeur Sourire – Sister Smile – back in 1959. The song describes how Dominique – 'pauvre et chantant' – poor but fond of singing – travels about the place, spreading the good word about God wherever he goes. The song's drawback is that the chorus goes 'Dominique, nique, nique', sung cheerily in time with the rhythm. Back in the innocent days of 1959, this didn't mean anything at all. Unfortunately, there is a modern slang verb *niquer*, which means, roughly, 'to bonk'. This puts a whole new spin on the 'Dominique, nique, nique' line and can make life tough for any Dominique who has to put up with all his friends singing it at him all the time at embarrassing moments.

Of course, any embarrassment caused to the Dominiques of the world by Sister Sourire's song pales into insignificance when compared to that endured by France Gall back in 1966. At the time, France Gall was only eighteen and clearly quite astonishingly innocent. A distinctly malicious Serge Gainsbourg duped her into making a record entitled 'Les sucettes' – lollipops – a song which appeared to be just a childish hymn to lollipops, barley sugar and other sugary delights. Unfortunately, the words of the song could be interpreted – apparently by absolutely everyone on the planet *except* France Gall – to mean something quite astonishingly rude. Poor France Gall seemingly only discovered what the words really meant after she had sung it on national TV in, what's more, a particularly twee and childlike way.

As we were getting ready to head back towards Paris, two text messages arrived in quick succession. They were from friends who had been in that chilly garage the night the quest began. The first was from Siggi and Christine. It read simply: 'Alors – as-tu encore coulé?' – so have you sunk again? Sunk again? The cheek of it! My poor boat had only capsized (and didn't actually sink thanks to the fine workmanship shown in its construction) because the least nautical German of all time had mistreated it so despicably. The second text, from another couple of so-called friends, inquired whether I had given up on the quest and, if so, when they could expect their Champagne.

I couldn't let them get away with that!

Rather than just text back, Inès and I set off back round Melun in search of postcards to send. We found the perfect card. It was a black-and-white close-up of a large white rabbit with the hard, penetrating stare of a contract killer. There was a caption on the back reading 'Je vous ai à l'œil' – I've got my eye on you / don't mess with me. We bought two and sent them straight off to our friends with identical, defiant messages about how well things were going on and pointing out that I had now finished the first stage of the quest. Each card finished with the words: 'A votre place, je ne compterais pas trop sur le Champagne' – I wouldn't count on the Champagne if I were you.

Part 2:
The Paris Area

15

In order to best carry out our exploration of the Paris area, we had borrowed our daughter Sarah's flat while she was away. As you come in, you are left in no doubt that you are in a true Parisian apartment building. In the entrance hall you are faced with a flight of rickety spiral wooden stairs with an even more rickety, but surprisingly well-polished, wooden hand rail. Narrow, frosted-glass windows with brass latches let some light into the gloomy stairwell. Seventy-two steps and four floors up, you come to a small flat which is instantly recognizable as being of nineteenth-century Parisian vintage: creaky parquet floors, tall double windows with brass handles, a shallow stone sink with elderly taps set on the wall above and an inwardly curved wall at the end of the kitchen where the staircase carries on up outside. The view from the window is also typically Parisian in that it is of the grey, lead-covered roofs of the buildings opposite.

On our first evening we had great fun cooking on the little stove, eating our supper while gazing at the roofs and the street opposite and then washing up in the ridiculously impractical sink. During supper we had been vaguely aware of the general background noise typical of apartments anywhere: the muffled sound of next door's TV, a loo flushing upstairs, a couple laughing as they walked up the stairs past the front door . . . But it was only when we went to bed that we were suddenly reunited with a forgotten, but far from missed, enemy. The building, like many other Parisian ones, was fitted with a *vide-ordures* – a refuse chute.

Some things should never, ever have been allowed into Parisian hands, and none more so than the *vide-ordures*. If operated by a responsible person, it would be a useful, practical device: used by a Parisian, it becomes an anti-social menace. A refuse chute is usually located on a wall of the kitchen but can occasionally be found outside the flat on a service landing. In either case, it consists of a metal trap door which, when you pull it open towards you, reveals a metal container about the size of a small shoe box. You put your kitchen rubbish into the container and then push it closed against the wall. This allows whatever you put inside to fall down a long, tube-like chimney leading straight into the bin which is waiting several floors below in the basement.

Used sensibly, the device need make very little noise and saves you having to take your rubbish bags down every day. Unfortunately, being installed in a Parisian flat, and thus, being used by Parisians, a *vide-ordures* is very rarely used sensibly. Of course, there will be rules restricting the use of the device late at night and forbidding putting any kind of glass down it at any time of day, but, these will be ignored by most residents as a matter of principle. This means that, at a time which is usually exactly forty seconds after you have contentedly dozed off, some person upstairs will have a sudden desire to get rid of the beer bottles they have just finished. Rather than wait till morning, they will bung them straight into the *vide-ordures*, oblivious to the lateness of the hour. You are thus wrenched from sleep by the clatter of empty bottles being flung into the metal container, followed by a loud clang as it is thoughtlessly slammed against its support and then a crescendo of horrendous clattering as two or more bottles bounce frantically from side to side as they hurtle down the pipe towards your floor and then on down to the basement. If you are particularly fortunate, there may be another lot of bottles or even a few tins along a bit later.

The only thing that is possibly even more annoying than the clatter of bottles from above is when the person upstairs over-fills their container. When we used to live in a flat in Paris, the retired couple upstairs did this almost every evening. They would shove in their rubbish as hard as they could, slam the thing shut and then open it again to check whether it was empty. On seeing that it was still full because they had over-filled the rotten thing yet again, they would go on and slam it repeatedly and with increasing force until, at last, whatever it was finally wriggled free and slithered off down the pipe. They then generally gave the poor thing a few final slams just to be sure, even though they knew for a fact it was empty.

In the end, that evening we were lucky enough to get only that one cacophonous emptying of the *vide-ordures*, which, I suppose, is a small price to pay for the joy of waking up and having fresh coffee and croissants as you sit looking out at a Parisian street.

After our coffee we made the final approach to Paris on a journey that included two rivers and two counties. There is a new shuttle-boat line which has been set up to link the town of Maisons-Alfort in the Seine-et-Marne *département* with the Gare d'Austerlitz in eastern Paris. This bus boat is called Voguéo. The name comes from the verb *voguer*, which means to sail. We caught the boat at its terminus on the Marne just a few hundred metres from the point where the river joins the Seine for the run-in to Paris. This meeting of rivers here is unmarred by the which-river-is-it-really debate that so inflames passions upstream because there is no doubt in anyone's mind that the Seine here is the bigger player. The Voguéo craft is a small green-and-white catamaran with a central cabin and an open after-deck. The inside of the boat is brightly coloured and, as it's relatively small, feels welcoming and cheery, even on a quiet Sunday morning. According to the friendly chap who sold the tickets, in rush hour the atmosphere on the boat is especially warm and friendly – far more so than on a Métro or a bus – because the number of people who use the line is fairly limited and so the passengers get to know each other very well. There must be worse ways to get to work each day.

We rejoined the Seine at the suburb of Ivry on the left bank, which is where the Voguéo makes its first stop. Pulling away from the Ivry dock, the boat passed under the huge concrete bridge (called *le pont amont* – the upstream bridge) that carries the Boulevard Périphérique – the Paris ring-road – across the Seine. Given that this ring-road marks the outer boundary of the city, passing under the bridge and into Paris should have been one of the major moments of my quest. But the first glimpse of the capital that you get from this part of the river is less than inspiring. Here, to say the least, beautiful Parisian landmarks are conspicuous by their absence. To be fair, this shouldn't be all that surprising, because this area of Paris, bordered on the right bank by the twelfth arrondissement and by the thirteenth on the left, used to be one of the poorest quarters of the city.

To get an idea of how poor it used to be you need only turn to Georges Simenon's novels. Some of Inspector Maigret's most demanding adventures were set around here amongst the mean streets of foul, cramped houses where the *chifonniers* – the rag and bone men – had their yards. In Maigret's day, the banks were also home to gravel and stone yards where building material brought in by barge was stored ready to be taken away in carts to building sites throughout Paris. Incidentally, Georges Simenon famously said 'La vraie face de Paris, c'est le bord de la Seine' – Paris's true face is shown on the banks of the Seine.

While the rag and bone yards and the decrepit houses have long since been cleared away, the tradition for storing building materials along the quayside remains. On both sides of the river are extensive yards which are piled high with stone and bricks as well as massive, open-sided sheds stacked with sacks of cement. As we passed one stretch of the right bank, I counted fifteen cement-mixer trucks all parked in a line.

Rather than stay on the little Voguéo all the way to its final stop at Austerlitz station, we got off on the right bank at Parc de Bercy. I had decided that if ever a part of the Seine deserved being walked along as part of the quest, it was this final approach into central Paris. Walking this stretch would also give us the possibility of crossing the Passerelle Simone de Beauvoir, one of Paris's newest and most surprising bridges.

The Simone de Beauvoir footbridge is unusual in that it works on the same basic principle as the big staircase in the Château de Chambord, with its two concentric spiral branches: it is one construction made up of two parts which go two completely different ways but which take you to the same spot in the end. When you set out to walk across the bridge you can choose to take the high road or the low road. If there are two of you crossing together, you can have splendid, simple fun by each choosing your own part of the bridge to walk on. Inès picked the single upwardly curving central sweep and was rewarded in the middle of the river by a wonderful view of Paris. I chose the other possibility and took the left-hand of the two downwardly curving parallel outer paths. This alternative route allowed me to cross from one side of the bridge to the other underneath the central span without being spotted by

Inès on the upper deck. Thanks to this I appeared, as if by magic, on the opposite side of the bridge to the one Inès was looking for me on. Surely no other Parisian footbridge can offer such a degree of excitement?

You are very probably far more knowledgeable about these things than I am, but I find I am never completely sure exactly who Simone de Beauvoir was. Indeed on the rare occasion her name comes up in conversation, I generally panic and worry that, at best, I might be mixing her up with someone else. Of course, I wouldn't go as far as to confuse her with Simón Bolívar, even though that would be a perfectly understandable mistake to make, not least because there is a splendid equestrian statue of him only a short way downstream from the Simone de Beauvoir footbridge. There is no particular reason to have a statue of him there at all; it was apparently a gift to France from some South American nations who wanted to mark the centenary of the Liberator's death and they had to put it somewhere. More understandable would be to confuse one Simone with another and think people are talking about Simone Signoret. But again, I don't think I would do that, because I have seen her in various films (Signoret, I mean, not de Beauvoir. I don't think Simone de Beauvoir made that many films, at least, none that I've ever seen) and know that she was married to one of the top ten most brilliant Frenchmen ever – Yves Montand – and they lived in Place Dauphine behind the law courts on the Ile de la Cité. Incidentally, you can have pretty much whoever you like for the remaining nine most brilliant Frenchmen ever, providing that at least two spots go to Monet and that none of the other seven is given to de Gaulle.

And just to be sure that everyone is clear about Ms de Beauvoir, she was the existentialist one who wrote *The Second Sex* and spent much of her life with Jean-Paul Sartre. At least, I'm fairly sure that's who she was.

Once we had finished amusing ourselves on the bridge, we carried along on the left bank, walking along a broad expanse of quayside which is dotted with replica Chinese junks and lightships that have been transformed into night clubs and restaurants. After a few hundred metres we reached the Joséphine Baker swimming pool. This is a brilliantly pragmatic Parisian solution to the problem of where to site a swimming pool. Parisian reasoning – I'm starting to realize that I actually rather admire Parisians – seems to go like this: if you don't know where to put a large expanse of water, why not stick it in an even larger expanse of water? The first time they came up with this solution resulted in the Piscine Deligny. This was a large floating swimming pool that used to be moored on the left bank of the Seine in central Paris. Its main distinguishing feature was the fact that the swimming pool itself was completely upstaged by the open air solarium that surrounded it. For the Piscine Deligny's main claim to fame was that, in its heyday in the 1980s, it was the best place in Paris to encounter topless ladies on a summer's day and, it would seem, get to know them well enough to take them home. Having set Parisian pulses racing for many years, the Piscine Deligny was severely damaged in a storm and broke up and sank in July 1993.

The Joséphine Baker pool was opened in 2006 and is a clean, modern, steel-and-glass structure. I suggested to Inès that it was important to have a look at it as part of the quest because it was the only example we had seen of water within water and thus it was doubly pertinent. Inès wasn't convinced by this reasoning, but we went and had a look anyway.

According to the person I chatted to at the cash desk, it is their proud boast that they don't attract the same sort of clientele as did the old Deligny pool. Looking through the windows, I could see that the emphasis was on swimming and sport rather than on encountering members of the opposite sex. Despite its self-imposed clean-cut image, the pool's short life has been full of incidents. Notwithstanding the vast quantities of water both out-side the pool and in, it somehow contrived to catch fire shortly after it opened. How on earth it managed to do this is unclear; the person at the desk didn't seem keen to discuss it. Then, once the pool had been repaired, an error during a maintenance oper-ation nearly plunged it to the bottom of the river. Happily, it has been open without further incident since July 2008.

From the pool it was only a short walk to the Gare d'Austerlitz railway station where I was hoping to glimpse one of the Seine's less-well-known tributaries. Indeed, with all the fuss that I have been making about the Seine, you might be excused for assuming that it is the only river to flow through Paris. In fact, it isn't: there are supposed to be two others.

The first is the river Bièvre, which seemingly tries to con-sole itself over the fact that it is unknown to most Parisians by styling itself 'Paris's second river'. This is a proud boast indeed because, given the size of the Seine, a Parisian river would be hard put to come anything better than second. From some last-minute research I had done the day before I had got the impression that the Bièvre flowed into the Seine at a point on the left bank just near the Gare d'Austerlitz. But not a trace of it did we see. Further, more productive research has since revealed the fact that the unfortunate Bièvre was not only banished from public consciousness by being covered over along the whole length of its course through Paris in 1912, it was even denied the pleasure of pouring into the Seine. The poor Bièvre has now been made to flow straight into the main conduit of the Paris sewer system. This is hardly a dignified end for a self-respecting river but at least explains why we failed to find it.

The other Parisian river is somewhat better known, even though no one has seen it recently either. It is also surrounded by myth. In fact, it is so surrounded by myth that it is hard to be sure where the myth ends and reality begins, so much so that I am not completely convinced that the river really exists at all. It is called the Grange-Batelière, and the myths come from the fact that it features in *The Phantom of the Opera* by Gaston Leroux. In the book, the river is described as flowing under the Paris Opera, where it forms an underground lake. This is where the wicked Erik hangs out. No such lake exists, though a lot of people, notably those who have read the book, are quite convinced that it does. While there is no lake under the Opera there actually is a fair amount of water. The architect Garnier – who gave the Opera his name – had great problems with building the foundations due to the presence of so much water. It apparently took two years of pumping to get everything to dry out enough to even start building the walls. There is still a fair bit of water under the Opera to this day, as it seems that Garnier dealt with the problem by creating a subterranean cavern filled with water and which is intended for use in the event of a fire. This cavern may, or possibly may not, have fish in it.

Despite what *The Phantom of the Opera* would have you believe, the Grange-Batelière doesn't flow under the Opera but it does pass nearby on its way to the sewers into which it now flows just like the Bièvre. We had been told that the river goes right under the big Printemps Haussmann department store not far from the St-Lazare railway station. As it concerned an erstwhile tributary of the Seine, I thought it was worth the longish walk to Printemps to try and verify the rumour I had heard that you might be able to go down and see the Grange-Batelière from the shop's sub-basement. We walked all the way there but, according to the only shop assistant we tried who had any idea what I was talking about, health and safety laws don't allow that kind of thing any more. The river, again like the Bièvre, is now completely covered over. The only sign we could find that it ever existed is a small road near Boulevard Haussmann that was created when the river was covered over and which bears its name.

16

The important thing about Paris is that it is really quite small. Other cities sprawl endlessly in all directions, but Paris is clearly delimited; for all practical purposes, it is contained within the Boulevard Périphérique – the multi-lane ring-road. Paris is not like London, where someone who lives ten or even fifteen miles from the city centre will happily assure you that they live 'in London'; no one whose address doesn't end with a 75 post-code will ever say they live in Paris. It would be hard for them to claim otherwise, because, once you go beyond the Périphérique, you not only leave the city, you arrive in one of the three counties –Hauts de Seine (92), Seine Saint-Denis (93) and Val de Marne (94) – which ring the capital. If asked, residents of these counties start by telling you which county they live in, then, if you appear to know what they are talking about, go on to tell you the name of their town. Distances to Paris from other places in France are measured from a zero point marked on a stone in front of Notre Dame Cathedral. This reads 'Point zero des routes de France'. Nowhere in the city is further than seven kilometres from this zero point; it really isn't very big.

The city takes its name from its original inhabitants. Back in the Neolithic period, people following the course of the Seine (the very idea of such a thing!) came upon the Ile de la Cité, where Notre Dame now stands, and decided it was the ideal place to found a settlement. This original settlement grew into the town of Lutèce (Lutecia), a place inhabited by a tribe called the Parisii.

If you want to have an idea what Lutèce may have looked like, you need look no further than the Astérix books. In *La Serpe d'Or* – *The Golden Sickle* – Astérix and Obélix come to town to try and buy a new sickle for their druid. After a journey which is enlivened by brushes with ferocious brigands, they reach Lutèce, and we share their first view of the place. A clearly recognizable Ile de la Cité, linked by only one bridge to each bank, is packed with little wooden huts, chimneys smoking merrily. Even though it is just a small island settlement, Lutèce is clearly a whole lot bigger than Astérix's village. Indeed, Obélix is so stunned by the size of the place that he exclaims: 'Que c'est grand!' – it's so big! As Lutèce, along with all the rest of Gaul, except, of course, Astérix's village, had been conquered by 50 BC, the island has one or two substantial stone buildings built by the Romans which dwarf the locals' wooden huts. The name Lutèce may since have been lost in the mists of history, but at least the name of the original inhabitants lives on. Astérix's village, of course, didn't have a name at all.

Our exploration of the footbridges and swimming pools of eastern Paris had left us near Austerlitz station but with an appointment to keep later that day on the Pont des Arts, a footbridge that lies some way downstream. Having said how small Paris is, you might suppose that getting across it by river wouldn't pose much of a problem, but in fact there isn't all that much choice when it comes to trans-Parisian water transport. Faced with the task of getting downriver, your first thought might well be to catch a Bateau Mouche, one of the large passenger boats that take tourists on guided tours up and down the Seine. As a way of discovering the essential sights in a minimum of time, Bateaux Mouches have a lot to be said for them. Indeed, if you are prepared to pay more, you can even discover the city while enjoying a decent meal. But, for someone on a quest, such easy luxury doesn't seem appropriate at all. What's more, because Bateaux Mouches travel in a loop from one side of Paris to the other and back again, travelling on one would, for half the time, involve heading back towards the source. This is hardly in the spirit of a downstream quest. A final, minor consideration is the fact that Bateaux Mouches don't actually stop to pick up passengers along their way.

The only readily available river transport seemed to be something called a Batobus, a boat that travels up and down the river in the centre of the city; using ordinary public transport as part of the quest seemed perfectly acceptable. The Batobus – it is supposed to sound like *bateau bus* – looks very much like a small version of a standard Bateau Mouche: it is basically just a flat deck covered with seats and enclosed with a glass canopy. The Batobus has a route that it follows just like any other bus. This is made up of a long loop from the Jardin des Plantes natural history museum upstream of Notre Dame all the way down to the Eiffel tower. There the bus turns round and heads back upstream again. There aren't that many stops – just three on the right bank and five on the left – but they are almost all conveniently located for the major tourist destinations such as Notre Dame, the Musée d'Orsay or the Louvre. The stop to watch out for is the one rather optimistically called Champs-Elysées, which is actually a good ten minutes' walk from the avenue in question.

Incidentally, the idea of the *bateau bus* is not new. In the nineteenth century the Seine was one of the principal public transport axes of the city. In the course of one year, 1886, some eight million passengers were transported over a route that boasted over forty stops. The arrival of the Métro and bus networks put an end to the *bateau bus* until the idea was resurrected over a century later, albeit on a smaller scale. The original boats didn't disappear completely, of course: they evolved into the Bateaux Mouches.

Batobus's English-language slogan is 'Hop on: Hop off'. This is a fair bit simpler and catchier than its French one, which is 'Montez et descendez librement' – get on and off freely. Both slogans use four words to try and convey the same message but end up creating completely different impressions. The English one, with its repetitive use of 'Hop', has an attractive rhythm and conjures up an amusing image of someone leaping nimbly on and off the boat. The French slogan, on the other hand, is just a prosaic description of the rights granted to anyone who buys a ticket. You get the feeling that someone pinched the 'Hop on' idea from somewhere and only then realized that they were going to have to translate it into French.

Our nearest Batobus stop was further downstream, at Hôtel de Ville. To get there we walked over the Pont de Sully to reach the right bank of the Seine. Once on the quayside, however, we found that a large number of people had got there before us. They had all come, not to catch the Batobus, but to take part in one of Paris's best-ever ideas – Paris Plages. Every summer since 2002, a stretch of Parisian quayside is transformed into a holiday resort for a month with some three kilometres of it being closed to traffic and opened to short-term holidaymakers. The event was originally known as Paris Plage – without an *s* – a nod to the seaside town of Le Touquet, which has always styled itself that way because of the huge number of Parisians who used to go on holiday there. In 2006, in view of the success of the previous years' events, the city fathers extended the event to include a second beach on the nearby Canal St Martin. With this the name became Paris Plages, which it has remained ever since. Adding the *s* also helped to put an end to any possible conflict over the name between Paris and Le Touquet.

Parasol on Paris Plages – taken by Peter Eriksson

Paris Plages is easy to sum up: you either love it or you despise it. But there is much to love and not a lot to despise. For a start, its annual existence is the result of a fairly impressive operation. Some 2,000 tons of sand is brought in by barge and then spread out along selected lengths of quayside. In addition to all the sand, the organizers bring in and set out a selection of full-sized palm trees in huge pots as well as a considerable number of deck chairs, some hammocks, a vast array of sun loungers, a climbing wall, a dance floor, a swimming pool, some swings, a trampoline or two, a few places to play *pétanque*, some bar-football tables and much more. On top of this there are information booths, first aid tents, bars and cafés, a library . . . It is a vast and very well-run operation. Practically every activity (except eating and drinking) is free. If you ask nicely, they may even give you some sunscreen.

Of the people who speak disparagingly about the event, many haven't actually been and justify their not having done so by their belief that it is too crowded, or is full of yobs, or is dirty, or simply is not that interesting. It is true that it can get very, very crowded, especially on a sunny weekend afternoon. But if you go to Paris Plages in the morning, or on a cloudy day, you can stroll happily along the quayside, pausing occasionally to lie in a hammock or relax in a deckchair near someone else's children who are making sand castles. And then you can have a game of *pétanque*, enjoy an ice cream, have another pause on a sun lounger, order a beer, perhaps, followed by a game of bar-football before you wander contentedly back again. If you are feeling a bit hot, you can always cool off by walking through a series of very fine water sprays that don't look as though they are going to make you all that wet, but do.

Having been several years running, I believe that Paris Plages' only real shortcoming is the fact that most of the activities that I really fancy doing – learning to make smoothies, the handicrafts stand, the badminton courts and the trampolines – are exclusively reserved for children. Each year I am struck anew by how unfair this is: playing *pétanque* is all very well, but it can't possibly match up to a bit of trampolining.

In my role as a man on a mission I declared that we should have nothing to do with any of the attractions that we passed on our way to catch the Batobus; frivolous enjoyment does not sit well with a quest. But I am not made of steel: if someone offers the possibility to sprawl luxuriantly on a large comfortable bean bag, in the shade, beside a river, surrounded by beautiful architecture, while watching an entertaining selection of people taking part in their first-ever tai chi lesson, it would take a tougher person than me to say 'Non, merci.'

Some while later, revived by our rest, we set off to keep our appointment on the Pont des Arts. The Pont des Arts is a foot-bridge over the Seine which stands between the Ile de la Cité and the Louvre. It is quite simply one of the most wonderful footbridges across any river anywhere. If you are going to visit it – it is more than just a bridge so you visit it rather than just cross it – the best time is on a warm Saturday evening in July. The bridge itself is beautiful, but of course, you can't really appreciate that when you are on it. But when you walk across it in the summer, or indeed at any time of the year, you are treated to one of the best views in Paris and therefore, by defi-nition, in the whole world. Kenneth Clark started his book *Civilisation* by saying, when on the bridge, 'What is civilisation? I do not know. I can't define it in abstract terms – yet. But I think I can recognise it when I see it: and I am looking at it now.' What more could you ask of a view from a footbridge?

The present bridge was rebuilt in the early 1980s. The first bridge, built in 1804, had had a troubled life, being bombed in two World Wars and getting carelessly bashed by numerous passing barges (none anything to do with me). One of the incidents was so violent that a great chunk of the bridge fell into the river. Paris-ian attitudes to health and safety were clearly fairly relaxed in those days because, despite the fact that there was a sizeable piece of it missing, the bridge stayed open to pedestrians for quite a while before the municipality finally got around to closing it. A replacement bridge was opened by Jacques Chirac in the summer of 1984, just in time for our daughter Sarah to practise crawling on it, an activity for which the bridge is particularly suited as it is completely flat and made up of smooth wooden planks.

As we reached the stop at Hôtel de Ville – Paris's town hall – a splendidly ornate building that looks like an over-exuberant Loire valley château, the sight of it reminded me of a question which had been troubling me for months now. Some days later, in an attempt to find out, I sent a friendly email to the Hôtel de Ville, explaining that I understood that they had bought the source back in 1864 and was wondering what they had done with it since. This provoked a bluff, no nonsense reply which directed me towards the water page of the city's website but made no real attempt to answer my question about the source. I spent a considerable time reading the page in question, which taught me all sorts of things about Parisian water but absolutely nothing whatever about the source. Long years in France have taught me that, if you want to get anywhere with French bureaucracy, the things you need most are the three *p*s: politeness, patience and persistence. (Conversely, the three *r*s – rudeness, reticence and renouncing – will get you absolutely nowhere.)

So I sent another, slightly firmer and more specific email, thanking them for their reply and telling them how much I had enjoyed their website but pointing out that, interesting as it had been, it didn't actually deal with the source in any way, let alone the ownership thereof. This provoked a rather terse reply informing me that my inquiry had been passed on to the 'advisor in the mayoral offices who is in charge of water', who would give it his 'close attention'. I waited a couple of weeks and then, when I heard nothing, went round in person.

The Hôtel de Ville is well defended: casual visitors have to go through a security scanner before being allowed even to approach the reception desk. The interior of the building is apparently fabulous, with magnificent halls and ornate committee rooms, but the only way to see them is to book a place on one of the weekly guided tours. When I went, the ground floor was *en travaux* – undergoing building works – so a temporary reception desk was stuck in a corner in a small space surrounded by bare plywood walls. Despite the plain surroundings the bearded receptionist couldn't have been more helpful (thanks, no doubt, to my skilful use of the three *p*s). I showed him the email I had received, and he promptly pointed out that the *conseiller* who was supposed to be studying my request wasn't the right chap at all. After a bit of searching he gave me a new contact. My suggestion that I might be allowed to pop up and chat with the person there and then was politely, but most firmly, dismissed. One does not drop in unannounced on senior French civil servants.

So I sent another email, this time to the 'Adjointe au Maire en charge d'eau, assainissement et gestion des canaux' – the mayorial assistant in charge of all things to do with water. To my astonishment, the very same day, at 7.30 in the evening (I shall have to revise my view of French civil servants), I received a friendly and helpful reply. This basically said that, while the city of Paris hadn't actually done that much with the source since Baron Haussmann had had the idea of acquiring it, plans were currently afoot to cooperate with the local county council of Côte d'Or for a 'mise en valeur du site des sources de la Seine' – redevelopment of the site of the source . . . I shall go back in a while to see what they have done.

After only a short wait at the Batobus stop, a boat arrived, we got on and grabbed good seats by the window. The Batobus had a crew of two: a young, appropriately nautical-looking captain with a beard who did the driving and a pleasant-looking girl who checked the tickets and let people on and off. At each stop the girl's routine was the same. First, she would announce the name of the stop in French, English and Spanish, then throw in a sentence or two about whatever might be found nearby – 'St Germain des Près: the stop for the historic Latin quarter, so called because the students at the Sorbonne used to have their lessons in Latin.'

On the left, extending a fair way down the Ile de la Cité, we passed La Conciergerie. This used to be the Paris prison, back in the grim days of the Revolution, but is now better known to tourists as the home of the Sainte Chapelle, a thirteenth-century Gothic masterpiece with the most glorious stained glass windows you can find in France and probably anywhere else. Perhaps less well known is the fact that the Conciergerie also houses Le Palais de Justice – the Paris law courts. Relatively few Parisians have been inside, but I have been lucky enough to see several of the courts there in action – though I should perhaps point out that this is thanks to my job rather than because I had committed an arrestable offence – notably the Tribunal de Grande Instance – the High Court – and the Court d'Appel – the Appeal Court.

Once inside the Conciergerie, a flight of steps leads you from the principal courtyard into the main building. As so many cases are heard, you have to ask at the information desk for the particular court you are looking for. The nice receptionist, who speaks astonishingly fast, rattles off long and complicated directions – across the main hall, up the third set of stairs, down the corridor, past the second policeman, round the corner into another hall and it's the fourth door on the right – then promptly turns to deal with someone else. With that, you set off, hoping you are going to remember it all and, more importantly, wishing that you had thought of bringing a ball of string for the return trip.

The way to the courtroom takes you through one of the main halls called the Salle des Pas Perdus – the hall of lost steps – a magnificent vaulted hallway with arches and tall windows. As it is close to several courts it is believed to have got its name from all the people who spent time wandering restlessly back and forth, waiting for juries to return or for judges to finish their deliberation. It is also where they set up the lights and cameras whenever there is a high-profile trial going on. You press on in anticipation, thinking of all the TV dramas you have seen in which barristers in wigs, juries, spectators, subtle cross-questioning, the accused in the dock and a judge in full regalia feature strongly. When at last you finally make it to the court, it unfortunately falls well short of anything seen on TV. Imagine a small, mid-nineteenth-century village chapel that hasn't had a good clean for decades – dusty wooden floors, battered wooden pews set out in two rows of three, a raised dais with a wide table, a broken wall clock, grimy cardboard boxes abandoned here and there on side tables among piles of forgotten papers and the obligatory bust of Marianne on the wall.

Marianne is the symbol of the French Republic: you can spot a bust bearing her name in most major public buildings and in every *mairie* – town hall – in the country. All the busts are similar: they show an attractive woman wearing a *bonnet phrygien* – the woollen cap worn by women during the Revolution.

Early representations showed Marianne as fierce and warlike, brandishing weapons and leading the people into battle. Eugène Delacroix's picture *Liberty Leading the People* shows a good example of this. Over the years, however, she has lost her weapons, and her expression has softened considerably.

Busts of Marianne started to appear around the hundredth anniversary of the Revolution, when they replaced statues of the much less attractive Napoleon III. In the early years, the bust was just a simple representation of an unknown woman. Since the Fifth Republic it has become traditional to have the bust modelled on a popular (and attractive) woman of the time. This idea dates from 1968, when, unsurprisingly, they chose Brigitte Bardot as their first model. Since then, the model has changed several times and has included Catherine Deneuve, Laetitia Casta and currently Sophie Marceau, each of whom was chosen by a committee of French mayors.

There are around 36,000 *mairies* in France, but not all change their bust each time there is a new model. This is due both to the expense but also to a reluctance to flood the market with second-hand statues of Laetitia Casta.

Marianne also features on French stamps, the blue, white and red government logo and on French 10, 20 and 50 centime euro coins.

When the boat reached our stop we hopped off, as the sign had instructed us to do, and headed back to the Pont des Arts.

We wanted to be on the bridge that warm Saturday evening because we were inviting ourselves to our daughter Sarah's birthday party. We went expecting to find a single party going on somewhere on the bridge: in fact we found thirty parties. The Pont des Arts – strictly, as it is a footbridge, it should be called the Passerelle des Arts, but no one really bothers – has progressed from being the bridge most favoured by young couples for a romantic stroll to being the most fashionable place in Paris to have a party on a summer's evening. Young couples continue to come and stroll, of course, and often mark their passage by attaching a padlock to the bridge structure. Both sides of the bridge are weighed down by padlocks of all sizes, many bearing necessarily succinct, but undoubtedly heartfelt, messages written in felt pen. There are so many padlocks that the *mairie* periodically send people along with bolt cutters to remove them all. But, as soon as they have finished, the next lot of couples start replacing them.

Increasingly, visitors come armed not just with padlocks and felt pens but with blankets, cushions, ice boxes, food hampers and their close friends. Judging from the sight that greeted us when we walked on to the bridge that evening, you can come and celebrate your birthday or you can just come and have an *apéro* with your friends. That evening the entire walkway was covered with groups of people with only a narrow central space left for walkers. We picked our way past circles of revellers sitting on the ground while we looked for 'our' party. The average age on the bridge was clearly quite low but, reassuringly, there was the occasional group of people nearer our age.

A brief survey suggested that the older the participants, the better they were equipped and the more comfortably they were seated.

We had covered a good two-thirds of the length of the bridge before spotting Sarah. She has learned to walk since that first time she came on the bridge. As luck would have it, we arrived exactly at the moment she opened her present, and it warmed our hearts to see how pleased she was at the sight of it, especially as she hadn't spotted us at that point. Once noticed, we were collectively showered with hugs, *bises* and the last drops of the Champagne. There were even some slices of *saucisson* left. What more could one ask? It was all remarkably cheery, especially because, as each group of revellers is extremely close to the next lot, and there are large numbers of tourists constantly weaving their way through the crowds, when someone starts singing 'Happy Birthday to You', a surprising number of strangers tend to join in, some even singing in Korean.

And what of the view? When he stood in the middle of the bridge, Kenneth Clark would have seen: the Louvre, the Institut de France, the Eiffel tower, the Ile de la Cité with the towers of Notre Dame in the background, the Conciergerie with the Paris law courts, the Pont Neuf, the future Musée d'Orsay . . . and, of course, the Seine.

Civilisation? Most definitely.

17

You may recall that, on my very first visit to Paris, I had been stunned by the sight of a barge inexplicably crashing into the quayside. Having travelled the next stretch of river, I can only say how surprised I am that such incidents don't happen more often.

Through one of those peculiar, vague family relationships – my mother was friends with his mother, or something like that – we know Andrew, who lives on a barge on the Seine. Andrew doesn't live just anywhere, you understand; his postal address is: the name of his barge, Pont de la Concorde, Paris. As addresses go, this is both easy to remember and spectacularly prestigious. Living by the Place de la Concorde has the added advantage of being handy for the Champs-Elysées, or the parliament building should you need to go there or, more importantly, the Paris branch of WHSmith. Incidentally, building the Pont de la Concorde had begun in 1788, and the bridge had been half finished by 14 July 1789. After the storming of the Bastille, the bridge was finally completed using stones brought from the ruins. But not a lot of people know that . . .

Andrew's barge is a classic converted twenty-six-metre Freycinet barge where the original hold has been decked over and transformed into an apartment. When you go aboard and down the flight of steps, the wooden floor and long, narrow windows could be in some chic urban loft conversion and make the living area feel spacious and comfortable. There is, perhaps, a slightly damp, musty smell about the place due to the close proximity to the river. What really leaves you in no doubt that you are on a boat is a visit to the bathroom. Because the floor of the living space is actually below the waterline and because, when you pull out the plug, you want the bath water to drain out rather than the Seine to rush in, the bath has to be located on a high wooden pedestal so as to site it well above the level of the river. You thus have to climb up some steps to get into the bath, which gives bath time a somewhat regal feeling I am told. The loo, on the other hand, is at floor level, but is equipped with a peculiar arrangement of valves and a lever. This, once you have had a brief but slightly embarrassing training session, allows you to use it and pump it straight into the river. This is something that should perhaps be borne in mind if ever you get the urge to swim in a river downstream of a load of barges.

The location at Place de la Concorde is so sought after that each stretch of quayside is home to several barges, all moored side by side. Barges generally have their station in life: if your place is by the quay, or, more desirably, out by the river, you tend to return there each time you go on a trip. For those who have one of the inside spots, getting the barge out, or back in again after a journey, requires a fair bit of cooperation from your neighbours. What's more, if you live beside the quay, residents of other barges further out have a right of passage across your deck to get to and from their home, as, of course, do you if you come back from a trip and have to leave your barge further out. Understandably, you are expected to tiptoe when coming home late at night so as not to disturb those whose deck you are crossing. One unexpected advantage of this intimacy with your neighbours is that it does tend to keep burglars away. I stepped onto Andrew's barge one lunchtime to drop something off for him. As I did so, heads emerged from two nearby barges and I was asked quite sharply what business I had there. This seems far more practical than having to fit alarm systems or keep a guard dog.

An evening spent on his barge is wonderful: Andrew is a great cook and extremely generous with the wine. Towards the end of one of his meals you might well get the impression that the floor is moving up and down, whereupon you wonder guiltily if you have perhaps been overdoing the wine. It might not be the effects of the alcohol at all; it might just be that a Bateau Mouche or some other big boat has just gone past, and the barge is being rocked by its wake. This can come as a huge relief and makes a splendid excuse to drink more wine.

That particular evening we had been invited to a mobile drinks party. Once all the guests were on board and everyone was enjoying a glass of something on deck in the evening sunshine, Andrew set to work casting off ropes and starting the motor. It seems that back in the day when the barge was converted to include an engine, the previous owner just grabbed whatever was available. The barge's engine thus comes from an elderly Berliet truck, while the gearbox apparently had come from a tank. When the final rope was cast off, the engine noise was heard to deepen, and we were off.

We chugged steadily under the Pont Alexandre III, with the Grand Palais off to our right and the dome of the Invalides away to our left, with our host at the wheel in the little wheelhouse at the stern. Passing the Modern Art museum, we came to the Eiffel tower. Having seen the tower from the river on numerous Bateaux Mouches trips, I thought this might be a good time to see if I could have a go at the helm. I went aft to the wheelhouse, which proved to be a fairly stark place. It was a simple, varnished wooden structure containing a couple of gauges, a throttle and a huge steering wheel. Having shown me what did what, Andrew passed me the wheel. Unfortunately, as we had just swung past the Eiffel tower and under the Pont de Bir Hakeim, we had entered a long, straight stretch of river, and so there wasn't a lot of actual steering for me to do. All I really had to do was keep a watchful eye out for other boats.

One of the boats that we passed was the *Belenos*, a craft which has the job of cleaning up this part of the river. It is a catamaran equipped with a cunning mesh filter arrangement that skims floating rubbish from the surface of the river and dumps it in a storage bin at the back. Since it started operations in 1980 the *Belenos* has removed 400 tons of rubbish from the river every year, much of it plastic bottles and bags. According to an interview I read with the captain, while they still pull out loads of rubbish, there seems less tendency by local residents to use the river as a dustbin; the *Belenos* pulls out fewer cars, fridges and shopping trolleys than it used to. The captain said they once pulled a safe out of the water, though unfortunately it was empty. The name *Belenos* was chosen because he was the Gauls' god of health and of sources of rivers, notably that of the Seine. In the cartoon books, Astérix and his companions spend a lot of their time invoking his name – 'Oui, par Belenos!' – in their more exciting moments. Because the boat is quite large, it can't always get into confined spaces to pick up rubbish. To overcome this, the *Belenos* has recently acquired a smaller and more agile little sister who can nip in between parked barges or into other tight spaces to tidy up. This other, nimbler craft is called . . . *Sequana*!

After a few minutes, my enforced inactivity at the wheel due to the long, straight stretch of the river started to pall, and I asked Andrew if I could perhaps do a zig-zag or two to spice things up a bit. We had just got to the end of the narrow island called L'Ile des Cygnes, the one which boasts a small version of the Statue of Liberty at its end, and Andrew said that, if I liked, I could slow down and turn round and do a complete circuit of the island to give us all a good look at the statue. Cutting back the throttle, I turned the big wheel to the left, but nothing seemed to happen. I gave another turn to the left: the barge carried on as before. Ignoring the slight smile on Andrew's face, I wound on another couple of turns. The barge at last started to bear to the left. Once I felt that it was headed roughly where I wanted to go, I casually turned the wheel back to the right to straighten her up but the barge carried on turning to the left. More turns to the right, more urgently this time. The left turn started to slow, but then, rather than straighten up, the barge started to swing inexorably towards the right, heading for the opposite bank. 'She does that,' said Andrew calmly in the voice of one describing an unruly, but much-loved, pet, 'She takes a while to react, and then a bit longer to straighten up. It's because of her bulk. You have to be patient with her and anticipate it all a bit.' Getting her straight at last, we headed briefly along the island before it was time to turn again. This time, I tried to be more patient. It went better than the first time, but I still left a shamefully messy wake behind us as we headed past the island. At least it gave me a better understanding of how the barge captain had come to bash into the wall all those years before.

The statue of 'Liberté éclairant le monde' which graces New York Harbour was designed by Frédéric Bartholdi and given to the United States by the French people in 1886. The smaller version, which, thanks to my circuit of the Ile des Cygnes, we all had time to admire from various angles, is a quarter-size bronze version of one of the original plaster models. It was paid for by French expatriates living in the USA and put on the island in 1889 to mark the centenary of the Revolution.

You would think that one copy of the statue would be enough for any city, but, in fact, there are three others scattered about the place: two in the Arts et Métiers museum and one in the Jardin de Luxembourg. There is also the copy of the torch which has been adopted as a memorial for Princess Diana, whose car crashed in the underpass beneath it.

The fashion for spreading bits of the statue of Liberty around Paris is not a new one: before the statue was packed up and sent off to New York, the head was originally displayed at the Exposition Universelle in 1878.

I was hoping that we would press on as far as Asnières and the Ile des Ravageurs, site of an unusual cemetery, the last home of some 40,000 domestic pets. It is the most extraordinary place. You walk in to be faced with a fairly conventional-looking cemetery with parallel lines of headstones extending along the bank of the river. It is only after a few seconds that you realize that all the stones are much smaller than usual. Stone after stone bears the name of a much-loved pet, its dates and, very often a poem or a touching declaration of how much the animal meant to its owner. Many of the stones are decorated with flowers, some of them fresh. Opened in 1889 thanks to the efforts of an actress, Marguerite Durand, the cemetery can be a disconcerting place. At first sight it can seem a bit twee: the poems and messages can appear rather trite, and many of the stones are decorated with toys or models, some of which make you snigger. But after you have walked around for a while you change your mind: I have never seen so many heart-felt declarations of love and gratitude in my life. For over a hundred years, grieving owners have gone to huge trouble, and very probably great expense, to erect memorials to their friends, companions and substitute children and so to proclaim their love for them. Visitors who sniggered near the entrance can be seen wiping away a tear or two just a little further in. While cats and dogs predominate, there are also rabbits, a sheep, a racehorse, some ponies, Rin Tin Tin (how did he get there?), the very first St Bernard dog and the remains of a six-teen-year-old chicken called Cocotte, whose owner declared himself to be 'inconsolable' at her loss. There are also, appar-ently, a circus lion and a monkey or two, but we couldn't find them. While the cemetery commemorates dead pets, living animals aren't forgotten. A building at the far end was erected as a refuge for the numerous homeless cats that live amongst the headstones.

The trip with Andrew had taken us under the Pont Alexan-dre III. This is one of Paris's more notable bridges, not only because it is wonderful to look at, but more importantly for what you are specifically forbidden from doing underneath it. High up on one of the bridge's supporting beams is a small metal notice. Being small and inconveniently located, it is sur-prisingly hard to spot. To see it you have to be walking along the quay from the Pont de l'Alma towards Concorde on the right bank of the river, a walk which takes you through a rather gloomy tunnel under the bridge. As you pass through, you are more likely to look at the entrance to the nightclub that lies in an old boat shed to your left than up to your right into the bridge's eaves. I only looked up the first time because I wanted to be sure of keeping out of range of the pigeons that roost there in large numbers. Once you actually spot it and read its text, you will discover that a specific activity is forbidden underneath the bridge. Assuming that you have a sporting nature and want to try and guess what this activity might be, it is only fair to warn you that it is not probably something that you have ever thought desirable to do under a Parisian bridge, or indeed, under a bridge anywhere at all.

When seen from above, the Pont Alexandre III – the name dates from the signing of an alliance between France and Russia by Czar Alexander III and French President Sadi Carnot just before the Great Exhibition of 1900 – is a work of great beauty. The graceful 107-metre sweep of the bridge is set off by gilded statues on top of pairs of pillars on each end of the bridge. The statues are known as *renommées*, and represent Industry, Agriculture, Combat and the Arts. There are also a number of splendidly ornate lamps. All this makes it one of the most photogenic of all Parisian bridges. If you take the photo from the

left bank, you get the dome of the Grand Palais in the background, while a shot from the right bank will let you frame the Invalides between the bridge's pillars. You can't really go wrong.

And what about the thing you aren't allowed to do under the bridge?

It is . . . beating carpets.

I may have led a sheltered life, but I have yet to meet anyone who has expressed even the slightest wish to go and beat a carpet under a Parisian bridge.

Given the formal nature of the sign, this is probably just as well.

18

On the trip back to Andrew's berth we were overtaken by an inflatable boat travelling at considerable speed. It had the words 'Brigade Fluviale' – river police – down the side. First thing the next morning I set about tracking them down. Unlike the Hôtel de Ville, the Brigade Fluviale didn't seem to have an email address, even less a website, though I did manage to find a phone number. As a general rule, in France, when someone answers the phone in a government office, they just announce the name of whatever the organization happens to be – 'Sécurité sociale, Bonjour.' Occasionally they go on to give their name but more often prefer to remain anonymous. More peculiarly, having introduced themselves, they often feel obliged to reassure you that they might actually be going to pay attention to whatever you are about to say with the words 'J'écoute' – I'm listening. I always find this somehow bizarre: the person is there, with their ear to the phone. Why on earth wouldn't they be listening?

Just in their answering of the phone, the Brigade Fluviale marked themselves as a very classy operation. In a charming voice, the chap said, 'Brigade Fluviale. Bonjour; à qui ai-je l'honneur?' 'A qui ai-je l'honneur?' is delightfully old-fashioned and sounds roughly like a distinguished butler in a stately home answering the phone with the words 'Who may I say is speaking?' When I asked whether I could come round and ask them a few questions, I was politely advised to send a written request to their press office. Further questions revealed that it wasn't going to be up to the press officer to decide whether I was allowed to go but the Préfet de Paris. The Préfet is a top civil servant who is in charge of the Préfecture, the administrative centre of a given *département*. My casual request for a chat with the river police was therefore going to be considered by the head of the entire Paris police force. I felt that this wasn't perhaps the best use of the chap's time and said as much to the man from the Brigade. 'Ne vous inquiétez pas,' he said cheerily. 'Il est là pour ça!' – Don't you worry about that; it's what he's there for!

The river police's offices are, as you might expect from the name, on the river. A large, flat barge moored by the quayside a few minutes' walk from the Gare d'Austerlitz has been converted by having a number of temporary offices piled on top of it. I walked down a gangplank which led straight into a reception area and was instantly struck by two things: the floor was rocking slightly (that's something that doesn't often happen in my office), and the place was full of people, many of whom were a lot younger, and all of whom were in considerably better physical shape, than I am. I was also the only person present not wearing a blue jumpsuit and sporting an automatic pistol. (That's another thing that doesn't often happen in my office.)

I had never actually interviewed anyone officially before, so I had spent the previous couple of days preparing a list of questions that I thought might suit; I was meeting a senior police officer after all. In the end, I hardly needed to ask any of them. From the reception area I was led through a mess room with its well-equipped adjoining kitchen and out across another gangplank to a separate part of the barge. There, I was shown to an empty office, where I was asked to wait for the lieutenant who, I was assured, was due back any moment. As promised, barely a couple of minutes later, the lieutenant burst into the room and instantly set about greeting me, asking questions, telling me about the Brigade, answering the phone and replying to several emails ... all at exactly the same time. He explained that he had just returned from a training run but showed no sign of having taken any exercise whatever. These people were clearly even tougher than they looked.

The Brigade Fluviale was founded in 1900 by the then Préfet de Paris, Louis Lepine, who also came up with the idea of pedestrian crossings and created a dog patrol. If that wasn't enough, he also decreed that there should be one centralized lost property office in Paris, called, with impeccable logic, 'les objets trouvés' – *found* property rather than *lost* property.

Should you wish to join, you would first have to qualify as a normal policeman and gain some basic experience before taking the *concours* – entrance exam. The exam sounds particularly rigorous, seeing as how it includes tests in river regulations, first aid, swimming, underwater diving, boat handling and more. The nature of the tests explains the collective look of fitness and competence that reigns in their offices. They are all people that you would instantly pick to have on your side rather than against you.

At one point I asked about what I imagined was the toughest part of their job: fishing drowned people out of the water. Did it trouble them? As you might expect, the lieutenant explained that they become *aguerri* – hardened to it – though he didn't really talk about what it was like before you had acquired the necessary experience to harden you. I made the mistake of saying that I was pretty sure that I would be seriously shaken by the sight of a dead body, especially one which had spent some time in the water. To my horror, this was met with a cheerful offer to show me a film of his team fishing a body out of the river some time before. 'You get a really good idea of what it's like!' he assured me enthusiastically, like someone offering to show you his holiday movie of the Grand Canyon. It took considerable skill on my part to prevent him from actually showing it to me.

After we had been chatting for a while, the lieutenant said that, in order to have a better idea of what they do, I really needed to go out on a patrol with them. I was introduced to a major and his crew of three recent recruits. As before, my lack of blue jumpsuit and pistol made me stand out a bit. They took me aboard the *Ile de France*, an all-purpose craft which is designed to push or pull other boats out of trouble and is also equipped with a crane at the stern to lift things out of the water as well as a fire hose in the bows. The *Ile de France* is apparently the largest and best-equipped craft owned by any river police in Europe; a point of considerable pride. The trip was to form part of a routine patrol from their offices all the way down the river to the Eiffel tower and back, a circuit lasting a couple of hours.

Standing in the cabin, watching the helmsman coolly steering the boat with a wheel no bigger than a saucer – despite its size, the boat, with its four directional propellers, was amazingly light and manoeuvrable – I nearly spoiled everything with my very first question. I inquired whether they had ever fallen ill after swimming in the river. Unfortunately, I used the verb *se baigner*. A chill fell over the cabin at that point. 'On ne se baigne pas' – we do not 'bathe' – said the major, one hand drifting towards his Sig Sauer pistol, 'on nage' – we swim. *Se baigner* does mean 'swim' but applies more to people splashing about and having fun rather than *nager*, which is just the clinical term for propelling oneself through the water. They didn't actually throw me overboard and use me for target practice, but their collective demeanour suggested that, had they not been feeling generous, they could well have done. *Se baigner*: the very idea! And no, none of them had ever caught any bugs worth mentioning while *nageant* in the river.

I asked whether little rowing boats like mine were welcome on the river. For them, a small boat falls within the category of *menues embarcations* – very small craft – and as such are specifically banned from Parisian waters. I really liked the term *menues embarcations*: 'Come down to the garage to see my *menue embarcation*' sounds much more interesting than '*mon bateau*'. I then tried asking about stressful experiences that they might have had. I detected a distinct and collective reticence at replying to this, as though in some way it would be an admission of weakness. In the end, one of the younger crew members described how he had been called to assist when they had received reports that a tourist coach had crashed into the river. He was the first to dive down to find the coach and had gone in alone, believing that he was going to be faced with scores of dead bodies. In fact the bus had been empty when it fell off the quayside, though no one knew this at the time. Clearly, the anticipation of what he was going to find, even though it turned out not to be true, had been most unsettling. Then there was the question of suicides. These seem to fall into the 'damned if you do, damned if you don't' category. Arriving too late to save the person is obviously upsetting; arriving in time is not necessarily any better, because apparently the would-be suicide is very seldom pleased to be rescued and often takes their frustration out on their rescuer.

At one point I brought the discussion round to the local firemen and how they divide up the tasks between the two organizations, both of which have river patrols. Their reply was typical of inter-service rivalry, the sort of thing you get when you ask a soldier what he thinks of the air force, or vice versa. They made it clear that the fireman were decent enough chaps, but that the Brigade Fluviale was clearly the superior organization. To illustrate the difference between them, they explained that the firemen were always ready to race off and put out a fire on a boat, but generally they used so much water that, while they succeeded in putting out the fire, they often ended up sinking the boat. Even though they had probably heard this idea several times before, the entire crew fell about laughing at this point. Of course, they continued, only the Brigade is astute enough to turn up with pumps as well as a fire hose and so ensure that the fire is put out while also pumping out the excess water to save the boat.

Once back at the Brigade's base I went in search of the lieutenant to thank him for all his help. I found him in what appeared to be a filing room in the company of several of his colleagues and a large flagon of Sangria. The wine had been sent as a token of gratitude by someone or other, and the lieutenant had decided that everyone should have an aperitif or two before lunch. My morning thus finished on a strangely surreal note, standing in a gently rocking office, surrounded by police officers, who, for the first time in my life, were all warmly pressing me to have another drink.

19

It is difficult to further any sort of quest in August, because traditionally it is the month when the whole of France goes away on holiday.

Things aren't as bad as they once were. It used to be the case that every single factory would shut down for the entire month with all their employees having to take their holidays then whether they wanted to or not. With all the factories shut, all the offices that dealt with the factories shut too. And, of course, all the schools and universities were closed for the holidays as well. Hardly anyone was left at work. All the families that could afford to would then go away to spend the entire month by the sea, very often at the same seaside resort as the previous year.

A vast number of people still choose to take three or even four weeks off in August despite the fact that it is the busiest and most expensive period of the year to do so. For those who stay behind, things can become a bit frustrating, because local shops, hairdressers, cafés and restaurants often decide that, as almost everyone is away, they might as well close too. But, assuming you don't need to actually get something done like have your car serviced or find a plumber, staying at home in August can be wonderful. Public transport is almost empty, traffic flows freely, even at rush hour, and there are no queues at the canteen at work. You can even park for free in central Paris (and find a place to do so). I always spend August at work and find the whole experience so restful that I actively resent the approach of the end of the month when all these people that I have forgotten about start reappearing in the office and getting in the way, not to mention expecting me to actually do something productive.

Things started moving again at last around the beginning of September, when I spotted an advert for a cultural tour on the Seine pinned up in a dark corner at the back of the ticket counter of our local cinema. My obsession had by then reached such heights that the merest glimpse of the word *Seine* had me reacting like a pointer dog which had stumbled across an entire covey of partridges.

We had to meet up by a restaurant called La Maison Fournaise, which is in Chatou, a small town that lies to the west of Paris on the way to St-Germain-en-Laye. The restaurant stands on a long thin island that extends down the middle of the Seine, curving round towards the village of Bougival away to the west. What appears to be one single island is in fact made up of a series of independent, smaller islands interlinked by dykes. The two parallel halves of the river are thus completely separated one from the other over quite a distance by the resulting long, thin island.

La Maison Fournaise was much loved by the Impressionists – notably Renoir, who invited a friend there saying, 'I can't leave Chatou, because my painting is not finished yet. It would be nice of you to come down here and have lunch with me. You won't regret the trip, I assure you. There isn't a lovelier place in all the Paris area.' Even a century later, Renoir would probably still find the place a lot more attractive than his birthplace.

We spent some time exploring the island. A short way from the restaurant we came across an unusual boat club. The Sequana club is an extraordinary place: a group of volunteers, most of whom appear to be near or past retirement age, spend their evenings and weekends lovingly restoring antique rowing boats. If you ask nicely, one of them will give a very detailed guided tour of their two adjoining workshops, both of which are filled with elderly wooden boats in various states of repair. The place is enticingly filled with the smell of wood, glue and varnish. These boats have been restored to an astonishingly high standard and display the results of incredibly delicate and complex work. This is perhaps explained by the fact that among the club's members are a retired surgeon, a couple of precision engineers and a dentist.

We set off all the way down the left-hand side of the island on a stretch of river that forms the boundary between two *départements*. To our left, the side which is closer to Paris, was Hauts de Seine. Here, opposite Chatou, it is noticeably over-developed, as it is home to the large office buildings of the Rueil 2000 project, which do nothing whatever for the view. The island to our right in the Yvelines was visibly less spoiled. There, as we travelled along, we passed large numbers of fine, mature trees, a golf course, some attractive houses and a turtle the size of a soup plate, sunning itself on a log. There was a craze in France a few years ago for having terrapins as pets. Doting parents would buy aquariums for their offspring complete with a couple of greenish creatures the size of a matchbox that would swim about entertainingly and eat scraps of meat from the table. Unfortunately, terrapins grow. Once they had outgrown their homes, the parents could be seen – or, they hoped, not seen – creeping off to the nearest municipal pond or riverbank and pouring their pets off to a new life. It is thus quite common to spot a fair-sized turtle sitting by a fountain in a village square or sunning itself along a riverbank.

The first suburban train line out of Paris came past here in 1830 on the way to Le Pecq, a town that lies a short way downstream.

Rich Parisians were inspired by the easy access offered by the railways to build houses along the banks as weekend or holiday homes. You can still spot large family houses which look very much like those found in Deauville or Cabourg on the Normandy coast: two resorts also favoured by Parisians. Those who couldn't afford a house on the Seine just took advantage of the new train line to come for the day.

And it seems that the area used to be very rural indeed. This stretch of river became famous throughout the mid nineteenth century as a bathing place for Parisians. In those early days and outside the strict rules of the city, it seems that things were really quite relaxed and bathing dress was only optional. Only towards the end of the nineteenth century did bathing huts appear along the banks, and people were encouraged to wear swimming attire before entering the water. The island down the middle of the river is called L'Ile de la Grenouillère, its name a reference to the women who used to come and swim in the river. They were known as *grenouilles* because their shapely legs in action reminded people of swimming frogs. A less flattering possibility is that the word *grenouille* also used to be a disparaging term for a woman of loose morals.

As well as its reputation for being a desirable bathing spot, this part of the river was also known for the *canotiers* and for the *guingettes* that they frequented. It seems that, for once, Parisians had set out to copy the Londoners rather than the other way around. And what were the Londoners doing at the time that seemed so chic to Parisians? They were rowing on the River Thames. Rowing on the Seine at weekends suddenly became the fashionable thing to do and the *canotiers* – rowers – were born. Rowing boat hire firms sprung up along this part of the river to rent out boats to visitors, who came in large numbers. Having come all the way from Paris and spent a strenuous time rowing up and down the river while dressed in rather formal clothes, the *canotiers* obviously felt the need for a glass or two of something reviving, preferably followed by a convivial meal in the company of other, like-minded *canotiers*. And so the *guinguettes* were born.

To get an idea of what it was like at the time the Impressionists came to paint, you just have to take a stroll down the towpath on either side of the river. There you can find life-sized reproductions of the more famous pictures at the spots from which they are believed to have been painted. Sisley, Monet, Pissarro and Renoir were all attracted by the views, the rural setting, the *canotiers* rowing up and down and, most importantly, the quality of the light, to come and paint.

Like the *canotiers*, the easiest way to get an idea of what a *guinguette* actually looked like, as well as the atmosphere that could be found in one at meal times, is to look at some more Impressionist paintings. The best one to start with is Renoir's *Le déjeuner des canotiers*, not only because it shows a typically convivial meal at La Maison Fournaise, a well-known *guinguette*, but also because it shows the future Madame Renoir (and her dog) as well as Renoir's best friend, Caillebotte. In the background are two of the Fournaise children, and, behind them, you can just see some boats on the river. More prosaically, two things really made all this painting possible: the arrival of the railways and the invention of tubes of *gouache* paint. This provided an easily portable source of fresh paint in a multitude of colours.

To get a further sense of what it was like, you could always turn to some of Guy de Maupassant's works. Like the Impressionists, Maupassant discovered the river around Chatou and its *guinguettes* in the late nineteenth century and became such a fan that he included them in many of his books, notably *La*

Maison Tellier or *La Femme de Paul*. So keen did he become on rowing on the river and visiting the *guinguettes* that he actually acquired the nickname *le canotier*.

The nearby communities from which many of the tour participants had come – places such as Le Vésinet or St-Germain-en-Laye – are noticeably affluent and chic. A quick glance showed that the same could also be said for many of the participants. The men tended to have neat hair, glasses and wore carefully pressed casual trousers and polo shirts topped off with tasteful, pastel Lacoste sweaters draped over their shoulders and loosely knotted in front. None of them was wearing socks but they all had those trendy leather boat shoes that, should you actually wear them on a proper boat out to sea, guarantee that you would fall overboard in next to no time. Please pause now and spare a thought for such men: how on earth do they spot their own wives in a group of near-identical women? For most such women, like those on the boat that afternoon, look and dress identically. Any given one had shoulder-length, very clean brown hair held back with a *serre-tête* – a kind of smart Alice band – a kilt-like formal skirt, flat-heeled *mocassins*, a blouse or Lacoste polo shirt and a sober, high-quality sweater. A few were wearing make-up, but very discreetly applied.

Even if we hadn't already spotted them, the chic lot would have given themselves away as soon as they started asking questions; not because they dealt with obscure moments in the lives of Madame du Barry or Madame de Pompadour; it was rather the way in which they spoke. You can spot a chic French person (a proper chic person not just someone who is rich) by their vowels, vowels that are richer, rounder and more dragged out than a normal person's. Years ago, we lived in a flat next door to a whole family of such people. Of course, they were only living near us temporarily while they were waiting for their whopping great house to be done up. At the time they had four children, although by now they have probably got at least seven, who had names like Edouard, Arnaud and Charlotte. As they were exceedingly chic, their vowels tended to stretch out beyond all reasonable limits. This meant that, when they were on the landing getting ready to go out and doing a last-minute roll call of their offspring, the names would be drawn out endlessly, giving 'Edouuuaaaard ... Arnauuuuuud ... Charlooooote . . .' To imitate this properly, you have to make a round, open shape with your mouth and push your lips out. It's a bit like talking while yawning hugely. You could read most of a magazine in the time it took them to call out the four names.

20

I was back in my boat again. A few days before, I had gone down to fetch something from the garage and had glanced casually over at it. But, instead of a boat, all I could see was a storage bin. Somehow, over the weeks since we had brought it back from Montereau, it had become a handy place to dump everything that had been taken down to the garage to get it out of the way. There were some old towels, a pile of discarded magazines, a broken skateboard and the purple sleeping bag that, inexplicably, *still* hadn't been put back in its sleeve. This was no way to treat a boat.

So back to the river we went. I had rejoined the Seine a short way downstream from where the Impressionist tour had ended to meet up with my friend Stéphane, who regularly fishes along there. I was hoping that he would, amongst other things, tell me what kind of fish are to be found in the Seine. Stéphane is a carp fisherman. Carp fishermen are not the sort of occasional anglers who just turn up on a bit of riverbank at random, chuck in a hook with a worm on it and hope for the best. Carp fishermen do research. They are single-minded; they plan things. They come the day before and throw into the water great quantities of ground bait that they have lovingly prepared to a secret recipe to attract the fish and encourage them to stay in a particular spot. Then they come back and wait. And then, having waited, they wait a bit more. Apparently, Stéphane is the best sort of fisherman, the sort who catches the fish with care, takes pains not to stress it too much as he lands it, measures it, weighs it, photographs himself with it and then very carefully returns it to the water. What's more, it is Stéphane's proud boast that he always gives each fish he catches a kiss before returning it to the water. I don't know much about fishing but I'm fairly sure not all fishermen do this.

A few hundred metres down from where I relaunched the boat near Bougival I spotted Stéphane standing on a small jetty by the bank. There were fishing rods and gear of all sorts spread out around him. With very little prompting, Stéphane launched straight into an enthusiastic description of enormous carp and huge catfish and produced a series of photos of himself in the company of vast, surprisingly content fish. Clearly, being caught by Stéphane is as unstressful as he claims. But some of the fish in the photos looked to be pretty much the same size as him. 'Mais, je parlais de la Seine,' I insisted, thinking that he was showing me pictures of fish caught in the Amazon or in some extreme region of the tropics. 'Mais, ce sont des poissons que j'ai pris dans la Seine' – they *are* fish that I caught in the Seine – Stéphane replied and pointed out the bridge at Bougival in the background of one of the photos. It seems, therefore, that while I was innocently tootling along this part of the river, these enormous fish were lurking in the water right beneath me just like the shark in *Jaws*. I wonder whether the people at the rowing club where we launched the boat have any idea what they are sharing a river with each time they go out in one of their sculls. The largest catfish caught in the Seine weigh between 50 and 80 kilos and can measure up to 2.5 metres in length. I have no idea whether carp or catfish occasionally feel the need to jump out of the water, but if one suddenly decided to do so while someone was rowing past, it could sink the boat with no problem at all. And I seem to remember Stéphane saying that catfish are carnivorous, but it is possible that all the beer and *saucisson* we consumed may have clouded my memory a bit.

As to species, as well as carp and catfish that he fishes for and which were introduced into the river in 1980 to eat other, less desirable species such as the dreaded American crayfish, which is forcing out the local variety, Stéphane explained that you can find trout, pike, perch and gudgeon both around Paris and further upstream. There is also something called a *sandre*, which translates as 'pikeperch', something I previously assumed was two different fish being referred to at the same time. You can even find eels in some places, not to mention the occasional ornamental Koi carp that has outgrown both its pond and its welcome. Downriver, where the Seine becomes tidal, there are mullet and bream to be caught too. Of course, being a carp fan to the soles of his waders, Stéphane was quick to point out that his beloved carp can also be found there because they are so clever they can adapt to all sorts of different river conditions.

Inès turned up as Stéphane was getting his rods ready to start fishing. It became quickly clear to both of us that he would rather be left to get on and do this on his own, so we piled into the boat and set off downstream.

When upstream, we had met very few boats on the river.

Here, we came across one almost as soon as we had left Stéphane. It was a small sailing dinghy crewed by what seemed to be a couple in late middle age. They spent some time happily, though somewhat inexpertly, sailing up and down our stretch of the river while we rowed along, exchanging a few friendly words with us each time they passed before heading off round the next bend.

A few minutes later, the sailing dinghy reappeared around a bend a hundred or so metres away and swung round to carry on up the river towards us. As it did so, it gybed dramatically, clearly to the complete astonishment of its crew. The boom slammed over to the opposite side with such force that the dinghy started to heel over. A younger, nimbler crew could probably have got their weight across to the other side of the boat quickly enough to save the day. But this couple were far too slow. Even from where we were watching, we could feel their rigid indecision. Their little boat heeled over further and further with the couple's weight still located in precisely the worst possible place, until finally it capsized, flinging them into the water under the sail. Even then, it should have been OK. I can still hear Hubert, my gravelly-voiced instructor in Salcombe all those years ago, drumming it into us that, in circumstances like that, with the boat lying on its side, you had to swim round to the other side, get on to the centreboard, and pull the boat back up. What you should never ever do was to stay on the sail side and try and get back into the boat from there. Unfortunately, this, we were fascinated to see, was exactly what the duo set out to do. Together, in what passed for a frantic scramble for participants who were old, stiff, cold and wet, they tried to pull themselves back aboard their boat the wrong way. But it didn't work. All that happened was that they turned the whole thing right upside down and got a second ducking for their pains.

Still gazing from a distance, we realized that they had given it their best and only shot. As it had failed, they seemed to have resorted to the 'give up and hope for the best' strategy. This, on a cold day, was probably not their best option. With that, I bent to my oars (I have been longing to write that), and we set off to lend assistance. Despite my best bending, it took a good couple of minutes to get there: a long time for people in the middle of a cold river. Reaching their boat, we realized that the couple were a fair bit older than we had thought and, perhaps because of this, seemed to have given up completely. They were just floating there in their lifejackets, not doing anything, not even trying to gather the baler, sponge and half-empty water bottle that were drifting rather pathetically around them.

I called out cheerily, offering them a hand. They barely replied; the husband just flapped his hand weakly. Always keen to avoid being accused of piracy, I asked rather formally 'Est-ce que je peux monter à bord?' – permission to come aboard? Visibly shaking himself into some degree of alertness, the man muttered 'Seul un anglais poserait une question pareille à un tel moment' – only an Englishman would ask a question like that at a time like this. Giving him my best reassuring grin I shipped the oars, whereupon Inès and I grabbed hold of the upturned hull and started pulling. We quickly realized that, being a lot lighter than theirs, our boat was in no way designed as a recovery barge. Rather than pull theirs up, our heaving was just tipping our boat over. Before we knew what was happening, an alarming amount of river water was sluicing over the side, soaking our feet and setting my rucksack afloat. Inès flung herself across to balance our boat while I hung on to the dinghy. We tried again, this time with our transom up against their boat. With Inès balancing our boat, and water sloshing around our legs, I was able to carry on pulling. At last their dinghy started to swing upright, but when I pulled harder, it nearly put our boat under the water again. Rather than risk capsizing us as well, I clambered on to their centreboard and carried on heaving from there. With Inès pulling from our boat and me slipping around on the centreboard like a damp mountain goat, the dinghy slowly righted itself. Flinging myself inside just as it rolled upright so as to avoid being plunged backwards into the river, I still managed to scrape both knees and bang my head on a thwart.

Once the boat was upright, with me sprawled inside and Inès hanging on for dear life, the accursed thing tried to sail away all by itself. Rubbing my head, I managed to free up the sheets and bring the boat head to wind a few yards from our two chilly pieces of flotsam. Leaving them where they were for the time being, Inès fetched their baler and I set about emptying out the worst of the water. 'C'est bon! Vous pouvez monter à bord' – it's OK now, you can climb back in – I called to them a couple of minutes later. But they didn't react at all. As I was a fair bit colder and wetter than I had envisaged being when I got up that morning, I felt justified in telling them rather sharply to 'Secouez-vous' – snap out of it – and swim over to the stern. This they listlessly did until they were both hanging on the transom like elderly seals waiting to be fed. Two things became clear at that point: neither of them was going to get in under their own steam, and I wasn't going to be able to haul them in by myself.

'Je vais t'aider' – I'll give you a hand – Inès offered, tying our boat to theirs and climbing in. We heaved each of them into the boat, helped by Inès intoning 'Ho hisse!' like a seaman toiling on a rope. Shortly afterwards, the couple found themselves lying, like two recently caught tuna fish, side by side in the bottom of the boat. As they were gathering their wits and struggling upright, we straightened out their boat, sorted out the sails, put the mainsheet in the man's hand and climbed back into our boat. I fear I may even have patted him on the head as we left.

Now, I have read books and seen films where someone saves another person in a daring rescue and I know exactly what should happen. Some kind of token should be snapped in half and exchanged – 'If ever you need help, anything at all, show this half, and assistance shall be forthcoming.' Failing that, some small mark of gratitude (I believe an Italian sports car is the preferred choice) should be delivered to the rescuer's home. But the poor couple were beyond all that, so they just sailed away upriver in silence, and we never saw them again.

At least we still have their sponge . . .

21

The stretch of river I rowed down between Bougival and St-Germain-en-Laye is famous for a magnificent pumping system known as the 'Machine de Marly'. When Louis XIV had the château built in Versailles, he specifically requested that there be a large number of fountains, failing to notice or more probably care that there wasn't a river or decent source of water within miles. The King wanted fountains, so fountains he should have. The nearest potential supply of water was the Seine, several kilometres away and more than a hundred metres below the Versailles plateau. To overcome the problem of getting water from the river all the way up to feed the fountains, a vast arrangement of pipes was laid up the hill towards Louveciennes. There, they connected with a massive aqueduct that led off towards the château. But how do you get river water to flow uphill? Easy! At Port Marly, just upriver of St-Germain, they built a massive pumping station – the Machine de Marly – that sprawled halfway across the Seine. The principle behind the station was extremely simple: why not use the force of the river to pump itself up the hill? A huge series of paddle wheels were driven by the current and powered a system of pumps that sent the water off up the slope. But the pumps on the Seine weren't powerful enough to send the water all the way up to the top in one go. A second set were built about five hundred metres away to send the water the rest of the way up to the aqueduct. This second set was also powered by the Seine via a complex arrangement of levers.

Unfortunately, these levers clattered and creaked so loudly they kept all the neighbours awake. One of those who would later be kept awake, and complain about it most bitterly, was Madame du Barry, mistress to Louis XV. The whole system took about seven years to build and was inaugurated in 1684.

Unfortunately, even though I rowed past the very spot, I didn't see anything at all, because the pump was demolished in 1817. All that is left is the line of the pipes up the hill and the Louveciennes aqueduct, which is still a local landmark. Nevertheless, the fact that the pump hasn't been seen for a couple of centuries hasn't made it any less famous: indeed many people are quite convinced that it is still there.

We were both somewhat damp about the feet and legs after the rescue, so, just past the site of the Machine, I put Inès ashore so that she could walk back to the car. We agreed to meet up further down the river, in St-Germain-en-Laye. Once Inès had left, I rowed on down a stretch of the river which, despite its proximity to a main road, seemed astonishingly rural. Both the left bank and the bank of the Ile de la Loge, the long island which borders this whole reach, are set with trees and have very few visible buildings. A short way further on, I reached Port Marly and was delighted to row past the rowing club where we had launched the boat on that Sunday morning months before. I would have loved to have stopped to tell them how well the boat had performed since that day, but, unfortunately, as it was a weekday, there was no one around.

A few hundred metres past the rowing club, the entire character of the river changed rather alarmingly. Once I had reached the end of the island, instead of being in a quiet, calm, protected backwater, I was now out in the main river for the first time since leaving Montereau all that way upstream. And the Seine here is far, far wider than it was in Montereau. I suddenly found myself on a stretch of water a good 150 metres wide, a distance that seems enormous when seen from a small boat. And there was even more wind than there had been in the channel. And, what's more, there were waves. Waves! As if that wasn't enough, I could already feel that the current was much stronger. The quiet stretch I had come from had been closed to anything other than small boats, dinghies and rowing sculls. From here on, I was going to find myself sharing the river with boats of all sizes, especially the larger varieties of barge. In view of this risk of meeting something a whole lot bigger than me, it seemed prudent to stay close to the left bank, both to keep out of everyone's way and to give myself a vague sense of security.

The first real test of the boat's seaworthiness wasn't long in coming. Racing round the end of the island towards me came a huge bulk-carrier barge, so heavily laden its gunwales were almost awash. My first thought was that it seemed to be travelling straight towards me; my second was that there was absolutely nowhere to hide. The best idea seemed to be to get as close to the shore as possible, even though it was an unwelcoming, steep concrete wall. As the barge drew level, I turned the boat round so that it would be pointing straight at the approaching wake. Painfully gained experience over the years has shown me that wakes, like problems, should always be confronted head-on. Seen from the shore, the wake probably didn't look like much. Experienced from inside a small boat, with, what's more, your back to it so you don't know exactly when to get ready, it was far more spectacular; the boat pitched and bounced alarmingly. But more was to come, as I hadn't bargained on there being a rebound. When it reached the concrete wall, each wave of the wake bounced back and set off again back across the river, but at an angle to the way it had arrived. This meant that, as well as the waves coming from the front that I had been prepared for and which were busily making the boat pitch up and down, I was unexpectedly flung about from side to side by a load of new waves appearing from the shore.

I suppose that I could have turned round at that point and headed back into the safe, sheltered stretch. But that wouldn't really have been an acceptable option. I had taken up a challenge to travel down a river and so travel down it I would, despite the fact that the next bit looked like it was going to be a bit hairy. Thinking about it now, a good argument for turning back could have been based on the fact that, as on all my previous outings in the boat, I had neglected to bring along a lifejacket. But I didn't think of that at the time. In the end, I decided that the worst that could happen was that I would be tipped over by the wake of a passing boat. Thanks to Siggi's adventure back in Montereau, I was fairly sure that my boat didn't sink easily and I knew from experience that I don't either. So I did a brief review of all the things in my pockets to see if they would survive being unexpectedly plunged into cold water and carefully zipped my phone inside a plastic bag.

Having decided to carry on, I did my best to at least reduce the number of barges I would meet along the way by rowing much faster. Unfortunately, despite all my efforts, three more big barges went by, each loaded with sand or coal. I tried setting the boat at various angles to the oncoming wake and even, on one occasion, squatted down in the bottom of the boat in the hope of lowering the centre of gravity. It was difficult to tell whether the new strategies worked better than the previous one or whether I was simply getting used to finding myself a passenger on an aquatic roller-coaster every five minutes. Whatever the explanation, I found that, when the third barge went by, I was actually sufficiently relaxed to have time to read the information panel painted on its side. Thanks to this I can safely say that I have been shaken, but not stirred, by a barge which was eighty metres long, a distance which, to put it into some kind of perspective, is forty times longer than my boat.

Thankfully, before yet another barge could come along, I at last reached the quay which stands on the left bank in Le Pecq, just before the St-Germain road bridge. There, to my relief, Inès was waiting for me. Once I had clumsily changed my clothes in the car and put the boat away in the back, we were able to set off to keep our appointment up the hill in St-Germain-en-Laye: we were going to a grape harvest.

At St-Germain, the river comes within hailing distance of a proper vineyard for the first time since it left Champagne. Of course, you could argue that there are vines in Paris, up in the hills of Montmartre – and the Montmartre red wine, though ruinously expensive, is very good indeed – but they are surely much too far away from the river to properly count here. We had come that day because the grapes of the St-Germain vineyard were being harvested that very evening.

St-Germain-en-Laye is set on a plateau high above the river. The town is centred on the château, which was the residence of François I and later of Louis XIV, before he discovered Versailles. The gardens of the château are now a public park which extends away from the town centre towards a sheer cliff face that falls spectacularly down towards the river. Being set high up beside a sheer drop, the edge of the park affords fabulous views across to the towers at La Défense, with the monuments of Paris behind. More importantly, you can also follow a great sweep of the Seine as it swings by from Paris on its way west.

The King's carriage drive that leads from the château along the edge of the park and out towards the forest is still very much in use, though nowadays it is used by cyclists, walkers and joggers rather than by royal coaches. The round trip from the château to the end of the drive and back is four kilometres: a good distance to do on a Sunday afternoon after a heavy lunch. There is a stone balustrade that marks the edge of the park.

When we looked over the balustrade, we could see a small vineyard on a terrace down below where large wicker baskets filled with grapes were standing at the head of each row of vines. It seemed that we had missed the actual picking, which must have taken place earlier in the day. There were about a hundred people gathered near the balustrade, but practically none were taking any interest in the grapes; they were all more interested in a nearby marquee, apparently waiting for some kind of presentation to begin. We waited with them for a while, until we spotted the tractor coming up from the vineyard, laden with its baskets of grapes. Slipping away from the crowd, we went and asked the tractor driver if we could perhaps taste a grape or two. He was clearly delighted to share some of his stock with us. 'Enfin, des gens qui apprécient nos raisins, ça fait plaisir!' – at last, someone who appreciates our grapes. And quite delicious they were too.

At that moment the presentations began with a series of speeches made by local worthies. As is often the case with French official speeches, the beginning of each was devoted to endlessly listing the important people present: 'Monsieur le Préfet, Monsieur le Maire; Monsieur . . . Et Madame . . .' If a speaker gets really carried away with his own importance, he can even go through the list again at the end of his speech, thanking them for listening. I often get so irritated by such a tedious list of worthies that I can't be bothered to listen to the main part of the speech at all.

When the last speech was finally over, waitresses appeared

with trays of nibbly things and glasses of the local red wine from the previous year's harvest. The wine was surprisingly good: a strong, deep red with lots of fruit. There was much appreciative sniffing and slurping and exclaiming about how good it was, and not just by us. But I was keen to sample one or two of the nibbles as all the rowing had left me, once again, feeling hungry. But to do that we first had to get to them. As always in this kind of event in France it was *les retraités* – pensioners – who were causing all the trouble. I have never been to any kind of affair in France which didn't feature at least a couple of *retraités* standing foursquare in front of the table of canapés. The *retraités* near us had installed themselves in the best spot – they have a gift for finding it that is quite astonishing – and were not only attempting to hoover up all nibbly things within reach, they were ensuring, just by their presence, that no one else got a look-in. Hard-won experience shows that, at this kind of event, if you want the chance of getting anything to eat yourself, you have to put courtesy and fair play to one side and elbow your way into the throng.

Like many things in the fine-food line, canapés are a French invention. The French also came up with hors d'œuvres, foodstuffs which closely resemble canapés, so closely in fact that, in order to decide whether you are being offered one or the other, you need to know whether there is a meal coming up afterwards or not. If there is a following meal, you are faced with hors d'œuvres – an independent starter which is literally 'outside the works' of the meal. Conversely, if what you are eating is all you are going to get, then they are cànapés. Thus, canapés should be viewed as an accompaniment to drinks, but not to aperitifs. Canapés are very often based on small pieces of white bread which, like the bread used in fondues, has been allowed to go slightly stale before cooking so as to make it stronger. The name 'canapé' comes from an extension of the word for 'sofa' in recognition of the fact that something is laid upon a piece of bread in much the same way as a person lies on a sofa.

Section 3:
From Greater Paris to the Sea

22

Summer was almost over, and my challengers demanded an update on the quest. I told them how well things had been going so far and how much fun I had been having, notably with the Brigade Fluviale. When asked whether I reckoned the next part of the journey would be easy to accomplish, I foolishly replied that I was sure that it would. In support of this, I pointed out that I had already completed two of the three stages along the river and cheerfully described how easy it had been. What's more, along the way I had discovered vast areas of France I hadn't seen before, tasted quite a lot of Champagne, met some surprisingly friendly people and frequented a memorable series of bars and restaurants. There are worse ways of spending time. When Inès reminded them that this meant the date of their own trip was fast approaching, their smiles froze rather. Were they looking forward to indulging in pudding and jelly washed down with warm beer?

But now the boastful things that had been said were coming back to haunt me: I was starting to realize that completing my quest wasn't going to be half as simple as I had hoped. A belated map check had shown 300 kilometres of increasingly broad, increasingly bendy river stretching away to the distant sea, a length too dangerous to explore in a small rowing boat and which, at least on the stretch immediately after Paris, was devoid of any kind of public transport. And I had completely exhausted my small repertoire of friends who have their own boat.

Reducing the problem to its essentials showed that what I now needed to do was to find a complete stranger, or rather several such strangers, who were not only planning on travelling along at least part of the Seine downstream of Paris, but also, and possibly more importantly, could be persuaded to do so in the company of an unknown Englishman. I decided slightly desperately that the marinas along the river might be the answer to my prayer.

So, a couple of days later, on a sunny evening after work, I could be seen wandering along the quayside at the Port de l'Arsenal in eastern Paris in search of *la capitainerie* – the harbour master's office. The Port de l'Arsenal lies near the Place de la Bastille and forms the beginning of the Canal St Martin at the point where it leaves the Seine to wind its way north through Paris. It is a particularly pleasant place on a sunny evening. A long expanse of harbour filled with yachts and privately owned barges of all descriptions, many of them flying foreign flags, is bordered by stone quays with sloping lawns behind them. The quays that evening were filled with young mothers with pushchairs and small children taking a stroll before bedtime, while on the lawns were scattered numerous courting couples so engrossed in whatever they were doing that they were clearly oblivious to anything going on around them.

At the far end of the quay a long wooden ramp led me to the door of a narrow building with huge windows looking out over the harbour – I had found *la capitainerie*. I walked up a long flight of stairs into the room behind the huge windows to find a rugged-looking man in a blue shirt and blue trousers, who was concentrating on a series of video screens. These were showing various views of the harbour and its adjoining lock. When the lock gates that he had been carefully watching had finally closed, the man turned to see what I wanted. I launched into an initial explanation about who I was and what I was trying to do. This was met with no reaction whatsoever, a fact that I found somewhat unsettling. I carried on with my little speech and reached the bit where I asked if he thought it possible that any boat in his harbour might be going to head downriver. He barked 'Non' before I had even finished the question.

The following weekend, we set off to talk to the people at the next marina downriver from Paris to see if they could offer more help. I had noticed over the months that I have spent exploring the river that I had become much more skilled in interpreting body language. Some encounters, however, taxed my new-found skill less than others. The hefty bloke in the marina reception with a shaved head and a tight-fitting grey sweatshirt made his feelings clear right from the start. He took one look at us as we walked in and just stood there, leaning backwards, his mouth tightly closed and his arms crossed in front of him. I explained who I was and how I was trying to explore the river, but the arms stayed firmly crossed and the tightly shut mouth didn't waver. Inès had a try, approaching things from a different perspective and trying to play the 'eccentric English husband' card, but the man carried on resolutely leaning away from us. He clearly wasn't going to recommend me to anyone as a potential passenger.

The man's dismissive grumpiness had thankfully not been typical of the behaviour we had encountered since leaving the source. Unfortunately, this is not always the impression that visitors take home of those they deal with during their stay. Indeed, a lot of French people seem to strike visitors as unfriendly. One of the questions I get asked most often by pained visitors is: 'Why are French waiters – or, more particularly, Parisian waiters – so rude?' I suppose you could argue that, for a waiter to appear rude, they must behave in a sufficiently rude way for it to stand out relative to the average level of rudeness that you encounter in France during a typical day. Of all the people you meet in a given time, experience shows that a certain proportion – other drivers, passengers on public transport, colleagues at work, people in any kind of service industry – are going to be rude to you. Thus, in order for waiters to stand out, there must be more rude ones amongst them than this general average. But most of the waiters I have ever spoken to have been essentially very friendly.

So what might provoke your averagely pleasant, ordinary sort of waiter into anti-British rudeness? A possible answer lies in something very simple, so simple in fact that it just concerns a single word. That word is – *bonjour*. The lack of the greeting, or even the use of any other opening gambit in its place, simply won't do: there has to be an initial *bonjour*, or everything gets off on the wrong foot. If you, the customer, forget the *bonjour* and launch straight into whatever it is that you want to say – 'Which is the train to Marseilles, please?' 'Where would I find the cornflakes?' 'Can I have a cup of coffee?' – the person you are addressing will very probably ignore your question and hit you with a flat, more than slightly aggressive *bonjour* of their own. When you hear the tone of their *bonjour* and the way it is delivered, you are left in no doubt that you are being reproached. Feeling reproached, you may well feel forced to start the whole exchange again right from the beginning, but this time with an exaggerated *bonjour* of your own, and even back it up with a formal smile or perhaps a bow of the head to show how much you regret not having said it before. Alternatively, you might well think: 'Who the heck does this person think they are, giving me lessons in social etiquette?' and may even feel entitled to share this view with them. Doing that, however, will only end in all sorts of unpleasantness and, at the very best, won't get you the answer or the cup of coffee that you are looking for.

Wanting to check whether my *bonjour* explanation stands up to scrutiny, I have recently gone to the length of having a beer in several Parisian bars so as to be able to chat to a few waiters. How many people would show such selfless devotion to an investigation? In every case, the waiter agreed that it was very important for the customer to begin with a *bonjour* to get things off on the right foot. A recurring theme in my exchanges with the waiters was that failure to say *bonjour* was viewed as *mal poli*. This is a familiar alternative to the more proper term *mal élévé* – impolite. But the problem seems to go further than that. An unexpected discussion at the local florist led to the sales girl explaining heatedly that a failure to start any exchange with a *bonjour* was a clear sign for her that, in the eyes of the customer, 'Je n'existe pas' – I don't exist. In her view, a lack of a formal opening was not so much *mal poli* as a clear sign of contempt.

To be fair to the man at the marina that afternoon, after saying 'Non' more times than General de Gaulle, he did finally suggest that we ask at the nearby lock and even gave us vague directions as to how to find it. So, after a pleasant but fruitless prowl round the marina in search of some form of inspiration, we set off to look for the lock.

I can safely say that if there is one thing that is harder to find by road than a marina, it is a lock on the Seine. Clearly, everyone who actually uses the lock reaches it via the river. Boat users don't need signs to find it because the lock just appears in front of them as if by magic even when they're not even looking for it. The only person who needs to reach it by road is the lock keeper, and he doesn't need to be shown the way because he goes there every day and knows the road backwards. There are thus no signs on the road at all. Much frustrating trial and error interspersed with clear but completely inaccurate directions given by occasional local residents, including by one person who claimed to be unaware of any lock in the vicinity, even the one that proved, much later, to be just the other side of his garden hedge, finally found us beside the lock.

My first thought on seeing it was that they don't make locks like they used to. When I was a child, my dad used to take me on a Sunday morning to Godstow lock on the nearby Thames. A short walk down the towpath from The Trout led past the ruins of the nunnery (people will try and tell you that it isn't haunted, but it quite definitely is) to the lock, with its charming keeper's cottage and well-tended flower beds. When it was time to open the gates to let a boat into or out of the lock, the kindly old keeper would throw himself against a long wooden beam and so push the lock gate slowly open. Any offers of help, from portly gentlemen or small boys in shorts, were welcomed with a beaming smile. There was something intensely satisfying about heaving on the beam and stepping slowly along a quadrant shaped track until I heard the *thunk* of the gate reaching its fully open or fully closed position. I could then stand proudly and acknowledge the grateful salute from the person at the wheel of the boat as it passed by.

The people who built the lock at Andrésy had made it about fifty times bigger than it ought to be. They then fitted it with massive, automated gates, substituted an aerodrome-style control tower for the keeper's cottage and surrounded the whole thing with a high fence. Having done all that, they completely forgot to put in any flowerbeds. Inès and I walked, somewhat stunned, along the whole length of the fence without finding a gate. How the keeper, assuming there is one – the control tower had tinted windows so it was difficult to tell – reaches his place of work is something that probably only he knows. The control tower was too far away for us to be able to shout, and Inès reckoned that jumping up and down waving at it was probably not a very good idea. So, somewhat disheartened, we let the GPS take us home. Even it sounded fed up. It was clearly time to call for reinforcements.

My friend Andy wrote for a weekly newspaper called *French Week*. It occurred to me that I might be able to put some kind of plea for assistance in *French Week*'s personal column, so I rang and asked for his help. The following Friday lunchtime I positively galloped to La Défense to buy a copy of *French Week* at the RER bookstall.

Incidentally, in the very unlikely event that you should ever want to upset a French person, all you have to do is ask them why the place was named La Défense: they never know but hate to admit it. In fact, it is all thanks to a statue that sits, unnoticed, in the middle of all the office buildings. The statue was erected after the Prussians laid siege to Paris in 1870, the famous siege during which even the animals in the Paris zoo were eaten. Oddly enough, no one ever seems to notice the statue, which is strange, given that it is a sizeable, virulent green creation showing a forceful-looking woman doing her best to ward off further invaders. In this, unfortunately, she has been conspicuously unsuccessful. The probable reason why the statue didn't do better may well lie in the fact that it faces due west. This is precisely the wrong direction to have chosen because it is the one direction that no occupying army has ever come from.

Leafing through the paper on the way back to the office, I skimmed through the first few pages before stopping in astonishment at page six. For there was an entire article headed 'In

Seine Request'. Under the heading was a piece explaining who I was and what I was trying to do. The piece ended up with the following request: 'Charles is finding it more difficult finding craft with whom he can "hitch a lift" for a day or an afternoon. If anyone has any suggestions, or can indeed welcome him on board their own boat, please contact *French Week*.'

I laughed all the way back to the office, reading and rereading the piece along the way. Once back at work, I, yet again, drove my poor colleagues to distraction by brandishing the paper at them and forcing them to read the article. Now, if I were reading this part of the story, I might well be sneering somewhat sceptically at this point and thinking: 'I know exactly what's going to happen – just because he happens to know a bloke who writes for a newspaper, he is just going to whistle up a complete stranger, probably with a flash boat and a well-stocked drinks cabinet, who is going to pick him up at a convenient spot and drive him in comfort down the river. You see if I'm not wrong.'

Please don't bother thinking anything of the kind, because it wasn't like that at all. No one answered my plea at all. No one.

23

'Ecrivain anglais cherche à faire du "stop" sur la Seine' – English writer would like to 'hitch' down the Seine.

The quest had to continue. I posted my advert on a barge-user's website, accompanied by a few paragraphs explaining who I am and what I was up to. Having posted my message, I watched the site all the following day and was pleased to see the numbers of hits climbing steadily. And then at last came a reply. It was short and simple and from someone called Serge who had a twenty-eight-metre barge near Herblay – pretty much the next suburb on the Seine after leaving St-Germain-en-Laye, where the grape harvest had been – and said that he would happily take me for a trip downriver.

Serge is one of those calm, contented people who answer your questions in a friendly way but don't ask many of their own. Wanting to avoid any long silences, I think I may have asked rather too many questions, at least during the early part of the trip. The barge had been moored pointing upstream, so the first part of the journey involved a rather slow and laborious three-point turn in the middle of the river, a manœuvre that had to be accompanied by reports of our progress on the VHF radio to avoid any other river users coming racing round the corner unawares and bumping into us. Once the boat had been successfully turned round, Serge set off downriver at a comfortable ten kilometres per hour, a speed that covers distances steadily while allowing you plenty of time to look at the view.

Groups of attractive houses were interspersed with trees and even stretches of woodland, despite the fact that we weren't all that far at all from central Paris. We also saw dozens of moored residential barges. At one point, as we were passing a village that was spread out along the quayside, it took me ages to realize that the place we were passing was Conflans-Sainte-Honorine, a town famous for its population of resident bargees and somewhere I know quite well. The town lies at the confluence (as its name suggests) with the river Oise. Seeing a place from the river makes you realize that the impression you get of a town as you walk or even drive through it is completely different from the one you get from out across the water. When you walk down a pavement you are so close to the houses, shops and restaurants that you only really see the first floors of the buildings with their windows and signs. The rest of the buildings that lie above your head are generally out of your line of sight, and so you don't notice them. In fact, because you have never seen it, you have no real idea of the overall shape of a building, even less that of its roofline, nor that of any given street and the way in which it interconnects with its neighbours.

The view from a boat changes everything. As we passed Conflans that afternoon I could see the shapes of all the various houses that lie along the waterfront as well as the way in which the streets adapt themselves to the hill that rises away from the river. But being at a distance, I didn't really notice the shop fronts themselves and couldn't actually read the names on the signs from far away. What I did notice was the way the outlines of the houses differed widely along the main street as did the colours of their roofs. It was only when I spotted the church and the bargee's museum that sits on top of a hill overlooking the river that I realized which town we were passing. I shall look at it differently next time we go there.

Given the Seine's importance in French culture, it seems strange that its name doesn't figure in any common expressions the way other rivers do. Take the Rhine, for example, the longest river to flow at least partly through France. At one point the river flows up the right-hand side of France along the edge of Alsace, where it forms France's border with its neighbour Germany. The fact that Germany starts just on the opposite bank of the river leads to an expression for the country which is *outre Rhin* – on the other side of the Rhine. This is used almost as a euphemism for a country which, most probably due to its keenness on invading France, French people don't always seem willing to name overtly: 'the country which must not be named', if you like. Someone who has gone to Germany can thus be described as having gone *outre Rhin*. Or how about the Rhône? This figures in an expression that is used to illustrate the huge quantities of wine that are produced in the Beaujolais region just to the north of Lyons. To give an idea of how much Beaujolais there is (or even, surely not, to suggest that there appears to be so much of the stuff that some of it simply must be assumed to have come from somewhere else), people say: 'Il y a trois fleuves à Lyon: le Rhône, la Saône et . . . le Beaujolais' – there are three great rivers in Lyons, the Rhône, the Saône and . . . the Beaujolais.

And French river expressions aren't limited to local rivers. Following Napoleon's retreat from his unsuccessful campaign in Russia in 1812, his Grande Armée had huge problems crossing the Bérézina river. 'Ce n'est pas la Bérézina' has become a common expression for something that isn't as bad as it might have been.

Clearly the Seine has some catching up to do.

One interesting thing I discovered that afternoon was how barges fill up with fuel. Over the years I have filled up various boats on river estuaries and lakes and in each case it involved taking the boat to an aquatic version of a roadside petrol station. Once alongside one of those places you simply took a petrol hose, filled up the tanks, paid the man (usually quite a substantial sum) and headed off again. Barges must use huge quantities of fuel, and I was vaguely wondering how long a bargee has to stand beside the petrol pumps to fill up. It turns out that bargees don't do that at all. You apparently order a quantity of fuel from a fuel delivery service, which is then delivered to your barge, while it is sitting peacefully at its mooring, by a tanker truck in much the same way as central heating oil is delivered to a house. Alternatively, you can order your fuel from a tanker boat, which then comes along the river, moors alongside your barge and fills up your tanks as usual. According to Serge, there is one more possibility. If you are a commercial bargee for whom time is money, you can even arrange for the tanker boat to come alongside while you are actually travelling along the river. The two boats then continue along in parallel while the tanks are being filled with no travelling time being lost.

The next weekend was the Journée de l'Habitat Fluvial in Paris. I had been pointed towards the event by Serge, who had suggested that I might meet someone there who could take me some way down the river on another boat. It appeared to be some kind of bargees' jamboree, where barge residents from the greater Paris area came to meet up for a weekend on the Bassin de la Villette. The Bassin is a huge expanse of water in north-east Paris. It links the Canal St Martin – the one that starts in the Port de l'Arsenal, where I was given such short shrift at the *capitainerie* – to the Canal de l'Ourq, which heads north out of Paris. Setting out to explore, we first came across an extraordinary barge which proclaimed itself to be the smallest opera house in the world. The boat was called, somewhat unimaginatively, *La Péniche Opéra* – the Opera Barge. It was closed that morning but the sign on the deck recommended booking for performances, as the number of seats was limited. Who would have thought it? A short way down the quayside was another barge with an artistic bent, this time housing a theatre for children. This one was called *Antipode* and was home to a theatre company called Abricadabra. That the barge was in use with a play currently in progress was shown by a large sign placed prominently on the deck and which read simply 'Chut!' This – it is pronounced a bit like 'shoot' – is the French equivalent of 'Shush' and is usually directed at small children who are making a bit too much noise. Mind you, it can be used just as well with noisy adults.

It was clear that a broad selection of converted Freycinet barges had come up to Paris for the bargees' big event so that their owners and numerous hangers-on could meet up and chat. A large expanse of quayside had been given over to stalls for all the things that are presumably of interest to barge folk: boat insurance, boat builders, VHF radio manufacturers, engine specialists and whatever. Each time we paused in our wanderings to look at whatever was on offer, the stallholder almost always asked: 'Vous avez un bateau?' – do you own a boat? Each time we politely answered that we didn't, whereupon the stallholder would smile briefly and leave us in peace. At one point, between the stalls was something called a 'vide-tabernacle'. French jumble sales are often called *vide-greniers* – empty out your attics. Boats are not equipped with attics, whether cluttered or not, so their owners had been encouraged to empty out their *tabernacles* – apparently part of the barge's superstructure.*

The jumble stalls were filled with fascinating, impractical goods. There were pumps, lamps, brass riding lights (both green and red), cleats, bollards and lengths of rope on offer as well as several strange devices whose functions we could only guess at. There was even one stall offering some absolutely massive anchors for sale – at quite tempting prices, it must be said. I still regret not having bought one; I'm sure it would have come in useful for something one day.

But the stall that really caught my attention was the one with the propellers. Barge propellers being sizeable, weighty objects, they couldn't really be arrayed on a counter, so they had all been set out on the ground in front of the stall, perfectly placed to catch the sun as well as the eye of passing Englishmen. There were a couple of little ones, each about the size of a dinner plate, which were pretty enough, but the one I fell in love with on sight was one the size of a dinner table. It was made from gleaming, golden bronze and had five perfectly curved blades instead of the usual four. It was a work of art. I learned later that it weighed 200 kilos, took four people to get it out of the van and cost 15,000 euros. Even then, I still wanted it. But, at that moment, I was squatting down, stroking the propeller and imagining how nice it would look on our coffee table when the charming girl on the stall asked Inès the standard stallholder's

* Tabernacle, incidentally, is an unusual word which, in French, simply refers to a cupboard in a church which is used for storing religious artefacts. In Quebec, however, it means essentially the same thing but is definitely not a word to be used in polite society. Québécois includes several words of a religious nature that are used as surprisingly strong swear words. You might not think that you can stop a dinner party conversation in Montreal dead by just mentioning communion wafers or church storage units, but you can.

question: 'Vous avez un bateau?' This time rather than just say
'*Non*', Inès decided to explain that, while we didn't actually have
a boat that would need a 200-kilo propeller, her husband – that
bloke down there leaving finger marks on your polished bronze
– had built a wooden rowing boat in the garage. It is important
to note that I hadn't said anything at all at this point: not a single
word. For, at this, the girl looked me up and down, shaking her
head slightly, and asked Inès in that all-too-common, pitying
tone: 'Il est anglais?' – is he English?

How? How did she do that?

24

I felt stuck. At lunch with my colleagues the following week I went through my usual 'Do you know anyone who has a boat of any kind on the Seine?' routine, even though I had asked all of them at least once before. After a lengthy pause, Ghislain looked up and said, 'Oh. You mean a boat. On the Seine,' as though thinking about it clearly for the first time. I replied enthusiastically that this was indeed what I meant: a boat; on the Seine; yes.

'My father-in-law has a sailing boat in a club some way down the Seine from Paris.'

'On va l'appeler tout de suite!' – let's call him right away – I cried, desperate not to let this opportunity slip through my fingers. A couple of phone calls later I had an appointment to meet Ghislain's father-in-law, Bernard, not at a *sailing* club but rather at a *yacht* club, the following weekend. Saturday afternoon found me in the most wonderful boat club I have ever seen. A stretch of parkland beside the Seine contained a clubhouse, a boat compound and a vast, solidly built boathouse in which was arrayed an astonishing selection of boats. Bernard explained that the club had originally been founded between the wars by a clothing magnate called Armand Esder, a man so wealthy that he owned one of the six original Bugatti Royale Type 41s. Edser left the land and the buildings to the club in his will, which goes some way to explaining the comfortable, prosperous atmosphere that reigns there.

Bernard started off by showing me round the boathouse.

This had a magnificent selection of wooden sailing boats, not grown up enough to be properly called yachts, even though they had keels, but a lot bigger than the average dinghy. Most of the boats were antiques, many dating from the 1930s, and all were clearly lovingly maintained. Several boats were so gloriously woody that I found myself touching and sniffing them much more than would normally be considered suitable in polite society. Luckily, Bernard didn't seem to find this in any way surprising. Once we had seen all there was to see, Bernard kindly asked how I was getting on in my quest. Hearing that time was starting to be of the essence, he showed astonishing generosity to someone he had only just met by saying, 'Alors? On va faire un petit tour?' – so, shall we go for a trip. I positively galloped off to the car to collect some things I had brought in the hope that they might come in useful: my waterproof jacket, a bottle of water and a large packet of chocolate digestives. Armed with these, I found myself, only a few minutes later, standing gazing at a magnificent 1930s Finnish-designed six-metre Aile Class. My admiring reverie was interrupted by Bernard thrusting a bundled-up sail at me saying, 'Tiens. Est-ce que tu peux t'occuper du foc?' – here, can you deal with the jib?

And with that one sentence we crossed the line. It is a common feature of French life that, whether you know someone or not, as soon as you find yourselves in any kind of sporting situation together, you will very probably call each other *tu*. Sport, of any description, is a great leveller. But saying *tu* rather than *vous* is also fairly logical. Imagine finding yourself in a team game with a load of strangers. If you had to shout things like 'Would you be kind enough to pass me the ball?' or 'Should I kick this towards you?' it wouldn't do much for your chances of winning at whatever it was. So it is with *tu* and *vous*. Verbs in the *vous* form are more complicated to pronounce than those in the *tu* form. As well as creating an instant feeling of team spirit, using the *tu* form lets you get your message over more quickly and often less ambiguously. Passing the ball with a brief 'Tiens!' – here! – or 'Attrappe!' – catch – or an encouragement to 'Tire!' – shoot – saves time and lets you get on with whatever it is you should be doing rather than wasting time with the annoying extra syllable of the *'vous'* form. In any case, shouting 'Tenez', 'Attrapez' or 'Tirez' would sound completely ridiculous on a sports field.

However, some people seem to believe that the *tutoiement* should only last as long as the sporting encounter. Once whatever it is has finished, they will switch back to saying *vous* again. But not everyone changes back at the same distance – whether real or imaginary – from the sports arena. In the building where I used to work in La Défense there was a sports centre, complete with fabulous swimming pool. The company in question was extremely rich, so a fairly laid-back atmosphere reigned about the place. This was particularly noticeable among those who enjoyed the sports centre. On Friday lunchtimes we would play water polo or underwater hockey before going to the canteen for a leisurely lunch and then, finally, heading back to our offices to get ready for the weekend. But not all the players were regulars. Once the game was over, the more formal newcomers would switch back from the sporty *tu* to *vous* again. Some would change once dry and dressed, others, when they had left the sports centre. The oddest was the chap, a pleasant, prematurely bald fellow with the air of an enthusiastic tortoise, who got dressed by putting his socks on first. Once he was wearing just his socks and nothing else whatsoever, he would switch to saying *vous* while chatting to his erstwhile team mates.

So, having happily switched to saying *tu* to Bernard, I found myself, a few minutes later, perched on the Aile's deck. Sitting there, surrounded by a flat expanse of flawless varnished wood, was a bit like being in a giant Spanish guitar, though, of course, without the strings. My hand proudly on the tiller and the boat rocking gently beneath me, I surveyed the river, occasionally glancing knowledgeably up at the masthead to check the burgee.

If only the boat had been in the water at the time, it would have been just perfect.

Unfortunately, rather than bobbing about in the water, the boat was rocking about several feet off the ground. An Aile is too large to be rolled down a slipway like a dinghy, so, to launch one, you attach it to a large electric crane on the quay, which then hoists it into the air, swings it out over the water and then lowers it carefully in. That day, the crane managed only the hoisting-into-the air part before giving up. 'Ça arrive!' – it happens – Bernard called reassuringly up to me. Unfortunately, after much poking about in the innards of the crane while I enjoyed a slowly rotating view of the river, Bernard was forced to accept that the crane's problems were worse than usual, and thus the trip would have to be called off. 'Et moi?' – and what about me? – I called down to him from my wooden eyrie above the quay. 'Je vais chercher une échelle,' he yelled and went off to find a ladder.

25

The previous week had been unseasonably cold for early autumn. What's more, it had rained pretty much non-stop for several days, which meant that the river had risen well above its normal level. Despite the cold conditions, when an offer of a trip in a boat arrived, I jumped at it; the quest must go on, whatever the weather! The invitation came from Dimitri, who was the friend of our friend Sylvie, and he was nobly offering to take me out on his boat on a day when most boat owners were huddled inside in the warm.

Arriving at Dimitri's house in Villennes-sur-Seine, my immediate impression was that it couldn't really have been much closer to the water even if it had tried; there was just the width of a wooden terrace separating one from the other. Even on a damp, chilly day the view was pretty amazing: a long island some fifty metres away opposite the house extended off in both directions and was dotted with trees and nice houses, most of which had docks or jetties in front of them. If the view was good in autumn, in summer, sitting out on the terrace in the evening must quite simply be idyllic. This stretch of river between the house and the island was in fact just a minor branch of the Seine: a much wider main part flowed out of sight on the other side of the island.

Standing on the terrace, a warming cup of coffee in my hand, the sight of the river nearly in spate raised the question of flooding. The river had already risen sufficiently high that Dimitri was forced to describe some of the nearby docks and jetties that apparently lay out of sight under the water. His own jetty was relatively safe as it floated freely, as opposed to those of his neighbours, which were fixed on pilings. But it only needed the water to rise another twenty centimetres or so for it to be over the edge of his lawn. If the river rose another metre beyond that it would be time to start carrying the furniture upstairs. Dimitri seemed quite philosophical about this risk. His view appeared to be that if the cost of living somewhere so wonderful was that their home got flooded occasionally, then *soit* – so be it. Thankfully, their house hasn't been flooded since they have been living there, but the highest flood mark he showed me on the garden wall had come worryingly close.

In anticipation of the cold, I had piled on several T-shirts and sweaters before I left home and then added a fleece and an anorak on the top of all that before getting aboard the boat; I have been out on boats in the cold before. While warm, I was left with sleeves so thick that I could barely bend my arms. Dimitri's boat was a small cruiser of the sort known as a Bow Rider whose most noticeable feature was the whopping great outboard motor on the back. There were seats for the skipper and one passenger behind a windscreen and another lot of seats in the bows. Once aboard, we set off, travelling upstream at a leisurely pace past a series of houses, all of which had docks and boats of various sizes in front of them. The fact that the river was flowing fast was made all too clear when we got to the first bridge. Even though we were on the smaller arm of the river, water was sluicing through the arches towards us at a tremendous rate. The state of the river also meant that all sorts of rubbish had been washed downstream, and we saw dozens of plastic bottles, branches and even some sizeable logs that had been swept off the banks higher up.

A little further on we passed a rowing club, much like the one where we had had the launching ceremony for the boat that day, and where, despite the uninspiring conditions and the alarming state of the river, people were actually setting off in a four. Sooner them than me, I thought, wondering whether they had any idea about all those huge fish lurking beneath the surface.

A couple of kilometres upstream we reached the outskirts of a town called Poissy – a place best known for the manufacture of automobiles – where we swung round into the main part of the river and headed back downstream. This leg of the journey started with a long bend where there were no houses on either side, just trees, bushes and fields. Either there was no speed limit on that part of the river or Dimitri just thought he'd take advantage of the fact that we were the only people in sight. Whatever the reason, he wound the throttle of the big outboard wide open and sent the boat racing down the river. Since setting off we had been standing up looking over the windscreen rather than sitting down in the seats, because the view was better that way. More importantly, that was clearly the cool way for a couple of guys in a boat to cruise the river. Unfortunately, once we started belting along at high speed, it became a different sort of cool because we were almost completely unprotected from the wind. Travelling at fifty or sixty kilometres an hour in a car doesn't seem like any speed at all, but on a river, in an open boat, on a cold autumn morning, it is teeth-chatteringly exhilarating. Had I known Dimitri even a little bit better I would have been yelling 'Yahoo!' at the top of my voice. There was one troubling moment as we hurtled down the river when I remembered all the logs and branches that we had seen earlier. Hitting one of those at speed would very likely have sunk the boat outright or at least caused it to lurch and fling us overboard. Either way, being catapulted into icy water right out in the middle of a large, fast-moving river with not only no lifejacket but also so much clothing as to make swimming virtually impossible, would have been memorably unpleasant. It seemed fruitless to dwell on this prospect, so I just gripped the top of the windscreen and enjoyed the ride.

There is clearly a stronger feeling of community spirit among boat-owning river dwellers than you find on the average residential street. Each time Dimitri spotted someone he knew we stopped to exchange a few friendly words. One of the people we chatted to was a young chap who appeared to be a baker with an unusual commute to work. His house is on an island a short way downstream from the main one opposite Dimitri's house. This is called L'Ile du Platais and is home to a large number of houses, mostly made of wood and all noticeably smaller than those on the main island. And it seems that not all were built with planning permission. In any case, L'Ile du Platais is an odd choice for somewhere to live because there are no bridges whatever linking it either to the mainland or even to any of the neighbouring islands. The baker, like everyone else on the island, thus has to do his shopping, go and see his friends and, most importantly, travel to work every day by boat. Unfortunately, being a baker, he tends to get up a fair bit earlier than most people: apparently he sets off to work at 3.30 a.m., travelling a kilometre or so from his house to the quay in the centre of the village, where he leaves his boat near the bakery. Being up and about in the early morning must be bad enough, but the idea of travelling in a small, open outboard-motor boat on an icy winter's morning in the pitch dark doesn't bear thinking about. And, for much of the year, the return trip must be pretty much as bad.

At several points along the way we passed mature trees, which seemed to have large black birds roosting in them. Closer examination showed the birds to be not crows, as I had first supposed, but cormorants. (This is one of the few French birds' names that I don't usually get wrong because it is *cormoran*. Another that's even harder to get wrong is *héron*.) Despite the speed of the boat and the bone-chilling cold I still managed to wonder how on earth web-footed sea birds manage to roost on a branch. How on earth do they grip on? You never see ducks perched up trees . . . do you? Dimitri explained that cormorants don't just have simple webbed feet like ducks and geese, they have clawed webbed feet.

The most common theme of all the conversations, however brief, that Dimitri had with his friends and neighbours along the way was the height of the Seine. 'Ça va monter jusqu'où?' – how high is it going to go? – was asked at some point in every discussion. When it comes to floods, everyone's first thought is of the great flood of 1910. All along the Seine in and around Paris you can spot little plaques mounted on walls and bridges which show a short horizontal line and the date 28 January 1910. And the worrying thing about these plaques is that you often have to look *up* from wherever you are standing in order to spot them.

The 1910 flood really was the big one. It had been a very wet autumn and the water table was completely saturated. When it started to rain heavily on 18 January, there was nowhere for the water to go. Torrential rain fell upstream of Paris on the basin of the Seine, the Marne and the Yonne, all of whose levels started to rise dramatically. The flood water from all three rivers ended up heading down the Seine straight for Paris.

The river level in Paris in those days was traditionally measured with reference to a statue of a soldier on the side of the Pont de l'Alma. This statue is called the 'Zouave' – a soldier from the North African regiments of the French army of the nineteenth century. The statue was chosen to highlight the name of the bridge: Alma was a battle in the Crimean war at which Zouaves showed great bravery. By checking the water level with the Zouave, Parisians could gauge how worried they ought to be. As a general rule, if the Zouave's feet were in the water, it was considered time to start worrying. By the time the 1910 floods were at their worst, on 28 January, the water level had reached the Zouave's shoulders. To get an idea of the enormity of this, you need to know that the statue is five metres high. The statue has been raised since the flood of 1910, so the fact that its feet are getting wet is actually worse news than it used to be. The true height of the Seine in Paris is now

measured on a vertical scale that is fixed to the Pont de la Tour-
nelle, which lies a short way upriver by the Ile de la Cité.
According to the news on the day I travelled with Dimitri, the
Zouave's feet were nearly in the water for the first time for
several years.

In January 1910, huge expanses of Paris – some forty kilometres
of streets – were underwater. There are incredible photos of
the time that show people going to work in rowing boats,
horses and carts awash to their axles, or gentlemen in frock
coats and top hats being carried to the office on the shoulders
of wading porters. Even more distant areas such as the courtyard in front of St Lazare station are actually at the same level
as the river front and ended up being flooded by water that had
flowed there through the Métro tunnels. This was, and still is,
a considerable source of worry for the Métro company.

Rue de Seine during the great flood of 1910

Paris, and certain low-lying suburbs upstream, which at the
time were home to some 200,000 people, were affected for

over a month. It was hardly surprising, therefore, that, once things had returned to normal, the first thought was to launch a huge flood defence project. In London, flooding is expected to come from the sea, so flood defences are based around the Thames barrier, which is intended to act as a dam and stop water coming upstream. In Paris, the flood water comes from the other direction, and so any barrier would just make things worse, especially for those further upstream.

Rather than a barrier, the flood defence plan for Paris has involved building embankments, raising the quays and the bridges and, most importantly, creating overflow reservoirs to collect water upstream. There are four of these reservoirs, which are actually just huge lakes, located well upstream on the Seine, the Marne and the Aube. All the lakes are carefully managed to make sure they are empty by the start of each winter, ready to be filled up with excess river water in time of flood. The reservoir-lake system can cope with all but the severest floods, but there is still a risk that a similar series of events to those of 1910 would cause Paris to flood again. However, a flood on the same scale would have far more disastrous consequences, mainly due to the fact that far more of the lower-lying land near the river has now been built on.

I never discovered how Serge or Bernard had viewed our respective encounters, much as I would have liked to know what they had each made of it all. The trip with Dimitri was therefore unusual in that I actually managed to get some feedback about it. Some time after our trip, we were all invited to supper at Sylvie's place. Wanting to get the maximum amount of revealing information, I waited carefully until the evening had reached that special point where everyone has drunk enough to be chatty but where it hasn't got so late that people are starting to fall asleep. I'm not sure how well I judged it. I started off by asking Sylvie what had inspired her to give a hand with my quest. Her reply surprised me somewhat. She claimed that she had really just wanted to do her bit to bring an end to the Hundred Years' War. Now, history has never been my strong point but I am fairly sure that it has already finished, indeed that someone put an end to it quite a while ago. Nevertheless, Sylvie's altruistic aim had clearly been to improve Franco-British relations by any means within her power and, in this, not least in so far as Dimitri and I had both agreed to come to supper together after our trip on the river, it must be said that she succeeded admirably.

Dimitri himself proved modestly reticent about giving his view of things, so it fell to Emmanuelle, his wife, to give us a few details. It seems that one of the reasons that led to the invitation was the fact that I am English. There! I always knew it would come in handy one day. Dimitri likes things English; indeed, he apparently has such an affinity for anything English that, when he and Emmanuelle were first going out together, he explained his excellent command of the language by the fact that his mother actually was English. You can readily understand her shock when, some time later, Emmanuelle was finally introduced to the lady in question and discovered that his mum wasn't English at all but was actually from Le Havre! More prosaically, Dimitri was seemingly just pleased to share his passion for boats and the river with someone who seemed as enthusiastic as he is. In this, he was not disappointed, because I am told that I looked blissfully happy throughout the trip.

If I had only known this at the time I really would have yelled 'Yahoo!'

26

Time was moving on. Much of the year that I had been allocated to complete my quest seemed suddenly to have slipped by. I had managed to come up with a plan for travelling down a part of the Seine which lay a fair way further downstream, but my immediate concern was how to deal with the part much nearer to home. Unfortunately, that is precisely where the problems lay. The first problem was the fact that the Seine downstream of greater Paris is alarmingly broad and, what's more, is frequented by even bigger barges and boats than the ones I had seen so far. At the speeds they travel, these huge barges throw up wakes large enough to swamp a small rowing boat. The stretch before St-Germain-en-Laye had been bad enough. The next bit would be much worse. The second problem was that there didn't seem to be anyone anywhere who had a boat and was prepared to take me on it.

So, it all boiled down to a simple choice: it was my boat, or nothing.

The decision was quickly made: the quest must go on. I would follow the river downstream from where I had been suspended so frustratingly in Bernard's boat and look for any stretches of river that were protected by islands or which in some way would prove welcoming for small boats.

We rejoined the river at Les Mureaux, the boat sitting patiently in the back of another big car borrowed from work. This, I am starting to realize, is one of the boat's principal qualities: it can wait for ages without showing any signs of impatience or boredom. It will put up with the longest journey, hardly ever asking: 'Are we there yet?' or demanding that we stop for the loo. How many car passengers are that easy? We followed the river as best as we could, but, at first sight, below Les Mureaux it didn't look encouraging at all. Barges of all sorts were thundering in both directions, while the bank was unattractively adorned with oil storage tanks and the scars of heavy industry. A little further on was the huge power station at Porcheville. You can see its chimneys from miles away, which makes it a useful landmark when you are travelling on the A13 motorway west of Paris. If you are heading towards Paris, seeing it is a sign that you are about to enter a frustrating bit of motorway where a speed limit is rigidly imposed just at the time that you are keenest to press on and finish the journey. It is simpler travelling west: the sight of the chimneys just reminds you that it is time to start preparing for the *péage*, for the first motorway toll booth lies just after the next hill.

Les Mureaux is one of a sneaky breed of French place names that are a trap for unwary foreigners, a trap into which I have plummeted on numerous occasions. Any place name that starts with *Le* or *Les* has to be treated with care, because the name changes according to the way you refer to it. If you go to Paris, it is easy: you just say, 'Je vais à Paris,' while coming from it is 'Je viens de Paris.' But if you were going to Le Havre, you can't say – although I have done it on many occasions – 'Je vais à Le Havre,' because you have to remember the *Le* at the beginning. The *Le* is not a fixed part of the name: it changes when circumstances require it. Going to Le Havre should therefore be 'Je vais au Havre,' while arriving from it is not 'J'arrive de Le Havre' (though I've said that too, many a time), but 'J'arrive du

Havre.' If the name starts with a *Les*, like Les Mureaux, you will have to watch out too, saying 'Je vais aux Mureaux,' rather than the seemingly more reasonable 'Je vais à Les Mureaux.' Happily, any place name that starts with *La*, like La Rochelle, for example, is free of traps because you can just stick *à* or *de* at the beginning without changing anything.

I couldn't say I fancied rowing past a power station, not least because it is one of the ugliest things along the river. More importantly, the prospect of inadvertently becoming the subject of newspaper headlines along the lines of 'English rower sucked into power station cooling duct – homemade boat reduced to matchwood!' didn't really appeal. The boat, at least, deserves better.

So we pushed on downstream and, just a short way west, were astonished to stumble upon a rower's paradise. It was an odd place to find paradise. On the left bank was a town called Mantes-la-Jolie. This is a sprawling, over-developed place, so sprawling and over-developed that only a very small area can decently live up to its name and be described as *jolie* – pretty – even by its more loyal inhabitants. Opposite, on the right bank, is Limay, an unremarkable dormitory town for people who commute into Paris. An island called l'Ile aux Dames extends a fair way downriver between the two banks. Driving past on the main road, we caught sight of what seemed to be an interesting bridge on the Limay side.

We found ourselves in a small square, which got in our good books right from the outset by having a perfect parking spot beside a grassy bank, where steps led down to the water. Behind us, a line of attractive houses faced the river. More importantly, to our left was the Vieux Pont de Limay, a twelfth-century marvel which used to stretch all the way from the Limay side, across the Ile aux Dames all the way to Mantes on the far bank. It is one of the oldest river bridges in France. Unfortunately, like many bridges in this part of the country, it was partially destroyed in 1940 in an attempt to slow the German advance. Unlike most other such bridges, however, it has never been rebuilt. There is thus a missing span between Limay and the island and so, rather than proving a means of crossing the river, the bridge now has to content itself with welcoming fishermen and people out for a riverside stroll. But the bridge is also home, more permanently, to a family who are lucky enough to live in a house which stands on its own, right on the first span. This is La Maison du Passeur, which was built around 1750 to house the *passeur*, a man who collected a toll from people who wanted to cross the bridge. It is charmingly irregular, with none of the main walls looking square or even straight. The more I looked at the house, the more I wanted to live in it.

And just a few hundred metres downstream was another bridge. This one is a more recent stone bridge which carries the main road to Mantes-la-Jolie. Between the two bridges is a calm, sheltered stretch of river which, despite its inauspicious surroundings, manages to have splendid views on all sides. And it was the perfect spot for a row about. What's more, as well as the two bridges and the houses on the Limay side, there is a fine view of what I took to be Mantes-la-Jolie's cathedral on a hill on the opposite bank. In fact, it turns out that it is called La Collégiale Notre Dame. This is a thirteenth-century Gothic church which is very easy to visualize if you haven't seen it. All you have to do is imagine a smaller version of Notre Dame in Paris but with slightly narrower towers, and then mentally chop off the spire at the back. There! That's exactly what it looks like.

It was the work of moments to get the boat out of the car, carry it down the steps and launch it from some handy rocks. I amused myself first by rowing contentedly upstream, through one arch of the Vieux Pont, before coming back through another. Then there was the space formed by the missing span. In some strange way, passing through this was even more exciting than going under any of the intact ones. Having gone under all the spans several times in various combinations, I headed off downstream to enjoy the views from under the road bridge. Once through one of the broad, sweeping arches of the lower bridge I found myself on a new stretch of the river with views down to a boat club away in the distance. I wasn't the only one enjoying the river: several canoeists came by all in a line and exchanged greetings and enthusiastic comments about the river.

I went back to fetch Inès and gave her a guided tour of the two bridges. Now, what is it about going under a bridge in a boat? Stick anyone in any kind of craft and send it under a bridge and they will always react the same noisy way: the urge to call out and listen to the echo is overwhelming. Over the years I have been under countless bridges in all sorts of boats, and, in each case, as soon as we started to go under the bridge, everyone on board started making a noise. There are those who shout out words, those who scream, those who bark, and those, like Inès who sings very nicely, who sing single notes or snatches of tunes. I confess that my own preference is to shout a single, sharp 'Oh!' Once you have made your noise, you then have to make it clear to those around you that you are actively listening. To do this you have to tilt your head on one side and engage in a brief pantomime of listening and being astonished by the result. But you have been under bridges before and there was an echo. There is an echo under this bridge too. Why on

233

earth should you be surprised? In any case, anyone who is near you is certainly not paying you any attention at all, because they are engrossed in shouting and doing a listening pantomime of their own.

Each of the bridges at Limay that day had its own acoustic character. But then, not all bridges sound the same. Some types of arch resonate far better than others. A particularly satisfying one was a railway viaduct we had been under in a canoe not long before. Its broad, very tall arches, when Inès sang underneath it, gave a first echo which came off the sides and then, a fraction of a second later, another came from the roof of the arch. It kept us amused for ages.

When it was time to carry on downstream we pulled the boat out of the river and prepared to carry it back to the car. And, to my surprise, a slow-burning marital irritation suddenly emerged. The problem lay in the fact that, when you stick a boat in a river, it gets wet. What's more, when you pull the boat out and set about carrying it back to the car, it is still wet. And all that water has to go somewhere. If two people carry a small boat, one will naturally be at the back and one at the front. With my boat, the person at the back has the easier job, because there are two nicely rounded handholds cut in the transom. Whoever is at the front, where there are no handholds, has to grab on as best they can to either the edges or to a kind of triangular bit of wood that makes up the bow. I had always politely let Inès have the nice handholds at the back. Unfortunately, when the boat is wet, the water trickles down the sides, then runs along the bottom to a sort of mini-keel at the back – I seem to remember that the instruction manual called this a 'skeg' – from where it drips onto the jeans and feet of whoever is carrying it. This seems to be true whether you walk the boat forwards or backwards. Once both of us were back at the car, about to put the boat away, things unexpectedly came to a head. Inès suddenly declared that the novelty of visiting chunks of rural France with soggy jeans was fast wearing off, and a change of carrying strategy was perhaps called for. 'Essaie et tu verras' – try it and you'll see – Inès challenged. So we stuck the boat back in the river, gave it a few moments to get nice and wet, then heaved it out and carried it back to the car, this time with me at the back. It was true! River water dripped all down my shins and into my shoes. There is nothing like the prospect of spending time in cold, wet jeans for producing a good idea. From that moment on, we carried the boat with one of us on each side, so keeping both of us well away from the drips.

Thanks to our experiment, I drove damply on downriver keen to explore one more bit of the river before we reached that evening's destination a few kilometres further on, near La Roche Guyon. Before Mantes and Limay, the Seine had been very built up and industrial; less than ten kilometres further downstream its whole character had changed completely. Here there were fields on both sides of the river and the banks were wooded, with only a few houses scattered amongst the trees. Near a village called Mousseaux-sur-Seine we found a track leading down to a very rural stretch of river, where another long island created a good spot to row in safety.

The banks along this part were thickly wooded, but, at one point, a slope led down to the water, the sort of incline that is worn down as the cows or sheep grazing nearby keep going to drink from the river. At the bottom of the slope was a stretch of gravelly beach on which a large number of shells were scattered about. Not having seen any shells along the river until now, I rowed over to investigate and, poking amongst them, found several freshwater mussels. The French are well known for their passion for free food from the wild – chestnuts, mush-rooms and cockles are regular favourites – but, while I am happy to imagine someone eating oysters raw on a beach, indeed I have seen several people do just that, I can't really see anyone voluntarily eating a raw mussel. And it would have had to be raw, because there was no sign of ashes or any indication that a fire of any sort had been built nearby. While I was sifting through the shells a voice from up the bank behind me said 'C'est là où Monsieur vient dîner' – that's where Monsieur comes and has his supper. I looked up and saw an elderly chap in a worn blue suit under which a grey cardigan was drawn tightly over a generous stomach. He was leaning heavily on his stick just at the top of the slope and pointing at the shells with his free hand.

Several guided tours of Versailles over the years have taught me that 'Monsieur' was the name by which Louis XIV's younger brother, Philippe Duke of Orleans, was known. I had considerable difficulty imagining that a French duke would have come all the way from Versailles just to eat raw shellfish on a riverbank, not least because he died in 1701, so I smiled at the old chap and said, 'Monsieur?' in an interrogative way.

'Oui, Monsieur le ragondin,' he explained. 'C'est là où il vient manger.' Ah! That made more sense. A *ragondin* is a coypu, a beaver-like creature which was introduced into France by fur breeders at the beginning of the twentieth century. As is the way of such things, coypus wasted little time before escap-ing from their farms, since when they have been breeding copiously (coypusly?) throughout France. You can find them all over the place. There were a couple which used to live by a pond behind Inès's parents' house. We used to go and watch them grooming themselves in the sun on late summer eve-nings: they looked like small, friendly beavers. Remembering them fondly led me to say enthusiastically to the old chap: 'Oh oui! Ils sont mignons.'

He clearly disagreed, sneering: 'Mignons? Pas du tout! Ce sont des sales bêtes' – cute? Not at all! They are filthy creatures. 'Venez avec moi: je vous montrerai' – come with me and I'll show you – the man said and stomped off down the bank.

I followed him down the path to where there was another, more dramatic, slope of tumbled-down earth by the water. The man explained that, up until a couple of months before, this had been a solid piece of bank, but when a couple of coypus had moved in and started digging their earth they had brought the whole thing down. Coypus dig galleries that extend up to four metres underground and are responsible for a considerable amount of erosion along the river. 'Et ce n'est pas tout' – and that's not all – went on the old chap, warming

A coypu spotted along the way – not as innocent as you might think . . .

to his theme, 'Ils transmettent des maladies.' He went on to explain in more detail than I would have liked how coypus spread things such as Lyme's disease to humans. He clearly didn't like the creatures at all and got very agitated as he talked about them. One of the things that really seemed to irritate him was the fact that they cut down loads of plants to eat but leave about threequarters of everything they cut. Judging from the way he said: 'Gaspiller comme ça, c'est scandaleux!' – wasting food like that; it's outrageous – he had clearly known hard times at some point in his past.

I thought it might be wise to change the subject, so I asked what other creatures could be found along the bank. The man immediately dropped the subject of coypus and started talking enthusiastically about wild goats. It seemed that, if we were really lucky, some way further down the river – it wasn't clear exactly where – we would see a number of goats which apparently lived wild on an island.

That was something that we would definitely be looking out for.

27

We pushed on to La Roche Guyon, where we were going to stop for the night. La Roche Guyon is often described as one of the prettiest villages in France, and rightly so. It has glorious, quiet streets set with half-timbered houses and a magnificent market place which lies under a beamed ceiling supported by stone pillars. On the floor above the market place, held up by the pillars, is the local *mairie*: a most practical use of space. The village even has a ruined castle perched on the hill behind and, more interestingly, something called *une chapelle troglodyte*, a chapel that is actually set into the cliff.

Just a short way downstream of La Roche Guyon, the Seine passes into its final *région* before reaching the sea. Crossing the boundary line takes the river from the Yvelines, where we live, into Eure, where it remains nearly to Rouen, at which point it flows into Seine Maritime. And as it crosses the Eure county line, the Seine also leaves the Ile de France region, where it has spent the past hundred kilometres or so, and enters Normandy. More specifically, the river arrives in Haute Normandie (as opposed to Basse Normandie, which lies further to the west).

Départements and *régions* are very important in France: for many people they are their spiritual home. In the same way that, in the UK, a Yorkshireman is, and will always remain, first and foremost a Yorkshireman, French people retain a strong affinity with their regional roots. At work I have about thirty colleagues, all of whom have lived for some time in the greater Paris area. Of these, I can only think of two who would actually claim to be Parisian. All the rest, if asked, 'Where are you from?' would reply with the *département* of their birth. In many cases, this is the *département* where their parents still live and the place where they return on holiday. It is not just that each colleague came originally from a given *département* and then moved to Paris to get a job; it is much stronger than that. Each person came from somewhere and they still think of it as home, somewhere to go back to, one day. This is a topic that crops up a lot in conversations at work. Because the subject seems so important, all my colleagues are aware of where each other comes from; it is one of the first things that a new arrival is asked. Once they know where everyone is from, occasional references will be made to their regional stereotypes – Bretons can be stubborn, people from the Auvergne are thought to be stingy, etc. – or people will assume that a given colleague will be supporting a particular side in a sporting tournament.

Some are more active in their affection for their roots than others. One who comes from Aveyron is so proud of his *département* that he has put up magnificent posters of dairy cows (Aveyron is famous for its cows) in his office, together with photos of major local landmarks such as the Millau viaduct. Another colleague, who currently lives in central Paris, just has a photo of some obscure village on her wall. When asked where it is, she just replies 'C'est chez moi' – it's home.

What with all the rowing and exploring, it had been a long and strenuous day, and all we could think of was carrying on to find somewhere to have a reviving meal. But where was the best place to eat round there?

As a general rule, there are few pastimes as pleasant as wandering aimlessly along the streets of a French town, stopping at each restaurant to gaze at the menu posted outside. It is something that you can do at any time of the day, whatever the weather, regardless of whether you actually have any intention of going in and eating. Indeed, it can be most enjoyable especially when you *aren't* planning on going and eating: at moments like that, it becomes an activity akin to visiting an art gallery. No other activity offers such a pleasurable combination of mild exercise and reverie. What's more, it is pleasing on so many levels: you can spot a restaurant that seems to offer particularly good value for money ' – '16 euros for four courses and a cup of coffee!' – or one whose arrays of gleaming plates and glasses set out on spotless tablecloths beg you to come and enjoy them at suppertime. Or you can just read dreamily through the names of the dishes: 'Pressé de pigeon au chou et au foie gras confit' or 'Canard de Challans à la Montmorency' – pressed pigeon with cabbage confit and foie gras; Challans duck in Montmorency sauce – and savour some of the more imaginative choices of vocabulary: 'Mousserons des prés' or 'Effeuillé de cabillaud' – meadow mushrooms; finely flaked cod. For me, it gives a rewarding sense of purpose to what, otherwise, might just be an indolent stroll down a street.

Pleasant as this activity is – and I enjoy it so much that I have been known to cross a busy road in both directions at nine in the morning just to be able to spend thirty contented seconds gazing at a series of 'entrée, plat et dessert' that I have no intention of eating – you can't enjoy it to the full if you are tired, hungry and want to find somewhere nice to eat in a minimum of time.

We could have picked a restaurant more or less at random,

but that rarely guarantees you the sort of meal you are looking for. Instead, in view of the urgency of the situation, we tried Inès's 'ask the local gourmet' strategy. This theory is based on a surprisingly reasonable premise: if you want to get a useful recommendation about something, you are best off asking someone who is visibly an expert in it. After all, if you are looking for advice about hairdressers, it would seem a good idea to start with someone who has well-cut hair. For views on restaurants, Inès believes that one should only ever ask someone who visibly enjoys good food. A good place to start is often the local baker, or preferably the local *pâtissier*. It's easy enough to ask them. If you go in to buy bread, or possibly a cake or two, you can start off by chatting about the weather, or what a nice town it is, and then, if all seems to be going well and they haven't already moved on to serving someone else, you can casually ask where they would go for a meal nearby.

Assuming you have found someone who strikes you as both a potential gourmet and giver of advice, the vital question to ask them is 'Et vous, vous iriez où?' – and where would *you* go? If you don't ask them where they would go, they may well just suggest somewhere smart or expensive simply because they think that's the sort of thing you are looking for.

Looking to put the 'ask the local gourmet' strategy into practice, our first stop was at a *boulangerie*, but the *boulangère*, while her *pain au chocolat* was delicious, had the rather ascetic look of someone who didn't see the point in wasting time in restaurants. We crossed over the road to the *charcuterie*, even though there wasn't really anything we wanted, but there was a long queue. This was particularly frustrating, because Inès reckoned that the *charcutière* looked to be a fount of valuable culinary information. So we carried on to the *maison de la presse* – the newsagents – to buy a magazine. And there we struck gold. Even I could see at a glance that the newsagent was someone who liked her food. What's more, there were two other customers in there who also looked as if they knew a good restaurant when they saw one. Inès first asked the newsagent for her views, then skilfully drew the others into the discussion. Two things became quickly clear: we should on no account go to La Croix d'Or, but the brasserie just down on the left by the river was the place to go. 'On y mange très bien' – it's somewhere you can eat really well – the newsagent assured us. 'C'est là où vous iriez?' – that's where you'd go? – Inès asked the others, just to make sure everyone agreed. 'Absolument.'

By the time we had finished supper, which, as predicted by our advisers, had proved 'très bien', it had got completely dark. It can only have been the fact that we had eaten and drunk more than usual that can explain what happened next: I was suddenly struck by the realization that I had never rowed the boat in the dark. 'A quest that only takes place in daylight is a poor sort of thing compared to one that you have followed day and night,' I thought. And with that, there was nothing for it; I was going to have to give it a go.

So, by the lights of the restaurant terrace, we carried the boat from the car park, across a broad stretch of grass and down a steep bank. Being right down by the water's edge put us well out of the range of the restaurant lights, and so we found ourselves in complete darkness. After a couple of minutes, our eyes got used to the dark and we realized that, even when it appears completely dark on land, you can somehow still manage to see the river: there is a sheen to the water which means that you can always tell where the river stops and the bank begins. You can even pick out patches of reeds and clumps of weeds simply because they appear matt in contrast to the shine of the water.

The desire to go for a row in the dark didn't exceed my

fundamental sense of self-preservation, so I went back to fetch a lifejacket from the car, reflecting ruefully that this was something I hadn't got around to doing on any previous occasion, even along the memorable stretch before St-Germain-en-Laye. I also dug out a long length of rope from the boot. Armed with these, I made my way back to the boat, slipped it into the water and rowed tentatively away into the darkness.

Once I had rowed some way from the bank I stopped and set about taking stock of things. Sitting alone in the dark in a small boat on a huge expanse of unfamiliar water is an unsettling experience, mainly because there is nothing to see except a few stars and some street lights far away in the distance. As your eyes have little to contribute, all your other senses start clamouring for your attention. I first noticed the smell: the river had a slightly oozy odour that probably came from its muddy banks. The water also seemed to feel warmer than it would in the daytime, but that was possibly because the night air was getting chilly. I thought briefly about tasting it but couldn't see any point, as it would surely taste much the same as it did in the daytime, not that I had actually tasted it since way upstream of Paris. But the sense that really started working overtime in the dark was my hearing. Drifting in a small boat in the pitch dark quickly convinces you that a quietly flowing river makes far more noise at night than it does in the daytime. For a start, you can hear the water itself – whether it is the ripples against the shore, the soft lapping against the hull, or the drips falling from the oars. After you have been rowing slowly and drifting about for a while you start to notice other noises. I'm not talking about the distant laughter from the restaurant, the occasional, somewhat echoey barking of a dog or the sound of a train far away beyond the opposite bank. I'm talking about the rustles from the bank and the odd, unexplained splashes:

the splashes close by the shore, and, more importantly, those out in the river close to me.

Reason – not something that is in great abundance when you are on your own in a boat in the pitch dark – says that the noises near the shore must just be water voles or frogs or some other small creature of the night. But what about the splashes near me? And some of them seemed to be quite close by. Well, they must have been fish, jumping. I've seen fish jumping several times in the daytime, but do they jump at night? They must do; what else could possibly be splashing about near me?

And the darker shapes in the water nearby. Could they really all be just weeds?

A slight change of plan seemed called for, so I called out and when Inès answered I rowed briskly back towards the sound of her voice. Once reassuringly back in contact with the bank, I tied the long rope to the boat and gave Inès the other end to hold. That was much better. There was no question of it being a lifeline – the very idea of such a thing – it was just a means to prevent me from inadvertently rowing too far away and worrying her unnecessarily.

Once back out on the water, I was able to potter about at the end of the rope and discover other aspects of rowing about in the dark. The main thing you notice is that the simple act of rowing itself is surprisingly noisy. It wasn't that the rowlocks squeaked as they turned but rather it was the movement of the oars between the jaws of the rowlocks that made the noise. I had never previously wondered what they meant in the Hornblower books when they talked about muffling the oars of a boat when out on a night raid. It only took a few minutes of nocturnal experimenting to show that all you have to do to deaden the noise is to put some cloth wadded up between the oar and the rowlocks. That worked a treat. Apart from the sound of the water dripping off the oars, I could then row slowly about without making a sound. This was surprisingly entertaining and kept me amused until it was time to head off to bed.

28

It was around this point in my quest that it occurred to me that I might have been thinking a bit too narrowly. All this time I had only been looking for types of boat in which to travel down the river. But perhaps I was missing a trick? Surely other forms of transport allow one to travel down a French river? A bit of lateral thinking seemed to be called for.

So, what other means might be possible? Kite surfing, perhaps? Or a flight in a Sunderland flying boat? Or being towed along on the fin of an amenable dolphin? Before I could get too carried away with investigating any of these, a much better suggestion came along: how about an amphibious vehicle? There was even a French amphibious vehicle club, the AVAF. The club's motto is the catchy 'L'originalité des véhicules amphibies est d'avancer là où les autres s'arrêtent' – the clever thing about amphibious vehicles is that they carry on where others stop.

My conversation with Christophe, the president of the AVAF, started off along fairly typical lines – who I was and what I was looking for – before broadening out to become a beginner's guide to amphibious vehicles. It seems that true, old-fashioned amphibious vehicles are extremely rare; indeed they are so rare they are the sort of thing that people should have bought a long time ago as a hot investment. It appears that some models are so sought after they have to be locked away to avoid their being stolen. There is even a man in Paris who, Christophe assured me, winches his amphicar back onto the deck of his barge each time he uses it to be sure of keeping it out of harm's way.

More interestingly, you might well have assumed from the name 'amphibious vehicle' that the things in question are equally happy on land or in the water. 'Que nenni!' as the French would have it – no way; think again. Amphicars are amphibious in spirit, but considerably less so in practice. After each immersion in water, however brief it has been, a truly devoted owner will happily spend the rest of the day stripping down, cleaning, greasing and most importantly, drying their vehicles (sometimes with hair dryers) to stop them being attacked by rust. Is it just me, or doesn't that reduce their amphibiousness just a tiny bit?

Walking down the quayside on the outskirts of a village not far from Bonnières-sur-Seine some time later, I got my first-ever close look at an amphicar. It was bright red with grey upholstered seats, the beige convertible roof neatly folded down at the back. In front of the wheels, the bodywork was swept up sharply to give an adventurous, capable look to the car. Unfortunately, the effect was spoiled somewhat once I got round to the front and could see the goggle-eyed headlights that gave the vehicle a vacant, slightly gormless expression. The rear had clearly been modelled on some American car from the 1950s, with wings formed with sharply pointed fins. Between the fins the boot lid was pierced with vents for cooling the rear-mounted engine, whose exhaust pipe poked pragmatically straight out through the back of the bodywork. Though it seemed vaguely improper to peer under someone's rear end when you have only just been introduced, I bent over and could clearly see two painted propellers lurking between the rear wheels.

Christophe and friends in their element

At a nod from Christophe I opened the door and slid into the driver's seat, where I was instantly struck by a faint odour of damp and upholstery polish. My hands comfortably on the steering wheel, I looked optimistically at the dashboard in search of something visibly amphicar-ish. But there was nothing that shouted out that I was in an amphibious vehicle rather than any ordinary, non-floating car from the 1960s. There was a central ignition key, the usual gauges, a choke – something that I hadn't seen for years – and a fairly conventional-looking gear lever. I even spotted a foot-operated dip switch, another thing I hadn't seen for years. It reminded me vaguely of the cars my parents had had when I was young. I felt at home straightaway. I moved over to the passenger seat to allow Christophe to take the wheel, whereupon, with only a couple of turns of the ignition key, the engine started, and we drove of down the slipway.

There are two ways of entering the water in an amphicar.

Charles Timoney

There is the spectacular, splashy, show-off way where the amphicar is driven down the slipway straight into the river at a speed sufficient to create a wave of water that sweeps over the bonnet, washes halfway up the windscreen and produces gasps of delight and astonishment from first-time passengers. This, you may not be surprised to learn, is what I was fervently hoping for. And then there is the reasonable way. This involves driving very slowly down a slipway and then, just as the front wheels touch the water, slowing down even further so that the amphicar creeps into the river with barely a ripple.

Clearly mindful of his car's age and fragility – it was built in 1963 – Christophe opted for the reasonable way. But no matter. The lack of any kind of wave or drama was far outweighed by the sheer joy of being driven in a car – a car, what's more, with the roof down on a sunny, late-autumn afternoon – down a slipway straight into a river.

The change from land to water travel takes place fairly seamlessly. The car has two gear levers: one for a traditional, four-speed gearbox, which is used for road travel, and a second lever, which, once the road lever has been put into neutral, allows you to activate the twin propellers. At the bottom of the slipway, as it enters the water, the front of the car rises up, then, with a vaguely disconcerting wallow, the back floats up too. At this point Christophe operated the two gear levers, and a wake started to form behind the car as the propellers took over propulsion from the wheels. It is against all reason. You are clearly in a car, for the steering wheel and the dashboard are right there in front of you, yet, just as clearly, you are no longer on a road but floating serenely down a major French river. It is quite simply, wonderful.

I swopped places with Christophe and took the helm, or rather the steering wheel, of the first river craft I have ever been on with indicators and a rear-view mirror. And a horn! And, of course, a handbrake, even though pulling on it, or obviously pressing the brake pedal, would be a complete waste of time if you were hoping to slow down. With the window lowered you can lean over the door and look down at the river, only a few inches below. There is a chrome strip running down the side of the car which more or less marks the waterline, though, with the engine at the back, the rear of the car tends to sit lower than the front. The fact that the steering wheel steers the car in the water just like it does on land is, I suppose, quite logical. Nevertheless, something feels peculiar about it, perhaps due to the fact that it all seems improbably easy. The car is light and relatively easy to manœuvre: it is certainly a whole lot quicker to respond than Andrew's barge.

A word of advice may be useful at this point: it is not half as funny as you might imagine to ask an amphicar owner what would happen if you were to open the car door. It does not go down well at all, though I imagine that's exactly what the car would do if you were silly enough to try.

If being stared at and even pointed at by complete strangers is your thing, then an amphicar is definitely for you. I can't remember the last time I took part in an activity that caused heads to turn the way they do when you tootle along a river in a small red car. Later, when we drove back up the slipway, passers-by clustered round the car and bombarded Christophe with questions. Judging by the ease and friendliness of his replies, this is something to which he is well accustomed. Once we were back on the quayside, I offered to help with all the cleaning, drying and greasing that I assumed would be required but was told that there was no need because the car would be going back in the water that afternoon.

Of course, fun as it was, the car isn't perfect. At the risk of sounding like one of the blokes on *Top Gear*, I have to say that a far more exciting amphicar could be produced if you took something like an Aston Martin as your starting point. Beefing up the propulsion system so that it would exceed the rather pedestrian seven miles per hour offered by the amphicar's old Triumph Herald engine would be fun too, as perhaps would the addition of sonar and a couple of torpedoes. Now that really would turn heads.

29

Some weeks previously, there had been a programme about the Seine on one of the main French TV channels. Before it had even started, the programme gave me an insight into just how much I had been pestering everyone I knew about the quest. Three different people rang up in quick succession just as the evening news was ending to warn me that it was about to start. They weren't the only ones to have thought of me: the last phone call was interrupted by our next-door neighbour, who, as the phone was engaged, had rushed round to make sure I was watching.

The programme studied the river from a variety of points of view and included interviews with river users and dwellers such as bargees, restaurateurs and lock keepers. At one point the presenter went for a boat trip down the river in a cabin cruiser with a recently retired chap called Dominique, who had spent a lifetime on and around the Seine and had decided to devote his retirement to sharing all his knowledge with anyone who wanted to come on his boat. Clearly, this was a person I had to meet! Having tracked him down, I had made an appointment for a trip with him that day, just beyond the town of Vernon.

Vernon is the largest place between Mantes and Rouen but doesn't get much praise from the Green Guide, which casually dismisses it as no more than 'interesting'. Nevertheless, Vernon is famous for several things, notably its watercress, which was much sought after in the thirteenth century by the then king, and all-round good chap, Saint Louis. Somewhat more recently Vernon has become much better known for the Vieux Moulin, an old mill that sits on the remains of a medieval bridge. The original bridge has long since been replaced by a series of other structures, each of which was destroyed or bombed in various wars. The current bridge is thus at least the fourth to have been built on the same spot. Only a few of the original medieval bridge supports remain, two of which are straddled by the mill. The Vieux Moulin is typical of the region in that it is built *à colombages* – a half-timbered structure where all the supporting timbers are visible in the walls and are painted a contrasting colour. In the sixteenth century several similar mills, each perched above the water with a large water wheel extending underneath, stood at intervals across the old bridge so as to get the most out of the river's strong current. The bridge and its mill have been painted by numerous artists over the years, notably Monet, whose painting *Maisons sur le vieux pont à Vernon* shows it to have been even more dilapidated in 1883 than it currently appears.

There is a famous French song that all children are taught: 'Sur le Pont d'Avignon' – 'On the bridge of Avignon they are dancing, they are dancing . . .' And it turns out that the connection between bridges and dancing continues outside the South of France. The Vernonnais seem to have enjoyed their dancing in the past. However, while in Avignon the famous song shows that the locals used to enjoy their dancing on, or possibly under, their bridge, here the locals had to do theirs on a barge moored beside the mill, because there wasn't any room on the bridge itself.

And so to our appointment with Dominique, who was bang on time, as were we, at the agreed spot. Dominique's boat was a large cabin cruiser, the sort of thing you see pottering down the Thames on a sunny summer afternoon. A key feature of the Astérix books is that Obélix's massive strength is explained by the fact that he fell in the cauldron of magic potion when he was small. Despite the fact that he is not an obese man with pigtails and striped trousers, Dominique likes to explain his passion for the Seine by the fact that 'Je suis tombé dedans quand j'étais petit' – I fell in it when I was small. Whatever the explanation, his knowledge of the river and its surrounding countryside around where he lives is, to say the least, encyclopaedic. We found out later that Dominique was born nearby in another *Maison du passeur*, much like the one we saw in Limay.

While we were looking round the boat, Dominique explained that he had bought it despite the fact that he didn't like its name – *Las Vegas*. In England, many sailors believe that you can change a boat's name provided that you carefully explain the reasons behind your choice to the boat itself. In France, yet again, they do things differently. It seems to be a strongly held belief that you should never change a boat's name at all. 'C'est sacré' – it's sacred – Dominique said. As he seemed a bit shy, Inès broke the ice by suggesting various outrageous names that the boat might have had and asking whether he would have kept them regardless or whether he would have felt forced to go against tradition and change them. It worked a treat, even though some of her suggestions seemed to surprise Dominique a bit.

On the way along the river the day before, near a village called Vétheuil, we had come round yet another bend in the river to be faced with white cliffs in the distance. In prehistoric times the Seine was some hundred metres higher than its current level and vastly wider and faster-flowing. Around what is now Paris the river had cut progressively into beds of cobbles in the hills. These, when swept along in the water, gave the river huge powers of erosion. Because of this the Seine cut great swathes out of the limestone hills that make up the outer reach of the present bends and so formed a series of white cliffs. Around Vétheuil, only the points of the hills have been eroded, which has created a series of vertical white lines on the hillside like some enormous barcode. But downstream from where we set off with Dominique the cutaway parts become much larger and more extensive, and you start to wonder whether you have travelled all the way to Beachy Head without realizing it. In each case, while the outside of the bend is hilly and set with cliffs, the land on the inside is flat, given over to agriculture or, in some places, dotted with old quarries that have been transformed into boating lakes. At several places along the trip downriver we saw cliffs that have been eroded into points or tall pinnacles of chalk. On the higher pinnacles we spotted climbers hanging from ropes in amazingly precarious positions, busily

banging in new pitons on their way towards the top. This sort of thing didn't appeal to Dominique: 'Jamais de la vie vous me verrez là-haut' – you'll never catch me up there.

The river Dominique showed us had something for everyone. There were fabulous houses in huge gardens at intervals along the banks, while on some of the numerous islands that we passed there were some much smaller homes that were really no more than wooden huts. It seems that people who want to live along the Seine but can't afford to buy a plot go and check the *cadastre* – the land registry – to find out who owns untended pockets of land on the islands. These people, whom Dominique referred to as *petits malins* – cunning little guys – then go and offer a peppercorn rent for a bit of land, saying that they want to use it for recreational purposes at weekends. Once their offer has been accepted, they set about building a house, generally without telling the landowners. Even if the landowners, who often live far away, discover the house, there is not that much that they can do about it.

About halfway to Muids, on the apex of yet another extreme, horseshoe-shaped bend in the river – I'm sorry to keep going on about these but if only the river had been a bit straighter I really would have been at the sea long ago– we passed the small town of Les Andelys. Seen from the river early on a sunny afternoon, it was undoubtedly the prettiest place we had seen on the river since leaving the source. On the outside curve of the bend, Les Andelys is lucky enough to have another set of white cliffs cut into the hills on either side of it, which frame the view of the town quite pleasingly. From the river you can see a series of large houses in fine gardens along the river with the church visible just behind. Clearly, whoever founded the town thought of everything: as well as being attractively framed by cliffs, they chose to build the town just opposite a small wooded island in the river. This gives the people we could see on the riverbank something pleasing to look at during their afternoon stroll.

And there are not just cliffs behind Les Andelys. This land was once owned by the English. High on a hill to the right of the town is Château Gaillard, the ruins of a twelfth-century castle that was built by Richard the Lionheart. By building the castle at Les Andelys – in, apparently, the staggeringly short time of just a year – Richard hoped to keep the French king, Philippe Auguste, from claiming what is now Normandy for France. You can still see the remains of the fortifications there. Richard died in 1199, ironically enough fighting the French elsewhere, whereupon his brother, the dreadful King John, who also features strongly in Robin Hood tales, inherited the throne. It was during John's reign that Philippe Auguste decided to lay siege to Château Gaillard as a first step to reclaiming Plantagenet lands. After a siege that lasted for seven months, the castle fell to the French in 1204, and Normandy was reclaimed shortly thereafter.

Past Les Andelys, we wove our way through a series of rural islands, most of which were densely wooded. These, we learned, were home to all sorts of animals, notably *chevreuils* – roe deer, *biches* – red deer – and *sangliers* – wild boar. Oh yes, and a fair number of foxes. When short of food elsewhere, or when being pursued by hunters, all these creatures are capable of swimming across stretches of river to find refuge on the islands. But things on the animal front got a lot more exciting a bit further on, because we came upon the very herd of wild goats that the coypu-hating old chap up river had been talking about. At least, I assume they were the same ones – I really can't imagine that there can be two herds of wild goats on two different islands along the river. Dominique brought the boat close to the bank, and we could see at least twenty goats happily grazing a short way back from the river. 'Personne ne s'en occupe' – no one looks after them – he explained, pointing out in support of his argument that one of the males had extremely long, untended horns.

At one point when talking about the river – which it is only fair to say he did rather a lot – Dominique claimed that the Seine and the Loire had much in common. Now, I have seen a fair bit of the Loire: I have canoed on it, swum in it, waded across broad stretches of it and even built some splendid dams on it. Having done all that I can safely say that the Loire doesn't look anything like the Seine, not least because it is shallow and has loads of sandbanks. I put this view rather firmly to Dominique, who, unfortunately, was completely unimpressed by my reasoning. He patiently explained that, while the Seine appeared at first sight to be deep and devoid of sandbanks, it would be a wholly different story if there weren't man-made weirs every forty kilometres or so along the river. These weirs apparently keep the river a good four metres above its natural level and so stop it running out to the sea like bath water down a plug hole. Without the dams, and their associated locks, the stretch of river we were on would be almost all sandbanks for six months of the year and we would very probably have to get out of the boat and push.

'Et, est-ce qu'on peut se baigner, ou est-ce que c'est trop sale?' – and can you swim in it, or is it too dirty? – was my next question. To this, clearly shocked that I might have implied a criticism of his beloved river, Dominique replied, 'Bien sûr on peut se baigner! C'est très propre' – of course you can! It's really clean. He quickly went on to point out several sandy beaches along the bank that he had personally swum from. However, after a thoughtful pause, he did go on to admit that he wouldn't necessarily have been so enthusiastic about swimming there even ten years ago. Before then – and it must be said that it wasn't all that long ago – all the sewage from towns like Les Andelys used to be poured straight into the river. Thankfully, there are now numerous state-of-the-art sewage plants along this part of the river. And, judging from what we could see as we travelled along in the boat, the water does look extremely clean.

Each time we came to one of the many islands that dot this part of the river, we would head up the narrower, quieter channel and leave the main channel to the bigger boats, some of which were very large indeed. We kept pace for a while with one large boat which had taken the other channel on the far side of the islands. Being on different courses, we would see the boat – a massive white tourist craft, about a hundred metres long, a couple of decks high and equipped with cabins and restaurants appearing and disappearing behind each island. Where the islands weren't too high, we had the unusual spectacle of a large boat seemingly drifting silently amongst the trees. When we were on a visit to Les Andelys some time later, two of these massive boats tied up at special jetties along the riverfront, one disgorging a hundred or so French pensioners while a similar number of German tourists poured out of the other. For an hour or so the town was host to a mass souvenir hunt. A group of a dozen or so elderly ladies clutching carrier bags came tottering past us on their way back to their boat and all wearing the most peculiar and unflattering sunhats. I made the mistake of saying to Inès, 'Look at all the noddies in their silly hats.' At this, the nearest lady spun round with a furious look and snapped 'Do you mind! I happen to like my hat very much indeed.'

30

It was while we were planning where we might go next that the phone rang. It was some friends from England. The line was indistinct and crackly, perhaps something to do with their using a UK mobile in France, but it seemed that they wanted us to go and visit a battlefield of some sort with them. Normandy is full of battlefields, so we encouraged them to come and pick us up, assuming that they were thinking of some local monument to Second World War action. Once they had turned up, we discovered that we had not only got the war in question completely wrong, we had also severely misjudged the century. For, instead of heading west from the Seine we found ourselves racing northwards towards a small village called Crécy-en-Ponthieu. This, as you will have guessed, is the site of one of the definitive battles of the Hundred Years' War (between France and England) – Crécy.

In all the years I have been in France, I have never heard anyone mention the battle of Crécy. And the village of Crécy-en-Ponthieu doesn't seem to make much of a fuss about it either. As you arrive, there is just a small sign that lets you know it is the site of a battle but doesn't tell you anything useful like who it was between, even less which country actually won. Luckily, Peter (he of the 'Chevrolet' cows) and Helen had planned this part of the trip before they left and actually had a map of the battle with them. Thanks to this, we were able to pick out the spots where Edward III and his son the Black Prince had arranged their troops, notably the bowmen who would inflict such losses on the French knights. The battlefield probably hasn't changed all that much since 1346 – there was still a broad, muddy slope where the French charge was launched and rebuffed. Nearby there was a tall wooden observation tower which gave excellent views of the battlefield. Strangely enough, all the people we met on our way to and from the tower were English. As we wandered the fields, I was surprised to notice that Inès didn't seem to be sharing our enthusiasm for the brilliant tactical use of longbows or our ridicule of the French knights' ill-discipline. I remember thinking that this was a bit peculiar: I had always thought she liked history.

The following day, 25 October – St Crispin's day – found us driving into the little village of Azincourt. Unlike Crécy, you are left in no doubt as you come into Azincourt that you are arriving on the site of a battle: the roads into the village are clustered with life-size cut-out figures of bowmen, knights, foot soldiers and crossbowmen. They are standing by houses, on verges and, occasionally, peeping out from behind telegraph poles. As we drove into the village we observed that we were far from being the only British people to have thought of visiting that day: we counted sixteen cars, fourteen of which had UK plates.

We didn't have time to visit the local museum but we did make good use of its car park and also studied the handy map of the battlefield that is posted outside. According to the map a walk from the museum towards the hamlet of Tramecourt would take us via the French lines to the site of Henry V's camp. It proved to be a bit further than we had expected, but at least there was an observation point with another map showing the battle lines. The battle took place around 11 a.m. on a cloudy October day and, as luck would have it, we were there at just the right time on a similarly cold and damp St Crispin's day. According to the description of the battle, at a crucial moment, the sun came out and briefly dazzled the French lines during an English attack. While we were wandering about trying to work out who had been located where, the sun contrived to come out and dazzle us too; it all helped build up the atmosphere. As well as the map of Crécy, Peter and Helen had come equipped with a copy of Henry V's speech before Agincourt. It is a sign of how engrossed we had become in reliving the whole event that it seemed perfectly natural to gather together and read the speech out loud. It is a wonderfully stirring and inspiring piece: if ever there was a text that would convince me to grab a sword and charge full tilt towards a heavily armed enemy, this is it.

Unfortunately, it became clear as the speech went on that, of the four people present, not all were equally moved. Indeed, we came to realize that there is a previously undocumented condition to which the French seem unfortunately susceptible. Its principal symptom is that, in certain circumstances, seemingly exactly those present that day in a cold muddy field, sufferers suddenly cry out 'Vive la France' in the most aggressive manner. Inès was clearly suffering from an extreme condition of the ailment, whatever it was, for she then launched into an impromptu rendition of 'La Marseillaise', singing it at such a volume that it drowned out Henry V's magnificent speech. It is little wonder that local residents slowed to stare as they drove past us: three English people stripping their sleeves and showing their scars and remembering St Crispin's day while a lone, diminutive French woman bellowed out '. . . aux armes citoyens . . .' so loudly that it blew the rooks out of a distant spinney.

Our friends were keen to start heading back, but, before setting off, I really wanted to buy some more postcards. After a bit of searching we managed to find some magnificent ones showing a group of English archers indulging in some particularly excessive victory celebrations. I reckoned that receiving a card like that would annoy all our friends greatly, regardless of nationality. I sent each card off with the same message: 'On avance bien! Pensez à préparer vos valises pour votre voyage en Angleterre – à bientôt sur la plage en Normandie!' – it's all going well! Start thinking about packing for England. See you soon on the beach in Normandy.

31

The dramatic event which turns the tide when all had seemed lost is known as a *deus ex machina* – in Greek tragedy it's when a god literally climbs out of the machinery and saves the day. My sister Alison, who is hot stuff at Latin, reckons that the phone call I got that day from a friend could best be termed a *deus ex navicula* – a god from the little boat.

The call in question started off uneventfully enough, but after only a couple of minutes my friend's use of the word 'Seine' made me snap into alertness and switch into intensive questioning mode. From this I discovered that his cousin Jean-François had seen an advert for a second-hand sailing boat – a First 29, I was told – at a knockdown price. The asking price was so reasonable that it had made it well worthwhile to come all the way to Paris to buy it and then take it home. The journey back was going to involve spending a week chugging up the Seine and then heading off up the coast a short way to Fécamp, a small port just west of Dieppe.

We talked some more about the boat and the journey, and then I asked 'What about the bridges? Isn't he going to have to take the mast down at some point?' I have never done that on a boat but I somehow imagined that it wouldn't be an easy task, especially for a chap on his own. 'Il n'y a pas de mat' – it hasn't got a mast – I was told. It seemed that one of the reasons behind the surprisingly low purchase price (though the word 'low' is relative since the amount in question would buy a decent sports car) was that the mast had been broken somehow by the previous owner.

The boat thus came with sails and a boom but that was all. Jean-François didn't seem to see the lack of a mast as that much of a problem. 'J'en trouverai bien un quelque part' – I'm sure I'll find one somewhere.

While I was still reflecting on what sort of bloke would buy a mastless sailing boat and then, having acquired it, actually set out on a long journey in it, our friend asked 'Alors, est-ce que ça t'intéresse?' – are you interested? Was I interested in what, exactly? 'Jean-François dit qu'il va s'emmerder tout seul pendant une semaine' – he says he's going to get bored witless all on his own for a week. If we wanted to do part of the journey with him, we'd be welcome.

We agreed that it would probably be a good idea for us all to meet over a beer or two to make sure we could survive being cooped up in a boat together. For few things are as taxing as being stuck in a confined, pitching and rolling space with someone you don't get on that well with. Turning up at the marina the next day, it was easy to spot Jean-François's boat as, obviously, it was the one without a mast. A First 29 is made by Benneteau, the French yacht manufacturer, the 29 in the name referring to the length of the boat in feet. It is big enough to sleep six people and is equipped with all essentials such as a sink, a small galley and, most importantly, a loo. Being designed for six meant that three people should be able to travel in comfort, especially along a river where there's no risk of sea sickness.

We stood on the quayside and had our first look at the boat. It looked clean and well cared for. The boom was lying down one side of the deck and there was a bicycle propped against the cabin roof on the other side. Jean-François had clearly come prepared. We walked to the stern and saw that someone had very artistically hand-painted the name 'Hirondelle' on the back. It somehow seemed important to get the encounter off on a proper nautical note, so I called out, 'Ohé, du bateau!' – Ahoy there! At this, the companion hatchway opened, and a chap with a large, reddish moustache, blue eyes and an affable expression emerged from the companion way. He looked to be about our age and appeared to be holding a crayon in his hand. Jean-François showed us where to climb onto the boat and then shook our hands warmly. 'Bienvenus à bord!' – welcome aboard!

I liked him instantly and, as we climbed aboard, shared an enthusiastic smile with Inès who, clearly felt the same. Stepping down the companionway steps I found myself in a well-equipped cabin with a small table set with bottles and some glasses. I had expected it to feel a bit damp but the atmosphere in the cabin was warm and welcoming. My suspicion that Jean-François had been holding some kind of crayon when he greeted us was confirmed by the fact that on a bunk bed along one side of the cabin were arrayed two pastel still-lifes and a splendid picture of a sunrise over the river. A small easel was squeezed in a corner of the cabin and had a partly finished still-life on it featuring some fruit, a chunk of baguette and a piece of cheese. None of the objects in question were visible anywhere in the cabin. When we admired the pastels, Jean-François explained that they were his 'Violon d'Ingres' – his hobby – and that he spent most of his spare time doing still-lifes just from memory. 'C'est plus pratique comme ça' – it's a lot easier that way – he explained.

The lack of a mast meant, quite obviously, that there would be no sailing on our way downriver. This was a pity, not only because sailing is fun, at least when it isn't raining too hard it is, but also because I wouldn't get a chance to use all the French nautical terms that I had worked so hard to learn over the years.

French boats are no different from English ones: every single bit of them has a name and, more importantly, a name that isn't used in any other field. This is particularly true of all the ropes. At least the idea of having loads of similar looking bits of cordage, all having different names, none of which (assuming your boat isn't fitted with a bell) is actually called 'rope', is common to both countries. In order for your skipper not to regret having brought you along, you have to learn the French for halyard, mainsheet, shrouds, warps, stays, cleats, shackles, jib, mainsail, spinnaker, tiller, rudder, bow, stern, port, starboard and, possibly most importantly, 'Shall I make something for lunch?' Of all this vocabulary, the only word that is the same in both languages is spinnaker, and not all French sailing boats even have one.

I remember spending the entire train journey from Paris to La Rochelle, where I was going to spend the weekend sailing with some colleagues, sitting beside one of them who was holding a picture of a sailing boat in full rig, reciting 'Les drisses, les haubans, les écoutes . . .' as my colleague pointed to each bit in turn. He also taught me the French way of remembering which is 'port' and which is 'starboard'. In English, you learn to say, 'Is there any Port left?' which also helps remember the colours of the riding lights because Port wine is red. On a French boat, left and right are *babord* and *tribord*. But which is which? To remember, you just need the word *batterie*, which sounds like *ba-tri*. Reading from left to right, *ba* is on the left of *tri*. Simple.

Being easily amused, however, my favourite boating terms are to do with jibs. A jib on a French boat is *foc*. This sounds just like *phoque*, which means 'seal' (the fish-eating mammal). But we haven't got to the amusing bit yet: to haul in the jib is *border le foc*. But *border* also means 'to tuck up in bed', which produces strangely pleasing images when applied to seals. Conversely, letting your jib out again is *choquer le foc* – but how exactly do you go about shocking a seal?

We weren't able to set off straight away, and, in any case, I had already explored the part of the river that Jean-François would be travelling down first. According to the map, the first unexplored town beyond Muids, where we had finished our journey on Dominique's motor boat, was Elbeuf. This lies about twenty kilometres upstream of Rouen and, according to Jean-François would be an excellent spot for us to meet up, because there was a quay on the river which was right on the main road through the town.

A couple of days later, we were dropped off in Elbeuf by our son Sebastian. He had been surprisingly willing to drive us there as it meant that he would be able to keep the car to go off and see some friends who lived nearby. Elbeuf used to be famous for the manufacture of bedsheets. The quality of its products was so high that, in the seventeenth century, the town acquired a royal warrant – 'La Manufacture royale de draps d'Elbeuf'. Even after the Revolution, Elbeuf maintained its reputation, earning a visit from Napoleon himself. Sadly, like so many others, the town was badly bombed during the war. Many of the *usines drapières* – sheet factories – were destroyed, and the few that survived closed barely a decade or so later, when production of cotton products shifted away from France. The town has managed to keep going thanks to the arrival of more modern but less picturesque industries such as chemicals and motor manufacture.

As we carried our things aboard, anyone could see that we had come thoroughly prepared for the trip. As well as sailing gear and our clothes, we had brought my folding bike. This, together with Jean-François's bike, would allow us to go off on forays into the countryside. We had also brought my boat: I thought a change of scenery would do it good. I was also sure that it would come in useful at some point and, anyway, any self-respecting sailing boat (even one without a mast) needs a tender.

Whenever you go to bed in a strange place, there is always an initial period of adaptation when you get used to all the unfamiliar sounds. When sleeping in a boat, this period of adaptation tends to last a fair bit longer. That first night, it wasn't so much the sound of cars on the road by the river or the striking of the church clock that took getting used to, it was all the noises that are peculiar to a boat. For a start, there were the waves rippling against the hull. The regular sound of their ripples is oddly soothing. Then there was the occasional long, droning rumble of an engine as a barge headed past upriver, followed by the arrival of the barge's wake, which slapped against the hull and set the boat rocking. But none of that bothered me at all. What I found distinctly irritating was the irregular tapping of a rope in the wind somewhere on deck and the squeaking of a fender stuck between the hull and the quayside. When it woke me up for the third time I decided that I would really have to go and tighten the ropes or I would never get a good night's sleep.

I opened the hatch above our heads and climbed out into the night air; the deck was cold under my bare feet and wet with dew. I paused for a moment to take stock of the surroundings, but there wasn't that much to see because of the mist that had settled on the river. In any case, downtown Elbeuf at 3 a.m. on a week-day seemed a fairly tranquil place with absolutely nothing moving on the quayside. I had just tightened the ropes and silenced the fender when there was a sound from a boat next to us at the quay-side. Turning to look, I could see a woman coming up the steps onto the deck. She saw me and, after a pause, waved and called a hushed 'Bonsoir.' I observed politely that she was out late, like me. 'C'est mon mari' – it's my husband – she explained. 'He can't bear the noise of loose ropes tapping at night. He's neurotic that way. The silly fool lies there grumbling, and the only way to get him to shut up is to come and fix it myself.' Clearly looking for some explanation as to what had brought me onto the deck at that hour, the woman said 'Et vous . . . ?'

Not wishing to admit that I was as daft as her husband, I just mumbled 'Euh . . . je voulais juste prendre un peu d'air' – er . . . I just wanted to get a bit of air. And, with that, I slipped quickly down through the hatch into the warm and now quieter cabin.

32

Rather than spend all the next day travelling along the river, Jean-François had suggested that we stop off in Rouen, some twenty kilometres downstream. This suited us perfectly. Rouen is the capital of Normandy and, more importantly, is the first place along the Seine since Paris to be awarded three stars in the Michelin guide.

We slipped our moorings and headed off downstream and, only a few hundred metres beyond the quayside, started negotiating the first bend of the day. As we swung to the right, some more white cliffs appeared on our left, as always on the outside of the bend. In the village of Orival where the river started straightening, many of the houses were built right up against the cliff face. The owners of most of these have taken advantage of the relative softness of the chalk to dig themselves cellars, their size limited only by the energy of the occupants themselves. There is one cellar that is so large it accommodated the whole population of the village during the Allied bombing raids on the nearby railway bridge. But, I suppose, the village was a lot smaller in those days. Things were also very different, because the locals used to swim along there before the war. Indeed, the stretch of road just past the bridge is still called Boulevard de la Plage. There even used to be bathing huts *à l'époque* – back in the day.

Heading to the right of another long island, we passed under another railway bridge, this one a magnificent structure called Le Pont aux Anglais. I was suddenly struck by the thought that surely you couldn't just park a boat somewhere in the centre of a city the way you can a car. Where exactly, I asked, was Jean-François planning to leave *Hirondelle*? With his habitual blend of vagueness and optimism, he replied 'Oh, on verra. Je suis sûr que l'on pourra s'amarrer quelque part' – oh, we'll see. I'm sure we'll be able to tie up somewhere or other.

Hirondelle emerged from the channel between the island and the quayside. 'On doit être dans le centre, non?' – we must be in the city centre – asked Jean-François in a tone that sounded less certain than I would have liked. When we said that we were fairly sure we were in the city centre because wasn't that the cathedral over there to our right, Jean-François brightened visibly. He then started looking keenly along the quayside, where a number of barges were moored, until he spotted an empty space, just long enough for the boat. 'On va le laisser là' – we'll leave her there – he declared in the tone of one who had been expecting nothing less. With that, we set about mooring *Hirondelle*, despite the fact that neither Inès nor I felt half as sure as Jean-François appeared to be about our right to just leave a boat wherever we felt like it. We were both wondering whether there would be the nautical equivalent of a parking ticket on the windscreen when we got back later on.

Rouen is known by its admirers as 'la ville des cent clochers' – the town of a hundred church towers. Somewhat unfortunately for the town, though, this is not its only nickname. Normandy is famously one of the wetter areas in France, and in this famously wet region Rouen stands out because it apparently enjoys an even higher rainfall than most of its surroundings. In view of this, the town is more commonly known, both by its critics and those who love it, as 'le pot de chambre de la Normandie' – Normandy's chamber pot. I can safely say that both nicknames seem to be well deserved. On the day that we spent exploring the town we saw a remarkable number of church towers; it also started raining just as we tied up and carried on raining for most of the time we were there.

Apart from its damp climate, the main disadvantage of the place, at least for English visitors, lies in the demise of a certain young lady called Joan. We had decided to start our exploration in the market square – La Place du Vieux Marché. Unfortunately, the first thing you see as you walk into the square is a large metal cross. This – 'La Croix de la Réhabilitation' – marks the spot where Joan of Arc's short but eventful life was brought to an end. I hadn't actually realized that she died in Rouen; I had somehow assumed that as she was the 'Maid of Orleans' she had probably died somewhere a bit nearer to home. What's more, visitors are left in no doubt of how she actually died: all the signs, as well as all the references in the guidebooks, make it gruesomely clear that she was 'brulée vive' – burned alive. And, of course, you are left in even less doubt about whose fault it was, although I really think that after 600 years, it must surely be time for someone to start forgiving and forgetting, if only a little bit.

The city seems to have more churches than it really knows what to do with. One church, previously known as L'Eglise St Laurent, has been transformed into something called the Secq des Tournelles museum. According to the sign at the entrance it houses a famous collection of wrought-iron objects. Now, it may just be me, but I can't say I jumped up and down with enthusiasm at the idea of a museum of wrought iron. But the Rouen weather was getting damper by the minute, so in we went. In the nineteenth century, Henri le Secq des Tournelles and his son Henry set about creating a collection of anything and everything made from wrought iron. On his father Henri's death, Henry (what fun they must have had when visitors called to see one or other of them) bequeathed the entire collection to the city of Rouen after he had happened to discover that some of his ancestors came from there. The collection opened in the church in 1921.

When you go in you are immediately struck by what a brilliant time the museum's creators must have had. They had been presented with a medium-sized, completely empty sixteenth-century church on the one hand and a massive collection of everything from gates, staircases, shop signs and lanterns all the way down to irons, belt buckles, scissors and surgical instruments on the other hand. They solved the problem by putting things absolutely everywhere. There are exhibits hanging from the roof, pieces mounted on the walls, huge things standing in the aisle and in the chapels and glass cases full of all the rest everywhere else. This concentration of exhibits caused some confusion: as we came in I stuck my umbrella in what I took to be an umbrella stand near the door but was sharply rebuked by the receptionist for misusing one of the exhibits.

Not for the first time, all this exploration had left us feeling a bit peckish, so we set off in search of something fortifying to eat. Not far from the Secq des Tournelles museum is a Bene-dictine convent which is famous for its biscuits. The nuns – the Bénédictines du Saint Sacrement – have created a small biscuit factory called Magdala right inside their convent. The biscuits are produced from the best local ingredients: eggs, sugar, flour, butter . . . But there is one unusual added extra. The nuns prepare the biscuits in reverential silence; during the preparation, as they do for most of their waking day, they pray. The nuns' motto is 'Prie et travaille! Mais prie d'abord' – work and pray! But pray first. It is this dash of prayer that is the added ingredient that the nuns believe makes each biscuit taste so special.

We bought a bag of biscuits – the first time a nun has ever sold me anything – and threw ourselves on them. I can't say that I could actually taste the prayers, but the biscuits were definitely uplifting.

Despite the reviving effects of the biscuits, all the rain was starting to get us down. We decided to abandon our idea of a walk beside the docks. Rouen docks have seen some notable departures and arrivals. One of the most famous departures was that of Giovanni da Verrazano, the Florentine navigator who settled in Normandy in the early sixteenth century. Verrezano was then charged by the French king to find the much-sought-after alternative route westbound to the Indies and China. Verrazano set sail from Rouen in 1524 in his ship *La Dauphine* with a crew of Norman sailors. In April 1524, rather than reaching the Indies, he ended up discovering an island on the east coast of what is now the United States. He called the place Nouvelle Angoulème and named the coast Arcadie. The name of the island was later changed, first by Dutch settlers to New Amsterdam and, later, by other settlers, to New York. While Verrazano's name is almost forgotten in Normandy, it is still well known in the USA notably thanks to the magnificent Verrazano Narrows suspension bridge which links Staten Island and Brooklyn.

Rouen's least welcome guests must surely be those who arrived in May 841. The area of France that would later become known as Normandy had led a fairly tranquil existence until around the beginning of the ninth century. Having never been attacked, the region was neither particularly well organized nor well defended. When Vikings first appeared and launched raids on the Normandy coast around the year 800, the lack of defences meant that they easily overran the surrounding areas. Reacting to this, Charlemagne – he who French children believe invented schools and despise in consequence – quickly organized a system of coastal defences. When the Vikings revisited the mouth of the Seine in 820, these new defences allowed the locals to drive them off with relative ease. The Norsemen returned to Normandy in 841, having spent the intermediate period completely revising their strategy. This time, rather than attack the well-defended area around the Seine estuary, their fleet headed straight up river towards Rouen. They reached it on 14 May, whereupon they set about relieving the city of prodigious quantities of loot before burning it to the ground. The Vikings continued to use the Seine as their route for attacking Normandy right up to the beginning of the tenth century.

Investigating the Viking attacks on Rouen ended up with me getting in touch with some people whose enthusiasm for their subject went beyond anything I had previously encountered. At lunch in Rouen that day, the waiter, overhearing us talking about the Viking raids, came out with an astonishing observation. 'Oh! Les Vikings – je les ai vus quand ils ont remonté la Seine' – I saw the Vikings when they came up the Seine. This was followed by a bit of an awkward pause while Inès and I both thought: 'The poor bloke must be losing it because there's no way he's twelve hundred years old.' Oblivious, the waiter carried on to explain, somewhat to our relief, that he had in fact been on the riverbank earlier that year when enthusiasts had recreated a Viking attack in a reproduction *drakkar*.

No more needed to be said: somehow or other I was going to have to talk to these people.

Some time later, after a considerable amount of searching, I could be seen strolling rather too casually around both home and office with a piece of paper in my hand. When anyone asked what I was holding, I replied, with studied nonchalance: 'Oh this? It's just a Viking warrior's mobile number.' One of the things I still find intriguing even now is how they originally all got together. That there should be a person somewhere on the planet whose dream is to become a modern-day Viking seems understandable; the world is full of people who are inexplicably enthusiastic about all kinds of odd subjects (not that I'd count myself among them, of course). But how did that first person find and gather together all the others? Whatever the explanation for their coming to meet up, there really are quite a lot of them. And they are all completely single-minded in their desire to crew a reproduction Viking *draki* (and not *drakkar* as I had foolishly thought) whatever the weather conditions. What's more, they do this dressed in the full Viking regalia of cloak, chainmail and helmet (without horns, of course – 'Evidemment, il n'y a pas de cornes – quelle idée' – of course there are no horns, the very idea of such a thing) with swords and staves also much in evidence. But here's the thing: give me the chance to dress up like that and sail up a river and I might actually go for it, not least because, in all the pictures I've seen of their adventures, they seem to be having a truly splendid time.

Their boat – called the *Olav Kyrre* – is magnificent. It is a faithful copy of one of the Vikings' more famous ships. The group didn't build it themselves but bought it from a place called Bjorkedal in Norway. They also have a large rowing boat with the splendid name of *Snorre*. When the wind direction allows, the *Olav Kyrre*'s crew can hoist the huge square sail and sweep majestically, and still somehow threateningly, up the river. However, once in the narrower reaches of the Seine, they have to resort to rowing with up to six oarsmen sitting along each side of the boat. And yes, they do attach their shields on the outside of the boat.

The only question that went down even less well than the one about horns on their helmets was when I asked whether the chainmail that they wore had been knitted by their mums just like the Monty Python mums had done for the *Holy Grail* film. The Viking didn't find that funny at all. 'Mais pas du tout!

On les a achetés à un costumier de théâtre' – Absolutely not: we bought them at a theatrical costumier's.

Incidentally, the real Vikings left their mark on many of the towns along the Seine. The names Elbeuf or Criquebeuf have nothing to do with *boeufs* – bulls. The *beuf* in the names comes from the Viking suffix *bo* or *bou*, which means 'dwelling'.

Back on the quay, I was relieved to see that *Hirondelle* was still there and more importantly didn't seem to have acquired any kind of parking ticket. Jean-François had got back before us and, keen to make his English guest feel at home, had already started to prepare some tea. The characteristic smell of a propane stove in action greeted us as we came down the steps into the cabin.

My suspicion that we hadn't really been supposed to leave the boat by the quay all day was heightened by Jean-François' reluctance to spend any more time tied up there. As soon as the tea had been poured, he advocated we push on to a village called La Bouille, which lay just a few kilometres away. This seemed a great idea, not only because it had stopped raining at last, but because it would take us under one of the most surprising bridges over the Seine. The Pont Gustave Flaubert stands on part of a new expressway leading out of the town over the river and is easily visible from miles around as it is the third-tallest structure in Rouen. As the expressway crosses the river in the area of the docks, one of the important considerations that had to be taken into account when designing the bridge was that it should allow seagoing ships to use the entire dock area. This meant that part of the bridge had to move somehow or other so as to let the ships pass. The designers rejected the usual solutions such as a swing bridge or a pivoting bridge and opted for a type of bridge called a vertical lift bridge. In this sort of bridge, a sizeable stretch of roadway can be lifted bodily into the air while remaining completely horizontal. As the expressway is a dual carriageway, the bridge has to lift sections of both carriageways at the same time. It thus has two pairs of tall grey pillars standing some eighty-six metres high near opposite banks of the river, each pair being topped off by an astonishing butterfly-shaped structure fitted with huge pulleys. Cables hang down from the pulleys to the roadway so that, when you want to open the bridge, you just winch on the cables and haul two sections of roadbed way up into the air (but without any cars on it, of course). It was opened in 2007, becoming Rouen's sixth road bridge.

I would dearly like to see the bridge in action, but 'C'est là où il y a le hic' – that's where there's a snag. The bridge was built at massive expense so that it could open to let ships pass; but in fact it is predicted to open only about thirty times a year – less than once a week, which means that you would have to be very lucky to see it in action. This all seems unsatisfactorily vague and uncertain: does the bridge open or doesn't it? If you seek clarification by asking one of the locals (and I asked several) you will only get *une réponse de Normand*. Normandy folk are famous for the vagueness of their replies, even to the simplest of questions. A basic question of the 'Is it or isn't it . . . ?' sort, the kind of thing that just expects a simple *oui* or *non* in reply, has them wriggling in spasms of indecision. Rather than commit themselves to anything remotely definite, the locals are believed to reply: 'Peut-être bien que oui; peut-être bien que non.' This sounds roughly like an English yokel saying: 'Happen it be, but happen it ain't,' in reply to a simple question such as: 'Is this the road to the market?' And you can't really ask for anything clearer than that.

33

Like other places that we would see further down the river, La Bouille is a long, thin village that has stretched itself out along the riverbank. It boasts some fine houses, many of which stand along the river, some shops, several restaurants and the most astonishing number of art galleries. We counted five, but there may well be others that we missed. Given that La Bouille's population is less than a thousand, that seems somewhat generous. Jean-François spotted a couple of still-lifes in the window of one of the galleries and promptly decreed that it was a splendid place.

We were sitting in the cockpit, having a convivial drink and starting to think about supper, when Jean-François noticed that there was a wedding just finishing at a nearby church and the wedding party was coming down to the riverbank near us to take some atmospheric photos of the happy couple. Having watched them for a minute or two, Jean-François decided that, while the couple looked nice enough, he was sure that the photos needed a little something extra. 'Il leur faut un peu de couleur locale' – what they need is a bit of local colour – he proclaimed – and that local colour was us! He quickly urged me to grab every bit of foul-weather gear I could find and follow him up onto the quayside. 'Allez-y, je vais vous regarder' – go ahead, I'll watch you – Inès said, sitting down on the cabin roof.

Despite the rush, I think I got the local colour bit down perfectly – a greasy blue and white woollen hat that I found in the steering locker, a bright-yellow oilskin jacket that Jean-François had brought along as a spare and my blue sea boots with the tops rolled down an inch or two, just to look professional, all topped off with the mainsheet, neatly coiled up over my shoulder. Dressed like that I was certain that no one would ever guess I was anything other than a local tar who had sailed these waters since before he could walk. Jean-François was similarly colourful if not, frankly, more so, sporting a very grubby woollen hat that was designed to stay on in the highest wind thanks to a string under his chin. Once up on the quay, we transformed ourselves instantly into rejects from *Treasure Island*, stomping about in our gear and exchanging heartfelt piratical cries. Having been brought up on Tintin books, Jean-François knew all the best of Captain Haddock's imaginary expressions off pat. 'Tonnerre de Brest!' he roared. 'Mille sabords! Bachi-Bouzouks!' It only took me a couple of minutes to pick them up and use them too to great effect.

The wedding party could not get enough of us: indeed, we ended up being in most of their photos. How we kept up the intrepid sailor routine without collapsing in hysterics remains a mystery. But if by any chance someone from that wedding ever reads this, I would love to have a copy of the photo of me with my arm around the bride while the groom has my coil of rope over his shoulder and Jean-François capering about beside him in his ridiculous hat.

The fact that we had been so readily welcomed by the wedding party was mainly thanks to the clothes we had picked. From the city-dwelling guests' point of view, the general grubbiness of our gear branded us as storm-hardened, seasoned sailors, a race of people who are probably not often seen in La Bouille. Had we wanted to pass ourselves off as professionals from a fishing trawler, again something not regularly spotted so far inland, we would have had to substitute oilskin bib-overalls in place of our jackets and add waterproof work gloves. Along the river, however, such clothes would look distinctly out of place. Most of the professionals of the non-seagoing variety I had encountered seemed to favour nothing more exotic than blue trousers and heavy blue sweaters, and this regardless of whether they worked on the deck of a boat or inside a warm office on the quayside.

And what of the non-professionals? *Les plaisanciers* – leisure sailors – who you see along the river are no different from sailors anywhere else: they tend to opt for jeans, tennis shoes and modern synthetic fleeces bought from well-known sportswear chains. On the other hand, rich people with large, expensive boats tend to stand out because they often try to look *authentique*. In order to achieve this, they will go and buy their clothes from the local *coopérative maritime*. This is a ship's chandler's, a shop which does most of its business selling shackles, rope and paint to professional sailors. But *coopératives maritimes* also have a lucrative sideline selling high-quality clothing to comfortably-off weekend sailors. They offer tempting arrays of warm woollen sweaters – generally navy-blue or red – long-sleeve T-shirts (often of the stripey variety) and waterproofs. These are often made by Armor Lux or Saint James, French manufacturers famous for their marine clothing. Thus, if you spot a middle-aged man in clean blue Aigle boots, ironed blue trousers, a *pull de marin* – a seaman's sweater with buttons along the shoulder – all topped off with a brand-new waterproof jacket bearing a French brand name, you can be fairly sure that he is heading for a large yacht which most likely goes to sea only on fine days.

But the sailors who are really worth keeping an eye out for are those in the French Navy – the Marine Nationale – because an article of their clothing can provide a source of good luck for anyone cunning enough to take advantage of it. French *marins* are easily recognizable by the red pompom that sits atop their hat. Tradition has it that if you manage to touch the pompom with your left index finger without the sailor noticing, then you will have good luck for a day. The luck available is precisely quantified: one touch gives a twenty-four-hour dose while touching three pompoms in a day, again without being spotted, ensures you will be lucky for three weeks. But no one seems to care about the not being spotted part any more. Any poor sailor in a Métro carriage or other easily accessible place will find his pompom being constantly grabbed from all sides by people so desperate for a bit of free luck that they are prepared to ignore one of the key elements of the tradition. No wonder their lottery numbers never come up.

La Bouille stands at the beginning of a continuous series of Omega-shaped bends that extend through what is one of the least-known national parks in the whole of France. This is called Le Parc des Boucles de la Seine, where *boucles* refers to the loops formed along the river. The area was declared a national park in 1974 and covers 80,000 hectares of farmland, orchards and forest and includes several châteaux and a couple of ruined abbeys. As on stretches of the river earlier on, each bend has white cliffs on the outside curve while the inner bank generally lies on a flat plain. The area is strangely isolated: right up until 1977, when the Pont de Brotonne was built near the town of Caudebec-en-Caux, there was not a single bridge across the river along the entire stretch from Rouen to the Pont de Tancarville, which sits at the beginning of the estuary. And the Tancarville bridge itself was only built in 1959: before that there were no bridges downstream of Rouen at all. Faced with a stretch of river a good 100 kilometres long without any bridges at all, how on earth did the locals cope? Simple: they created a network of river ferries. And they are still there. Within the borders of the national park there are seven river ferries, known as *bacs*. These come in two basic sizes: small and a bit bigger. The small ones, which can carry about ten cars, are located in the quieter, more rural reaches, while the two bigger ones, which can take a couple of lorries as well as some cars, serve to connect major road routes from north to south.

We were very keen to explore the park and so, the following morning, we asked Jean-François if he would mind very much if we left him on his own for a day or so while we went to look around. He wasn't likely to need us all that much, because he was about to spend the day not really going anywhere at all. This was strictly true because the bends downstream of La Bouille are so pronounced that, rather than heading west towards the sea, he was going to be shuttling back and forth endlessly from north to south. Jean-François accepted this argument as philosophically as he seemed to accept most things but just asked that we do a bit of shopping while we were away because supplies were running low. He went on to say that, in any case, he would be perfectly happy while we were gone, because he had an idea for yet another still-life and was keen to get started. Reassured that we weren't going to be leaving Jean-François completely in the lurch, we phoned Sebastian and asked if we might borrow the car for a bit while he was in the area.

Following the signs in La Bouille that had a little *bac* pictogram on them, we found ourselves at the head of a short slipway leading down to the river. There was a helpful notice explaining how to use the *bac* as well as a timetable of crossings and, most usefully, a white line painted on the road showing where it would be a good idea to stop if you didn't want to drive straight into the river. A couple of hundred metres away, on the other side of the river, there was a strange red-and-white craft lying head-on to another slipway. As sound travels a long way over water we could hear the metallic clanging sounds as half a dozen cars drove in a line down the slipway and onto the deck. Barely had the last car clattered on board when the engine could be heard accelerating and the *bac* reversed away from the slipway and set out across the river towards us. As it came nearer I could see that it was made up of a basic flat car deck with ramps at each end that could be lowered to allow the cars on and off then raised back up a few degrees for the crossing. There was a simple bridge structure about three metres above the deck which was made up of a glazed cabin stretching across the centre of the car deck, and that was pretty much all there was to it. There was a captain up in the cabin and a crewman in a dark-blue seaman's jersey standing at the front – it was too square to be properly called the bow – with his hand on a length of blue rope that stretched across the ramp in front of the leading cars. As it got closer to shore, the *bac* lined itself up with the ramp in front of us and, with a loud roaring of engines driving astern, slowed to a stop with its ramp scrunching up the slipway. Barely had the front touched land than the crewman flicked away the blue rope, somewhat theatrically, and waved the leading cars off. As soon as the last car was off, the crewman made a brief beckoning gesture, and it was our turn to drive on.

We clanked onto the metal deck and were guided to the far corner. The turnaround time was incredibly short: barely five minutes from the first scrunch of the *bac* arriving to the moment when it set off again for the opposite bank. Of the six cars on board that morning, I was the only person who bothered to get out of the car. On later trips I noticed that it was ridiculously easy to tell the tourists from the locals. The tourists invariably got out of their cars and looked both at the view and at the workings of the *bac* itself. They would rush about the deck, exclaiming to each other about the fresh air, the view, the river, that nice house on the hill over there or the amusing activities of a passing duck. The locals, meanwhile, just stayed in their cars, checked their phones, smoked a cigarette or read a newspaper, only glancing up when it was time to start their engines. One bloke I spoke to who was sitting in a car with local number plates explained his indifference to his surroundings by saying 'C'est comme un feu rouge, sauf que ça bouge' – it's just like waiting at a red light, except it's moving. We made a crossing on another route at the end of a school day and shared the *bac* with a vast number of schoolchildren on their way to catch the bus which was waiting on the far side: not one of them seemed aware of the fact they were on a boat. In this they were just like the children I see on the Métro or on suburban trains when I'm on my way to work: why should they care about their surroundings when there are texts to be sent, phone calls to be made and music to be listened to?

The Seine below Rouen is not just broad, it has grown into a proper seaway. This is something which can come as a bit of a surprise. After the crossing on that first *bac*, I thought I would spend a few minutes watching it shuttle back and forth across the river. Sitting on the slipway in the sun, watching the cars drive off on the far shore, I was suddenly snatched from my reverie by the sound of heavy marine engines. I looked upriver and saw a huge, ocean-going ship of several thousand tonnes rumbling past from Rouen docks on its way down to the Channel. Even though it was travelling relatively slowly, a ship that size kicks up a sizeable wake, which, if you are lounging about on a slipway down by the water's edge, can make you leap quite smartly for higher ground.

Captains of seagoing ships are not expected to know every twist and turn of the Seine, nor each and every shoal along the way. In fact, because of all the difficulties and potential dangers, they are not actually allowed to steer their own ships along the seaway which stretches from – obviously – the sea, all the way up to Rouen, the inland limit for large ships. Rather than the captain, responsibility for taking the ship along the Seine passes to one of fifty-eight river pilots – *pilotes de la Seine* – who are based at Le Havre, Caudebec-en-Caux and Rouen. Any ship over fifty-five metres long coming upriver has to pick up a pilot just outside Le Havre. It isn't necessary to stop for him, or quite frequently, her, to come aboard: the pilots have a number of powerful motor boats which look like the small RNLI lifeboats that are seen in the UK. The motor boat comes alongside, and the pilot climbs aboard up a rope ladder hanging down the side of the hull. Pilot regulations are very comprehensive: they specify how far in advance the captain has to inform them of his arrival, the radio frequencies to be used, the speed limit to be observed during pilot pick-up (nine knots) and, perhaps most importantly from the pilot's point of view, the characteristics of the ladder. The side of a ship is a sizeable thing, so ladder rung sizes and angles are specified to reduce the chance of accidents on the long, often slippery, climb up. Once aboard, the pilot takes over complete command of the helm and retains it until either the ship berths or when pilot change-over takes place at the halfway point up- or downstream at Caudebec-en-Caux. Each pilot thus specializes in a given half of the seaway. On non-French ships, all communication between pilot and crew takes place in clear, concise English.

Sadly, when I rang, and despite my manifest ability to speak clear, concise English, the river pilots proved unwilling to take an untrained foreigner out to sea and let him try to scramble up a long, treacherous rope ladder with a view to inviting himself onto the bridge of someone else's ship.

Even after we had crossed the river several times, the novelty of travelling on a *bac* never seemed to wear off. On every crossing I would get out of the car, wander round the deck and admire the view. The national park itself is a great place to wander, as there are great swathes of forest – the Forêt Brotonne – which are so extensive that, when exploring, we very rarely saw another walker. The more interesting trees, many of which really are worth a detour, are shown both on the local maps and by helpful signs along the tracks. At each *boucle* of the river, the flat land inside the bends is given over to agriculture. Here, there are orchards, a selection of slightly run-down farms, some smarter modern houses that are clearly inhabited by outsiders, some more orchards, fields of sheep, still more orchards, fields of cows, generous quantities of ponies, goats and geese, yet more orchards and a fair number of ducks. All these orchards produce huge quantities of delicious apples. But the odd thing about Normandy apples is the fact that you very rarely see a Norman actually eating one. This is because the poor folk don't often get the chance. Any available fruit are either chopped up on sight and put in a *tarte normande*, which, once you taste some, you agree is a very good thing to do with them, or they are used to make cider or calvados.

One of the key features of French cider is that it often comes in Champagne-shaped bottles which have corks with twisted wire closures. Removing the wire and popping the cork makes drinking it feel far more exotic and pleasurable than does stuff from a simple screw-top bottle. This bottle design can, however, lead to confusion, whether accidental or otherwise. A guest once turned up at our house for supper, produced a green bottle with a gold foil neck and, just as he was about to offer it, looked at it and exclaimed 'Oh! Merde! J'ai apporté du cidre, pas du Champagne!' – oh, no! I've brought cider instead of Champagne! I have never decided how much of an accident that actually was.

And what of calvados? This is a strong alcohol of the *eau de vie* type which is made by distilling cider. Calvados, more familiarly known as 'calva', comes in two main varieties. Basic calvados, which makes up seventy-five per cent of production, comes from cider produced from apples grown anywhere in Normandy, while 'calvados du pays d'Auge' is made, as the name suggests, from cider produced using apples uniquely from the Auge region of Normandy and also using a specific type of still.

So, having bought yourself a bottle of calva, what do you do with it? Well, drink it for a start: it makes an excellent *digestif*, or you can drink it as an accompaniment to Normandy cheeses. If you like, it can also considerably improve a plain cup of black coffee. But the very best way of consuming calvados is in the context of a *trou normand*. This is one of the better reasons for going to France, or, at least, for going and having a decent meal there. A *trou normand* comprises a quantity of apple sorbet, served in a glass or small dish, over which has been poured a generous measure of calvados. In more expensive restaurants, it is generally served, often without appearing on the menu, between the main dish and the cheese (which, of course, is served before the pudding). It tastes absolutely wonderful, makes a break from all the heavy eating, aids digestion and gives renewed strength to carry on. What more could one ask?

One of the highlights of the park is the ruined abbey in Jumièges. Jumièges, you may recall from my initial investigation of the Seine, is the only place downriver of Paris apart from Rouen to be awarded three Green Guide stars. Ruined abbeys are rarer in France than in the UK, notably due to the fact that there was no French dissolution of the monasteries. The few ruins that there are, are either the result of the local communities dying out or, as is the case with Jumièges, a casualty of the Revolution. Many religious buildings in France were declared national assets by Napoleon and promptly sold off to the highest bidder. Jumièges was bought by a wood merchant, who, rather than seeking to preserve it, actually blew up the choir to create a supply of building stone for other projects. Luckily, in 1852 the Lepel-Cointet family set about saving it. Thanks to them there is a sizeable amount of the abbey left, notably its two 'mango-chutney-pot'-shaped towers, which are visible from miles around. On a misty morning, it is a wonderful, atmospheric place to visit.

On the way back we stopped at a supermarket to get some supplies but, heading for the check-out, I saw there was a sizeable queue. It seemed that there was something wrong with the till and, as the girl at the cash desk couldn't fix it, she had called for the *monsieur*, who was apparently on his way. Rather than stand around waiting for the man to turn up, I thought I would use the time more profitably so I wandered back round the shop in search of an answer to a question which had been troubling me: 'Are there still any French brands or products that you find only in France and nowhere else?' On childhood holidays I remember being fascinated by all the local brands and products, none of which I had seen anywhere else – this was at a time when, if you saw a jar of Nutella in someone's house, you knew they must have been on holiday to Italy. There presumably was once a time when there were French brands in almost every field of consumer products, but along came global marketing, and now most of what you find in a French supermarket can be found anywhere else in Europe. And vice versa. But is there anything left that is exclusively French? The time waiting for the *monsieur* to fix the till showed that there still is. The products aren't that numerous, but if you look carefully, they are there.

The first aisle didn't produce much in the way of exclusively French things: just two sorts of chocolate biscuits – Péptito and Petits Ecoliers – some local tins of Cassoulet – surely you don't get that anywhere else? – and a French sugar brand called 'Daddy', which I occasionally buy because the name amuses me. There were also a selection of *biscottes* and *pains grillés* that form the basis of many a French breakfast but don't seem to be sold elsewhere.

But where I struck gold was in the soft drinks aisle. It started with the selection of *sirops*. While orange or lime concentrates are available everywhere, in France they really love their *sirops*. These are fruit or herb concentrates that you mix with cold water and then drink, generally on a hot summer's day. I first discovered such things at Inès's parents' house when one of her younger sisters offered me a *sirop de menthe*. This proved to be a very sweet, very green, minty liquid that, when mixed with water, made the water turn green and taste a fair bit mintier, but not, as far as I could see, necessarily that much nicer. Subsequent experiments have shown that it is a better idea to use very cold mineral water – people ask for a *Vittel menthe* in bars – and the drink can actually become quite pleasant if you use fizzy mineral water or even lemonade. But *sirops* come in all sorts of flavours. As well as mint you can find *grenadine*, *anis* – aniseed – *violette* – violet – and *orgeat* – barley, all of which seem to sell strongly. Having tried many of them over the years, I can safely say that you really have to be brought up with *sirops* in order to love them. But love them French people do. Our children were born in France, and this may well explain the fact that, hidden behind the cereal packets in our kitchen cupboard, there are at least four tall metal cylinders of different flavours of *sirops*. Sarah and Sebastian having outgrown them, the cans may well still be there the day we finally move. I'm certainly not going to be the one to finish them.

Further down the aisle from the *sirops*, there was some Cacolac – cartons or tins of chocolate-flavoured milk that are also especially favoured by children. There was also a brand of soda which, I am almost certain, is exclusively sold in France and which revels in the splendid name of Pschitt! This is apparently an onomatopoeic reference to the sound of a bottle of fizzy liquid being opened. And this was not the end of local fizzy drinks, for, a bit further down, I spotted some bottles of Ricqlès. This is a clear, very minty fizzy drink: minty drinks are evidently something of a favourite in France. Ricqlès was once sold under the arresting slogan 'Le glouglou qui fait glagla' where 'glouglou' is the sound of swallowing and 'glagla' is that of shivering. Ricqlès also makes another extraordinary liquid, one that I was offered on my first-ever long French car journey. It is 'L'alcool de menthe Ricqlès', a high-proof alcohol with, yet again, a strong minty taste. It comes in very small bottles, and you are supposed to consume it, when feeling tired or fed up in a car or possibly elsewhere, by shaking a few drops onto a sugar cube (you are expected to have some sugar cubes about your person for this purpose) and then crunching it. The resulting mix of alcohol, mint and sugar gives you a surprising kick and will definitely help wake you up or dispel long car-journey blues. If you ever get the chance, try opening a French car glove pocket: it can often reveal a little bottle of Ricqlès and a few sugar cubes, especially if the car's owner is anywhere near middle age.

The rest of my wander round the *superette* produced one or two other oddities that I think of as particularly French, notably green beans sold in glass jars. Why green beans need to be packaged in a glass jar has always puzzled me. People know what beans look like; they don't have to be shown them in a jar. Surely, a label on a tin, either with just the words 'haricots verts' or, if you really insist, with a picture of some of the things, would be enough? In the final couple of aisles there was nothing particularly interesting apart from extensive proof of the local obsession with sterilized milk and also of the odd enthusiasm for interleaved packs of loo paper.

By the time I had finished my investigation of the aisles, the *monsieur* had managed to fix the till, and so we were able to stock up with essentials and head back to *Hirondelle*.

34

Down the river from Jumièges lies the village of Villequier. For most French people the mere mention of the village conjures up the name of a famous writer and, unfortunately, of a tragic moment in his life. The writer in question was Victor Hugo, and Villequier was where his daughter Léopoldine drowned. I know this now – I confess that I didn't know it before – because it is almost impossible to mention the fact that you are planning to explore the Parc des Boucles de la Seine without someone instantly mentioning Leopoldine.

In 1838, during a family visit to the Vaquerie household in Villequier, Leopoldine met Charles Vaquerie and promptly fell in love with him. Being only fourteen, Leopoldine was quite reasonably considered to be a bit too young, so they had to wait until February 1843 before their families would allow them to marry. Sadly, their marriage would not last long. In September of the same year Leopoldine and her husband set out to row down from Caudebec en Caux to Villequier, but their boat capsized, and the Vaqueries and two other family members were drowned. They are buried in Villequier cemetery, and the Vaquerie house in the town is now a museum to Victor Hugo.

Having explored Villequier and much of the rest of the national park, we found ourselves at the local tourist office, looking for inspiration. The girl behind the counter offered several brochures, but the only one that really stood out was for the Bayeux Tapestry. I had seen it once before, when I was eleven. The thing that really stuck in my memory was the handheld commentary device. This gave visitors, even eleven-year-old ones, unaccustomed autonomy. Anyone who didn't want to follow the tapestry round the wall with their parents could jump to another point and hear the commentary there, or even, as I did, follow the whole thing backwards.

The tapestry wasn't the only thing on that holiday in France that seemed surprising to eleven-year-old eyes. But it was the time spent staying at Léah and Marcel's house – they who had the musical loo-roll holder in their Paris flat – that left me in open-mouthed amazement for much of the time. At supper the first night I was presented, out of the blue, with a strange green object on a plate. I stared at it in panic: what on earth was I expected to do with it? Learning that peculiar thing was called an avocado only solved part of the problem. And then there was all the handshaking – but, inexplicably, they didn't actually shake. And in many cases, most notably when being greeted by Léah herself, they didn't even grasp your hand, they just held it fleetingly. It was all very disconcerting. But the most notable moment of my first stay is something I can't remember at all. Léah decided one suppertime to give her young guest his first-ever glass of red wine. I definitely remember the sight of the glass, the red wine gleaming in the candlelight and the excitement I felt at being allowed to drink it, but, after that, nothing. I especially have no memory of the impassioned speech, Timoney family lore assures me, I made to all those present, in, what's more, almost comprehensible French.

I thus had fond memories of the tapestry (which, as everyone knows, is actually an embroidery) and was keen to see it again, but this time preferably in the right direction. And my companions seemed keen to see it too, although, it would turn out, for somewhat different reasons. Jean-François wanted to go mainly because his parents hadn't taken him to see it when he was a child, despite his apparently having begged to go, and the memory of it still rankled. Inès's enthusiasm was more puzzling. Given that the victory over the English in 1066 was won by the Normans – people from northern lands, rather than those born and raised on French soil – few French people seem to care much about the invasion at all. Indeed, on the rare occasions the subject comes up, they don't usually seem to feel that it had anything really to do with them. In fact, until that day, I had never heard any French person use the battle of Hastings as an example of a dramatic French victory over the perfidious English. So when Inès expressed a strong desire to go, then spent much of the trip using terms like 'défaite humiliante' – humiliating defeat – and 'on vous a battus' – we beat you – I couldn't understand where all this vehemence was coming from. It was only when we were nearly there that I finally made the connection with our irksome victory celebrations in Agincourt back on St Crispin's day.

Whatever the reasons behind our respective enthusiasm for being there, we found ourselves, a couple of hours later, walking past the Norman longboat which sits in the courtyard of the Musée de la Tapisserie de Bayeux. Once you reach the viewing room, you follow the tapestry in its glass case, all sixty-eight metres of it, all the way down one wall of the room and then slowly back on the opposite side of the wall. I'm not sure exactly how long the whole visit takes, but, despite being part of a slowly advancing, continuous line of people where the ones who are just in front of you at the beginning are still right there in front of you when you reach the end, you find the time flies by; the story is so gripping.

With hindsight, it would seem that on my previous visit I missed one or two key elements of the plot, because all these years I have believed that William of Normandy just woke up one morning in 1066 feeling a bit irritable, looked across the Channel at some smug-looking white cliffs, thought: 'Right, I'm having them,' and promptly mustered some troops and horses and sailed off. But it wasn't like that at all, even if you do allow for the fact that the tapestry was commissioned by the winning side and thus may give a slightly biased view of things.

The story starts off straightforwardly enough. Edward the Confessor, King of England, has no heir and decides to send Harold to Normandy to tell William that he, William, is to succeed him. Harold has considerable difficulty finding William, even managing to spend some time as a prisoner of Guy, Count of Ponthieu, along the way, but he meets up with him in the end. They become friends and go off to have various adventures together, including waging a campaign against Conan II, Duke of Brittany. It isn't clear what Conan did to annoy them: I suppose his name alone may have been all the provocation they needed. Only then does Harold get around to informing William that he is to become King of England. William, clearly unsure about how trustworthy Harold is, gets him to swear the most solemn of oaths on saintly relics that he really will honour Edward's wishes. This, in a formal ceremony, Harold does and then heads off back to England.

When about to set out on my quest, I wondered whether the journey would reveal an example of the English perfidy that the French are always talking about. Sadly, the actions which provoked the Norman invasion may well be one of the most blatant embodiments of *la perfidie anglaise*, for, once Edward died, Harold promptly abandoned his promise and had himself crowned king instead. This went down very well in England, but not so well in Normandy. That things were pretty soon going to start going badly for the English was forewarned by the appearance of Halley's Comet – shown in the tapestry as a star with streaming hair.

With that we come to my favourite bit of the tapestry. When William and his troops set off in their boats to cross the Channel, they took their horses with them. The horses had clearly never encountered anything remotely as much fun as a cross-Channel cruise; there is a wonderful panel showing them looking out over the side of the boats and positively beaming with delight.

The tapestry ends, predictably, with the battle and the death of Harold, whether from an arrow in the eye as is traditionally believed or from some other injury. It's impossible to tell on the tapestry which one he is. William became king, and England was now ruled by the French.

We didn't see much of Jean-François on the trip back. The tapestry visit had inspired him to spend most of the return trip trying to draw still-lifes that were supposed to look as though they had been embroidered. I am not convinced that he managed it, though I kept that to myself.

35

I never realized how much we missed when we used to hurry down the motorway.

For years we used to race along the *autoroute* to catch the car ferry from Le Havre to Portsmouth. When Sarah and Sebastian were younger, it seemed a much better idea to have the minimum of driving and the maximum of entertainment on our way to England rather than the reverse. To small children the six-hour crossing to Portsmouth seemed like a cruise. On a typical day we used to find the time to fit in a meal, a nap, some sunbathing on deck, a visit to the cinema as well as the occasional dip in the small swimming pool that was hidden somewhere in the basement. Our children raved so much about the cruise aspect of the trip to my parents that they decided it might be fun to try it for themselves. Having booked their crossing, my parents apparently boasted, tongue in cheek, to their friends that they had decided to spend part of their retirement by going on a cruise. 'The Caribbean?' their friends inquired. 'No – Le Havre!' Even though they weren't going anywhere exotic, they carefully booked the best cabin for both the outward and the return crossing and then set off for Portsmouth. But there was never any question of coming to see us; my parents' idea was to create their cruise by spending the whole time on the ferry without getting off in France at all. I have always imagined them standing on deck during the crossing, beaming with delight like the Bayeux horses.

For us, who used the ferry to actually take us somewhere

different, the time aboard was considered as being part of the holiday, whereas the journey to and from the ferry was just something to get over with as quickly as possible. There was never any question of dawdling along the way to or from Paris just to look at the scenery. Indeed, it never really occurred to us that there might be something nearby worth dawdling over.

Well, there is: it is called the Marais Vernier. This is an expanse of reclaimed marshland that lies on the left bank of the river just after you have left the Parc des Boucles de la Seine. It is easy to find it: all you have to do is find the Pont de Tancarville – the big suspension bridge that leads towards the port of Le Havre – and then not go across it. As a general rule, if you can see the left-hand end of the bridge anywhere in the distance, you are very probably in the Marais Vernier.

After exploring the Parc des Boucles de la Seine for a bit, we had gone back and rejoined *Hirondelle* at Caudebec-en-Caux, a small town just near the Pont de Brotonne. Jean-François had seemed very pleased to see us and reckoned that, thanks to all the bends, he had travelled about three times the actual straight-line distance between La Bouille and Caudebec. Luckily, he didn't consider the time wasted because he had nearly finished his latest still-life – this one of some apples, two oranges and a Chinese ginger jar.

After another cheery evening on board *Hirondelle*, followed by a long sweep round yet another *boucle*, Jean François dropped us off in Quillebeuf-sur-Seine so that we could do some more exploring, this time on the bikes. Quillebeuf, a village on the left bank (its name is yet another souvenir of the Vikings and apparently refers to a hut beside a spring), is a pleasant enough place, in a modest, somewhat inoffensive way, and extends along the bank of the Seine like many other villages we had visited. Unfortunately, it lies in one of the most ill-chosen positions of any place along the entire length of the river. Quillebeuf has whole streets lined up facing the Seine, and many of the houses on them appear, at first sight, to offer fabulous views. Unfortunately, the view from Quillebeuf not only includes the river, which is fine as far as it goes, but also takes in the structures on the opposite bank. Poor Quillebeuf's misfortune is to lie right opposite Port Jérôme, a huge installation which comprises not one but *two* oil refineries as well as a generously equipped petrochemical complex. From the window of the riverside café where we stopped for a reviving coffee all we could see was an array of catalytic crackers, storage tanks and distillation towers. Apart from that, the café was very nice indeed.

There wasn't much more to see in Quillebeuf, so Inès and I headed off towards the marshes on the bikes. The first thing we learned about the Marais Vernier was that it was created by the Seine. It seems that originally the river used to be even bendier than it currently is. However, thousands of years ago, the river was struck by the notion that it perhaps had just a bend or two too many and promptly set about abandoning one of its loops. (If only it had seen fit to get rid of a few more at the same time . . .) The raised escarpment that used to define the southern limit of the bend is still there, only now it forms the boundary of the marsh. By changing its course, the river created a roughly circular expanse of marshes between the escarpment and its current course. The original marshland was too wet to be useful until it was reclaimed in the seventeenth century by Dutch engineers, who were the world experts of their day. The engineers started off by building a first protective dyke known as the Digue des Hollandais, which now carries the present road across the marshes. They then went on to dig a series of drainage canals and ditches, all of which give the marshland its characteristic air. These straight, regular ditches created a pattern of long thin fields – known as *courtils* – which were originally used for growing crops but are now mainly used for growing hay or as pastures. The boundary ditches are all planted with elders, alders and willows, all of which are regularly pollarded.

Many of the farmhouses in the Marais are thatched and have walls *à colombages*, like the Vieux Moulin in Vernon. Once you have seen a few, you realize that spotting the difference between a working thatched farmhouse and one that has been bought up by outsiders is ridiculously easy. Outsiders do their houses up with care, often taking pains to use traditional, local building techniques. Working ones look generally decrepit and have outbuildings that have been patched up using old doors or bits of rusty corrugated iron. And in the remotest parts of the Marais you can still find some extraordinary structures. If you strike off down one of the paths that lead away along the ditches between the fields you come across thatched houses so old and neglected that their roofs have been turned green by all the moss growing in them. These old houses occasionally have outbuildings that are built out of *torchis*. This is a mixture of clay, gravel and straw – known in English as 'cob' – which is used to fill in the spaces in the half-timbered structure. Its use dates back to the middle ages. Where the paint and plaster has come off the buildings, you can easily spot the tell-tale signs of the straw sticking out of the gravelly walls.

The farmhouses we passed were also noticeably well staffed with cats. This slowed our progress somewhat, because, as happens when we go past any kind of habitation, each time Inès spotted a cat she would stop and talk to it. I still find this surprising, because, when we first met, Inès didn't like cats at all. She would explain her dislike and mistrust of them by showing me the long scar on her wrist that was inflicted by the white cat next door when she was little. What provoked the altercation remains a mystery: Inès has always claimed to have been the innocent party and explains the scar by the fact that white cats are notorious for picking fights. Over the years, however, we have managed to acquire a cat here and there, and the species has slowly progressed from least favoured to most favoured in Inès's animal hierarchy.

We currently have two cats whose only shortcomings lie in their names. The older one is known as Kiki, a name chosen by our children when they were a fair bit younger. As well as being a slightly whimsical female name, *kiki* can mean 'neck', as in the expression *serrer le kiki*, which means 'to strangle'. There is also *c'est parti mon kiki*, which is something you cry when getting down to something in a 'right, let's get on with it' kind of way. Unfortunately, as with so many basic French words, there is also a children's lavatorial sense to the word, in that children sometimes use it to refer to a man's 'thingy'. Knowing this not only allows you to imagine some interesting alternative interpretations for the expressions given earlier, it also explains why, when we introduce our rather distinguished cat to people as Kiki, they appear mildly taken aback. But the cat's name is Kiki and, inasmuch as she answers to anything, she answers to that. So rather than give her a completely new name, we have come up with a brilliant solution to the problem: we have taken to introducing her to visitors as Marie-Kiki rather than plain Kiki. In a Catholic country, any name that starts with Marie has an indisputable air of gravitas and quality. Where 'Kiki' provokes a wry smile, 'Marie-Kiki' makes people raise their eyebrows in polite, mildly interested surprise.

Unfortunately our other cat's name is more problematic. In France, any name given to a pedigree animal in a particular year has to start with the same letter. The year our second cat was born, the letter was D. Thus, the kittens in her litter were called Diabolo, Dragée and . . . Darling. As luck would have it, the one we liked best was Darling. But, as I tried to explain, increasingly urgently, on several occasions after we brought the kitten home, 'You can't have a kitten called "Darling". It is ridiculous.' 'Nonsense!' countered Inès, 'It will be fun.' The neighbours who live within earshot of our house know full well that I am English and may naively assume that a French wife calls her English husband 'darling' now and again (I should be so lucky). Knowing this, Inès delights in occasionally going to the back door at supper time and calling out: 'Darling! Viens manger tes croquettes' – come in and eat your crunchy stuff – fondly imagining the neighbours shaking their heads and saying to each other: 'Si ce n'est pas malheureux! Elle ne lui donne que des croquettes' – the poor chap: she just gives him crunchy stuff for supper, or even 'Darling! Arrête de faire pipi sur les rosiers et rentre tout de suite' – stop weeing on the rose bushes and come in at once. Oddly enough, since we have had Darling, we haven't been invited to any kind of social event by our neighbours. Though I am sure that is just an unfortunate coincidence.

Whichever way you walk in the Marais Vernier, the land is so flat you can see what's coming up for miles. This is not a place for hurrying, and, as you wander peacefully along, you pass apple orchards, fields with contented cows and dozens of trees full of mistletoe. While the kissing under the mistletoe tradition is known in France, it doesn't seem to be followed with the fervour that it is in England, and so a lot less of the stuff is harvested around Christmas-time. Incidentally, these contented cows are busily contributing to Normandy's justifiable fame for its dairy products. The local milk is known (at least in Normandy, it is) as *l'or blanc de la Normandie* – Normandy white gold. And the cream is even better known than the milk. And, of course, we shouldn't forget Normandy butter. Any recipe which includes the words 'A la normande' is going to involve generous quantities of cream or butter, and, very possibly, both. Normandy is not a good place to start a diet. It is rather somewhere you should consider starting a diet as soon as you leave.

At a village called Sainte-Opportune-la-Mare – so called because of its proximity to a small lake called, somewhat inaccurately, the Grande Mare – we came across an apple market. I had been puzzling about all the orchards we had been passing and wondering if they ever sold any of the fruit, so I was quite relieved to come across some for sale. The stallholders were local growers, and all prided themselves on the varieties of apples they had on offer. These were mainly 'old' varieties, the sort you very rarely see in supermarkets but which, according to the growers, deserve far wider recognition. The apples had wonderful names: Pigeonnet de Rouen, Gueule de mouton, Choupette – Rouen pigeon, Sheep's face, Sweetie – and one which pleased me particularly: Royale d'Angleterre – English royal.

There were also a couple of stalls from local duck farms. When it comes to ducks, French farmers seem to have the same attitude as that of English farmers with regard to pigs: there is very little of the animals that can't be eaten somehow or other. The duck stalls were laden with heavy glass jars full of *rillettes*, or pâté, but there were also things that seem, at first sight to be less appetizing, such as *gésiers de canard* – duck gizzards. I don't know what you expect to see when you hear the word 'gizzard', but the things in question are chunks of dark meat which, once heated up in a pan and added to a salad, transform it from a simple starter into a sumptuous main dish. Please don't bother wondering why I run for the hills when threatened with *andouillette* but throw myself upon duck *gésiers*: life just isn't as logical as it should be.

The word for an apple – *pomme* – features in a variety of French day-to-day expressions. *Ma pomme* can refer to oneself, and so be used as an alternative to *moi*: *c'est pour ma pomme* means that whatever it is, is for me, or is my responsibility; if someone keeps everything for himself, that would be *il a tout pris pour sa pomme.* The expression, seemingly, comes from the fact that a round apple looks like someone's head and, by extension, is supposed to remind you of the whole person. To see that this is so, you need look no further than an old, but still surprisingly well-known, Maurice Chevalier song called 'Ma pomme', which includes the refrain 'ma pomme – c'est moi'. Apples can also be used to give a notion of size. A small child, for example, can be described as being *haut comme trois pommes* – as tall as three apples. Finally, if someone faints, rather than using the verb *s'évanouir*, you could say that *il est tombé dans les pommes* – he fell in the apples – which gives a far more pleasing image.

It appears that there are far more apple enthusiasts in France who are keen to save old varieties than I had previously imagined. Indeed, we have a friend who recently declared himself to be a key member of an *association de croqueurs de pommes* – an apple munchers' club. The club has a conservation orchard which has some hundred different sorts of apple tree. Their annual show includes not only stalls offering arresting types of

apples such as Pomme annanas, Claque pépin, Reinette de Brabant – Pineapple apple, Rattly pips, Brabant russet – but also
cider-making demonstrations and selections of locally made
cheeses.

Later, walking along yet another narrow track by a drainage
ditch, contentedly munching my second apple from the market – this one called a Cabarette – we came face to face with a
hunter. I have to admit that *chasseurs* are probably not the
French people with whom I have the most affinity. Hunters
spend their time wandering about the French countryside,
armed to the teeth, blazing away with both barrels at anything
that moves, from unfortunate thrushes to deer and wild boar.
What's more, they generally try and justify this activity by
claiming to love nature. There are over a million licensed hunters in France – more than in any other European country.
Hunting thus comes second only to football as a popular
French pastime. Between them, France's hunters dispatch
some thirty million animals per year. The one we met that
morning was a fairly typical example of the species. In his fifties, with a hard, ruddy face and an aggressive moustache, he
had the look of someone who had tried having a kind thought
some thirty years earlier but had never seen the point of having another. He was dressed in camouflage fatigues, boots and
a green cap and had a long bandolier of multi-coloured car-
tridges for the pump-action shotgun he was carrying over his
shoulder. He also carried a hunting knife of a size that would
make even Crocodile Dundee sit up and pay attention. This
was not a person you should ever consider pushing past in a
queue at the baker's. While sneering at our city-folk clothing
and our inappropriate footwear, the man did at least return our
somewhat tentative 'Bonjour.'

As French hunters are so numerous, publishers have come

up with a wide range of magazines for them to read. The most famous of these is called simply *Le Chasseur Français – French Hunter*. Everyone, even non-hunters, seems to have heard of it, although I've never found anyone who actually admits to having bought it. *Le Chasseur Français* owes its nationwide fame, not to its articles on hunting, fishing or the training of dogs, but to its small ads. In the old days, these adverts were the only way for a lonely *paysan* to make contact with the wider world and so have any chance of meeting a member of the opposite sex who lived beyond the village boundary. The small ads section of the magazine used to be made up of pleas from lonely, unmarried rural types to meet desirable unattached ladies. Or even unattached ladies of any description. Traditionally, the adverts would read something along the lines of 'Paysan cherche jeune femme pour rencontre et plus si affinités' – peasant would like to meet young lady for encounter and possibly more. Others were more pragmatic: 'Paysan cherche jeune femme possédant une ferme' – peasant would like to meet young lady with her own farm. But the best-known story about *Le Chasseur Français* is about a single, possibly apocryphal advert. This is popularly believed to have read 'Paysan cherche jeune femme possédant un tracteur: envoyez photo du tracteur' – peasant would like to meet young lady with her own tractor: please send photo of the tractor.

In the interests of objectivity, I bought a copy of *Le Chasseur Français*. This is yet another thing that I probably would never have done in my life had I not set out on my quest. Indeed, the man in the local newsagents made no effort to hide his surprise when I asked for it, nor did the people sitting near me in the train, who watched me reading it on the way home. My first impressions were not that encouraging: it is a small, cheap-looking magazine. The cover of the edition I bought had a photo of a worried-looking rabbit sitting in a field – be afraid, rabbit: be very afraid. But its contents proved a lot more read-able than I had expected. While there were quite a few leading articles about how best to go about shooting various sorts of birds and mammals, there were some very interesting ones later on about gardening, cooking, pets and DIY. And what of the small ads? Well, *Le Chasseur Français* has clearly leaped into the modern era. Instead of requests for photos of tractors there are a lot of fairly conventional contact ads, as well as a surprising number of adverts offering the services of scantily clad girls, none of whom seem to be particularly interested in hunting or tractors at all.

36

There are two World Heritage sites that lie along the course of the Seine. One of them, appropriately enough, is the riverfront in Paris. As well as the second site, which I shall come to shortly, two further sites along the river – Rouen and the Fontainbleau forest – are currently being considered for inclusion. I must confess that when I first saw a sign proclaiming that this second site was on the list I was a bit surprised; the image that I had of the place in question was far from flattering. Indeed, if anyone had asked me to suggest a place in France that needed preserving for the good of humanity, I would never have come up with the correct answer. Nevertheless, I am always prepared to discover that I have been misinformed, so we headed off to have a proper look at the place.

In order to get there from the Marais Vernier we were going to cross the Pont de Normandie, the last and largest of all the bridges over the Seine. Not only would the bridge help us reach our destination, crossing over it would give us a real idea of how wide the Seine becomes just before it reaches the sea. I reckoned that we would get a much more vivid impression of the bridge and the size of the river on a bike than one would from a car. The Pont de Normandie is not a suspension bridge but a cable-stayed bridge like the magnificent Viaduc de Millau down in the Aveyron. Stayed bridges started appearing when some clever person realized that you didn't actually need to have the two great curving cables that make suspension bridges so recognizable: you could do without them altogether and just have the supporting stays connected directly to the bridge pillars. Stayed bridges are thus much lighter and somehow more minimalist than suspension bridges. Seen from a distance as we cycled towards it, the Pont de Normandie seemed to float in the air under its twin triangles of stays.

A muddy track led up on to the approach road to the bridge. As we had expected, being on a bike does indeed give you a much better impression of the scale and shape of the bridge than you would get in a car. You are also made much more aware how steep the approach road is. It is a six per cent slope apparently, which is quite steep enough when you are on a bike, especially when you have the wind blowing against you. Rather than the conventional pillars used on suspension bridges, which generally look like a huge letter H, each of this bridge's pillars is like a vast, extended capital A. From the head of each A the supporting cables extend down to both sides of the roadway. Cycling along, you get the impression that you are in amongst the rigging of some vast sailing ship.

While the roadway was still sloping upwards we arrived at the first of the two pillars, where we stopped to give it all the attention it deserves. Standing right underneath it, the shipboard impression is even stronger, with the pillar looking more like a huge mast than ever. Even though we were still some way from the middle, the view was spectacular. To the right, through the cables, we could see the Marais Vernier with the Pont de Tancarville in the distance. To the left, the side the cycle path was on, we could see the huge spread of the river stretching away to the sea with an expanse of mudflats exposed by the low tide.

We carried on to the middle of the bridge. A solid-looking chunk of the supporting structure has been generously covered with pairs of names, some scratched in the paint, others written in felt-tip pen. I'm not usually one to deface any kind of structure but, perhaps because we were in the middle of a bridge, sixty metres up in the air, it somehow felt that we were not really anywhere real at all and that thus normal rules didn't apply. Whatever the reason, I was suddenly struck with the overwhelming desire to sign our names. There was no question of scratching anything and we didn't have a felt pen so, in what I fervently believe was washable ink, and in quite small letters, I signed our names on the grey paintwork.

I had just put the pen away when a rather austere-looking middle-aged woman appeared on a bike from the opposite direction and stopped beside us to look at the view. I was relieved that she hadn't turned up any earlier, because she had the look of one who would disapprove strongly of any kind of graffiti, whether in washable ink or not. We exchanged a few polite but enthusiastic words about the bridge. Just before she set off, Inès remarked: 'Quelle belle croix huguenotte.' She was referring to the small, rather complex gold cross that was hanging from a chain round the woman's neck. A *croix huguenotte* – a Huguenot cross – is a dead giveaway to those in the know, because it marks the wearer as being Protestant. Of French Christians, the huge majority are Catholic, while only a relatively small number are Protestant. Inès's family form part of this latter group.

Protestant churches in France are known as *temples* rather than *églises*, and their services are called *cultes* as opposed to Catholic *messes*. I encountered my first *temple* when we were planning our wedding, many moons ago, and wanted to see what possible venues were available near where Inès's parents lived. Inès's dad, who was actually the son of a Protestant *Pasteur*, or vicar – though you would never, ever have guessed this from speaking to him – was keen for us to get married in a *temple*, the nearest of which turned out to be thirty kilometres from their house. The distance wasn't the only drawback: *temples* are immediately recognizable by their minimalism. Rather than the warm, golden-stone buildings with wonderful stained glass that are Anglican churches, *temples* can appear bare, almost to the point of being stark, and usually have clear windows. Clearly, the only two things that count in a *temple* are God and you. In the end, we decided that a civil service at the local *mairie* was much more the sort of thing we were looking for.

And that's about as much as I know about Protestantism in France. In fact, the only lasting impressions I have of it are based on my contact with elder members of Inès's father's family, who – even if they don't forgive me for saying this, they will at least recognize the reasoning behind it – were not always a bundle of laughs. In my admittedly very limited experience, elderly French Protestants have two things in common: a mouth which goes down at the sides rather than up, which can give a face a somewhat dour expression, and a desire to be thought of as *distingué* – distinguished. Indeed, 'Il est très distingué' – he is most distinguished – was the highest praise my father-in-law could bestow on anyone, although he rarely used it for anyone except obscure cousins of his who boasted an upside-down smile.

Croix huguenottes are generally made of gold and comprise a Maltese cross with *fleurs de lys* interspersed between the arms of the cross. The most recognizable part is the small, inverted dove of peace that hangs from the bottom of it. The cross worn by the woman on the bridge was particularly attractive due to the delicate detailing on the *fleurs de lys* and on the dove. She responded enthusiastically to Inès's compliment about her cross by saying 'Oui, et en plus, je l'ai achetée à Nîmes.'

The fact that she had bought it in Nîmes is important, because that is where many people believe that the first cross was made in 1688, shortly after the revocation of the Edict of Nantes. The Edict, dating from 1598, had granted a fair degree of freedom for French Protestants and had allowed them to live relatively peacefully in what was then a firmly Catholic country. Its revocation meant that they became far less welcome than they had been previously. The revocation of the Edict led to an exodus of Protestants, notably Huguenots, to more tolerant countries such as England. And here, for once, we get to a really interesting bit: one Huguenot family called de Chauncy fled from France during this period and made for England. They settled in Oxford and, over the years, their name became anglicized to Chaundy. During this time they lived hard-working, law-abiding lives to such a degree that they even became Freemen of the City. Three centuries or so later, a dashing pilot, arriving in Oxford from his native Scotland, met and married a beautiful Chaundy and, some years later . . . produced me!

All this means that, if French people ask what made me come to live in France, I can always say that all I have really done is to return to my family's roots.

Inspired by this thought, we carried on across the bridge and found that, unsurprisingly, whizzing down the far side was infinitely more fun than struggling up the approach road. On the way down, despite travelling at speed, we spotted what has to be the very last 'La Seine' sign along the river, still with its annoying three wavy lines. According to one of the many reference books that I have acquired while engaged in my quest, Le Pont de Normandie is the 257th and final bridge over the Seine. Since leaving the source I reckon that I must have crossed well over 200 of the 257 – many of the ones we didn't cross are railway bridges – although it never occurred to me at the time to count them.

Near the end of the bridge, we must have taken a wrong turning, because we found ourselves on a road called La Route Industrielle, which was even less attractive than its name suggests. But we didn't really mind how ugly it was because we were very nearly at our destination and World Heritage site: the city of Le Havre.

Le Havre? A World Heritage site? For me, Le Havre is a town best known for being home to a ferry terminal and a dockyard as well as for being surrounded by ugly petrochemical plants, many of which we had just cycled past.

If visiting Le Havre was going to prove to be as uninspiring as I imagined, one could argue that this would be at least partially the fault of the English. For a start the city pretty much owes its existence to the English in the first place. During the early part of the Hundred Years' War, there was much raiding of the Normandy coast, and especially up the Seine, by English ships. Charles V, seeking to defend the mouth of the river, fortified both the port of Honfleur – all that now remains of the fortifications is La Lieutenance, the former home of the King's representative – and the corresponding port on the other bank, Harfleur. When the war eventually came to an end, there began a relatively peaceful period, which lasted so long that all dredging of Harfleur harbour was abandoned, and so the port silted up completely. Harfleur village now lies a fair way inland, near Gonfreville L'Orcher, both its heyday and its demise being at least partially the result of English activities. It was this lack of a decent port at the mouth of the Seine that forced François I to build a new one, and he chose Le Havre as its site.

The other contribution the English made to the history of

Le Havre took place more recently. In the course of the Second World War the town endured 132 Allied air raids. The entire city centre was completely flattened, and 80,000 people were left homeless. However, it seems that there has been some belated debate about the need for many of these raids and the military advantage that they actually produced. The most destructive bombing raid on Le Havre – that of 5 September 1944 – took place ten days *after* Paris had been liberated and when the front had moved well away to the east. It was clearly necessary for the resident German garrison to be defeated, but the 5 September raid specifically targeted the city centre rather than the German emplacements near the docks. In the course of the raid 1,000 French civilians lost their lives, while apparently only nine German soldiers died. The reasoning behind the raid has never become clear. Possible explanations include a disastrous error of targeting, the accidental outcome of rivalries between Allied generals or the complete disregard of civilians to achieve a quick surrender. Whatever the reason, it seems that the long-awaited liberation of the city on 12 September was greeted with neither joy nor gratitude but with resignation – *enfin* – at last.

Whatever the explanation for its destruction, Le Havre needed to be rebuilt. Unlike other French towns, which were extensively and unflatteringly rebuilt after the war, Le Havre set out to rebuild its city centre in the most thoughtful way possible. That the centre of Le Havre ended up on the Heritage list is essentially thanks to the efforts of one man: the architect Auguste Perret. But it is only fair to make clear that the whole city is not designated. Even Le Havre's best friends would have to agree that the outskirts of the town, as well as most of the docks, are far from being beauty spots. Unfortunately, these are precisely the areas of the city that you tend to see when you travel to or from the ferry terminal.

Despite the pressing need for housing, Perret took his time and set about creating a completely new city centre using his favourite building material: concrete. At seventy-one years old, Perret was probably concrete's greatest fan of his day. All his designs were based on 'La poétique du béton' – the poetry of concrete. Perret believed that concrete was even better than natural stone, proclaiming: 'Le béton, c'est de la pierre que nous fabriquons, bien plus belle et plus noble que la pierre naturelle' – concrete is the stone that we make ourselves: it is more beautiful and more noble than natural stone. Concrete was clearly something of an obsession: I am not at all sure how often he was invited to dinner parties.

Perret's plan was based on the pleasing grid pattern of the city centre's original streets. Using a basic unit of 6.24 metres – the optimum length of the concrete beam of the day – he created a modular structure of interlinked buildings. When you visit the centre of Le Havre you are immediately struck by the uniformity of all the façades, whether shops, offices or apartments. All Perret's buildings manage to exude a feeling of solidity and quality that you don't generally find with modern structures: his poetry in concrete was obviously well thought out.

There was one place that was particularly worth a visit in Le Havre. We had been aware of St Joseph's church for the whole time we had spent in the city centre, as it has a tall central tower 106 metres high that we could see from everywhere we had been. The church is also apparently a useful landmark for ships returning to the harbour. When you get closer you see that the tower is set on a solid-looking blockhouse, which has narrow, unremarkable windows and appears to have been unflatteringly pebble-dashed. The fifty or so years since it was built have left it a bit grubby; indeed the whole thing looks far from inviting and we were actually in two minds about whether it was worth walking all the way round it to find the door. But we had come this far, so we thought we would go and have a quick look. This proved to be an excellent idea, because we happened to walk in at exactly the moment that a christening was ending. We thus found ourselves face to face with two beaming parents who were proudly clutching their newly christened offspring in their arms. More importantly we also found ourselves being offered *dragées*, even though we had nothing whatever to do with the christening party.

As a general rule, I can happily go for months without tasting any kind of French sweet. The only exception to this is *dragées*: if there are *dragées* to be eaten, I'm your man. The *dragée* is one of the wonders of France: it is an oval sweet with a hard outer shell which is filled either with an almond or, less often, with chocolate. They traditionally come in three colours – pastel-blue, pastel-pink and white – and are given as a formal gift to mark a special occasion. According to circumstances you generally receive a handful of *dragées* in either a little white muslin bag tied with a coloured ribbon or a small decorative cardboard packet. *Dragées* are quite simply delicious. If they are the almond sort, they crunch wonderfully, and you end up with a mouth-watering blend of crunched almond and sweet coating. If they are the chocolate variety, they are possibly even better. Their only drawback is that it doesn't seem the done thing to just go to a shop and buy some whenever you feel like eating one; you have to wait to be given them. Unfortunately, you are only given them on specific formal occasions and only then if you are lucky. You usually get your first taste of *dragées* when your friends get married. There don't seem to be any hard and fast rules about giving them at weddings: some couples give bags or packets of white *dragées* to everyone who attended the wedding as a 'thank you', as well as sending some to those who couldn't make it. Others just send a packet to those unfortunates who couldn't come in the way that a slice of wedding cake is sent in the UK.

Having received a packet of *dragées* from your friends after their wedding, there starts a rather miserable period where you won't receive any more sweets. What's worse is that you have no control whatsoever over the length of this *dragée*-free period. The fast will last until either another lot of friends get married or until your original friends have a baby and he or she is baptized. This can be a distressingly long time indeed.

As soon as I hear the happy news that someone we know is expecting a baby I start calculating roughly when the *dragées* should arrive. As with weddings, there are differing views on

the sending of sweets to mark a baptism. Whether they are given to guests as well as to those who couldn't make it, or just to some, the *dragées* will be pastel-blue for a boy or pastel-pink for a girl. If they come in a packet, this will be colour-coordinated to the sweets, as will the ribbon. I can't remember the name of the child who had just been christened in Le Havre, though I know we asked and then exclaimed politely at the answer, but I can safely say that it was a boy, because the *dragées* we were given were pale-blue.

Incidentally, in France you aren't only given *dragées* to mark human baptisms. A suburban train was named for our village a while ago, and all the locals were invited to go on its inaugural journey. A short naming ceremony in which a plaque was fixed to the front of the train was enlivened thanks to the efforts of a brass band. But what we and the other villagers liked best were the little bags of *dragées* that we were all given at the end.

If we hadn't gone into St Joseph's church that afternoon, not only would we have not been given some *dragées*, we would have missed a marvel: the interior of the church is one of the most extraordinary modern buildings I have ever seen. Walking in, you are immediately stunned by the concrete. I would never have imagined that I could enthuse about plain, dull grey pillars and X-shaped supporting beams but they are quite simply fabulous. All the concrete has been left bare, revealing the imprints of the original builders' shuttering – you can see the grain of the wooden planks they used and even the knot holes. This was another of Perret's obsessions: concrete must be seen to be concrete.

I am more than a bit worried that I am turning into a concrete-phile like good old Auguste but I have no choice but to go on enthusing about his work. The stained-glass windows, seen from the inside, are splendid, but the central, open octagonal tower that rises above you is breathtaking. And, of course, it is made from concrete. But the most unexpected things in the church are probably the pews. These are not wooden benches; nor are they made from concrete; they are flip-down seats that look like they were pinched from a provincial cinema. Odd or not, they somehow contrive to look wonderful too. I picked one in the front row, slouched back and gazed contentedly up the tower until it was time to go.

You may have assumed that we had abandoned Jean-François for ever when we set off on our bikes to discover the Marais Vernier. Not a bit of it: we were fervently hoping to see him again, and preferably that very afternoon. For, while we had been exploring Le Havre, Jean-François had, we hoped, been steadily motoring down the river behind us. Indeed, had *Hirondelle* been able to go a bit faster, we might well have seen her earlier on, passing under the Pont de Normandie as we were cycling over it. We had spent a long time studying maps with Jean-François and had come up with a plan according to which we would meet up at a marina just inside Le Havre harbour before embarking on the final stage of our journey.

So we cycled off through the city centre and out on to the sea front, from where we hoped to spot Jean-François coming. And, to our delight, there was *Hirondelle*, just a few hundred metres away, pitching a bit but heading steadily for the harbour entrance. The plan had included a promise that, if we saw any ships heading for the harbour exit while Jean-François was coming in, we would call to warn him but, thankfully, nothing seemed to be moving at all. Much cheered by the sight of *Hirondelle* approaching, just as we had planned, we raced back round the harbour wall and, ignoring the 'Accès interdit' signs, headed straight down on to the marina's jetty by the harbour mouth. There we stood, or rather, there we leaped up and down, waving as *Hirondelle* swung into view and came along-side.

As we set about tying the mooring rope to a handy bollard, Jean-François observed in his usual, untroubled manner: 'Je suis sûr que je peux le laisser là deux minutes' – I'm sure I can leave her here for a couple of minutes. It seemed unfair to point out the numerous nearby signs on the pontoons that forbade precisely that. Once we had made everything fast, we climbed aboard and produced some beer we had bought in town. Bottle in hand, Jean-François set about describing his journey down the last part of the river. I asked what the Pont de Normandie had looked like from underneath and was astonished to be told that he hadn't actually noticed the bridge at all because, at the time, he had been completely absorbed in a particularly tricky bit of his still-life.

A short while later, our son Sebastian drove up in response to an earlier call for assistance – our organizational skills, at least so far as this last part of the journey was concerned, were proving to be pretty good – and we set about putting Jean-François's bike back on the deck and packing all our stuff back into the car. My boat, however, was left where it was because it was about to take centre stage for the final part of the quest.

For the last time on this trip Inès and I cast off the mooring ropes and climbed aboard *Hirondelle*. At the tiller, and with no still-life to distract him, Jean-François headed carefully out of the marina and then swung round through the harbour entrance. Once past the harbour wall, we were at sea for the first time, and my boat got its first-ever taste of salt water. Jean François set his course for the north-east, the buildings of Le Havre off to our right. Away from the harbour, *Hirondelle* started pitching regularly as she met the swell coming in from the channel, my boat bouncing and swinging in her wake.

Jean-François held his course for about ten minutes, scanning the shoreline to our right, then observed, as ever in his characteristic mix of uncertainty and optimism, 'On dirait que l'on est là, non?' – it looks like we're here, aren't we? He cut the engine, and we drifted to a stop some fifty metres off a cobble beach where a small group of people in warm clothing were standing, watching us intently. 'Oui, c'est bien eux' – yes, that's them all right – I agreed. Heading to the stern, I unfastened the boat's painter and pulled it alongside. Jean-François leaned down and held the boat steady while Inès and I climbed aboard; seen from the waterline for the first time, *Hirondelle* looked far bigger than she did from a quayside. Jean-François passed me down the oars, and there was a brief moment of confusion as he let go of the boat and then changed his mind and set out to do a last *bise* to Inès and a final handshake with me, neither of which was easy, given the height difference and the fact that we were swinging against *Hirondelle*'s hull in the swell.

Our goodbyes and thanks precariously completed, I pulled away from *Hirondelle* and headed for the group of people waiting on the shore, Jean-François watching from the cockpit, his arm raised in salute. It wasn't far to row, but I took my time, wanting to enjoy for as long as possible this final short stretch of water that would bring my quest to an end.

All too quickly, the boat was cresting the surf, and, with a final scrunch, we were ashore on the cobbled beach.

Conclusion

Several months ago, I was standing by the source of the River Seine on the outskirts of St-Germain-Source-Seine in Burgundy: a man on a mission.

I'm now standing on a cobble beach, my back to the bracing wind, gazing at the Seine as it flows out between this spot and Villerville, some fifteen kilometres away on the opposite coast, to reach the sea at last. A mastless sailing boat can be seen chugging away to the north-east, a moustachioed man waving wildly from the stern. I have travelled the entire length of the Seine from source to the sea in the best part of a year. Of course, had I not stopped to explore along the way, or spent all that time messing about in boats, I could probably have done it in under ten hours. But where would have been the fun in that?

I'm standing on this beach at Sainte Adresse, the most northerly, and the most attractive suburb of Le Havre, with the great triangular estuary of the Seine stretching away to my left, and I'm holding a bottle in each hand. In my right hand is a small plastic bottle that, according to the label, originally held some *eau de source* called 'Cristalline'. It is still full of *eau de source*, but the spring this water came from was the one under the statue of Sequana on that very first day. In my left hand I have the bottle of Champagne given by Monsieur Joséphine in thanks for my efforts during the guided tour of his cellars. It is time to empty both bottles, right here on the beach.

It seems fitting to start with the water from the source. To applause from our friends – the very same ones who came up with the idea all those months ago in a cold garage – I ceremonially pour the water into the sea. It is a great moment. Mind you, had I just left the water to flow down the river in the normal way, it would have got here all by itself months ago.

Inès produces some glasses from somewhere and I pop the cork on the Champagne. Before I can propose a toast, someone asks the crucial question: 'Alors, est-ce que tu as vraiment voyagé tout le long de la Seine?' – did you really make it the whole way along the river?

'Oui, absolument; je l'ai parcourue sur toute sa longueur,' I reply with a slight, but proud, smile.

At this there is much chinking and toasting.

A while later, I finish my glass, turn to our friends and say: 'I hope you remember your promise. Now it's your turn. The ferry to Portsmouth leaves from just over there in two hours' time. It's time to go.'